IELTS

SPEAKING

雅思口语真经总纲 （第二版）

刘洪波 杨师 编著

中国人民大学出版社
·北京·

推 荐 序

在雅思培训行业，刘洪波老师推崇以评分标准为切入点进行雅思教学。在刘老师看来，研究评分标准，就是对考试目的的理解，就是帮助学生取得高分的途径。溯本求源，雅思的评分标准，体现了雅思考试对于语言交互性的高度重视，这也是全球的院校普遍认可雅思成绩的重要原因。雅思考试之所以权威，不仅仅是因为成绩准确，更重要的是，它对普通英语学习者以及众多的考试都具有指导意义。

雅思口语评分标准，强调"流利度和连贯性""词汇""语法""发音"。你还在担心自己的口语不够好吗？雅思官方已经给你指出了口语学习的方向。把这四条全部做好，或者努力做好其中的几条，即使你不参加雅思考试，这些也能成为你提高口语交流能力的利器。

毕业于中国传媒大学英语播音专业的杨帅老师，在口语流利度和发音方面，有着得天独厚的优势。听杨帅老师说口语，宛如听 CCTV 国际频道的现场播报。虽然英语没有普通话，但是这样的口音无疑令人艳羡。除此之外，杨帅老师英语基础扎实，对学术充满渴望。他的"每日背三句"展示了他在口语方面的功力、词汇的丰富和对语法的精益求精，难怪他能够五次斩获雅思口语 9 分。

杨帅老师用自己超强的实力和不懈的个人努力验证了雅思考试的权威性和科学性。而学为贵教育之所以能被雅思官方评为白金级合作伙伴，也是因为群英荟萃、学术领先。

很多人喜欢杨帅老师，很多人喜欢刘洪波老师，很多人喜欢学为贵的课，这也许就是真经派的学术魅力。

这本雅思口语书包括三章。第一章是考试介绍，解释了很多在雅思考试官方说明中没有详述的内容，是杨帅老师的亲身经历和众多考生的考试需求。第二章是官方评分标准。只有读懂评分标准，才能真正读懂雅思。第三章是素材大全。这部分内容完整覆盖了口语题库，并提供了回答示范。

你可以跟随本书的录音，体会雅思口语高分表现；也可以依照书中的技法，举一反三，征战雅思，斩获高分。本书的姊妹篇是《雅思口语：杨帅教你 900 句》。

在本书的编写过程中，励雅、陈彦伊、赵小锐、刘畅、谭乐、刘娟、付晓楠、田杨、冯涛、成岩、程玲、李慧芳、刘素良、焦磊、柏立明、焦鸿、曹爱丽、张靖娴、袁伟、李海静、刘伟、杨志、贾玉梅、李悦、张璐、焦丽娜、尚莉、袁乐、邓素娟、殷博、戚旗、史策、范欣南、张儒雅、胡瑞青、沈小燕、张强、董哲羽、何运娟、陈星樵、高尚勇、冯鑫、李前领也参与了资料收集及部分编写工作，在此一并感谢。

吕蕾微信公众号　　　吕蕾微博　　　　　　　　吕蕾抖音号　　　吕蕾小红书号
lvlei1973　　　http://weibo.com/lvlei1973　　wonderfullei　　wonderfullei

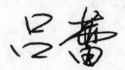

入重松通

输为放沟

诵型然辑

背句自逻

Part 2 话题一览表

- a time a child made you laugh P125
- a fashionable person P126
- a person who can speak a foreign language P127
- a person who can do well at work P128
- a person who always travels by plane P129
- a person whose job is important P130
- a family member P131
- a friend P132
- a famous foreign person P133
- a famous person in your country P134
- a helpful person P135
- someone who is older than you P136
- a creative inventor or musician P137
- a person who moved in with you P138
- a foreign country P139
- a place P140
- a street P141
- a street market or an outdoor market P142
- a café or restaurant P143
- a historical building P144
- a tall building P145
- a park or garden P146
- an important place P147
- a change that would improve the area where you live P148
- a long journey P149
- a long walk P150
- a paid job P151
- a skill P152
- a success P153
- a team P154
- a time when you felt surprised to meet someone P155
- a person who impressed you most P156
- a time that you and your friend had a disagreement P157
- a time when you were friendly to someone P158
- an artistic activity P159
- a natural talent P160
- an educational trip P161
- an article P162
- something you do P163
- an activity P164
- a (jigsaw) puzzle P165
- something you would like to do P166
- a situation P167
- something you've wanted to do P168
- a time when you were very busy P169
- a time when you got up early P170
- a positive change P171
- a time when someone or something made a lot of noise P172
- a time when you lost your way P173
- a time you got a little angry P174
- a time when you received good service P175
- a situation when someone gave you a piece of useful advice P176
- a habit P177
- a gift P178
- an electronic device P179
- a photo P180
- a piece of equipment P181
- an item P182
- a piece of local news P183
- an educational TV programme P184
- a movie P185
- something you would like to learn more P186
- a small and successful company P187
- a song P188
- a kind of weather you like P189
- an important invention P190
- a sport P191
- a historical event P192

目 录

第1章　雅思口语考试介绍 /1

雅思口语考试的时间和地点 /1

雅思口语考试的流程和内容 /2

　　口语"变题季"是什么意思？ /3　　如果对成绩不满意，可以申请复议吗？ /3

第2章　官方评分标准真经 /5

Fluency & Coherence 流利度和连贯性 /6

　　连贯性 /6　　流利度 /14

Lexical Resource 词汇资源 /29

　　三十组同义形容词 /31　　四十二个习语 /47

　　四十五个动词词组 /40

Grammatical Range & Accuracy 语法多样性和准确性 /52

　　四十九个语法功能句型 /53

Pronunciation 发音 /65

　　单个音 /66　　失去爆破（特殊连读） /70

　　连读（普通连读） /70　　重读和弱读 /71

第3章　口语素材大全 /77

Part 1 回答五大准则 /77

Part 1 练习方法 /78

Part 1 范例答案 /78

　　Work or study /78　　Relaxation /87

　　Hometown /80　　Family /88

　　Home/Accommodation /81　　Friends /90

　　Fruits /82　　Teachers /91

　　Transportation /83　　Festivals /92

　　Bus or taxi /84　　Flowers /93

　　Music /85　　Sunshine /94

　　Sports /86　　Rainy days /95

Sky and stars /96

Colours /97

Politeness /98

Concentration /99

Mirrors /100

News /100

Letters or emails /101

Magazines /102

Sleep /104

Cooperation /105

Maps /106

Shoes /107

Jewellry /107

Housework /109

History /110

Daily routine /111

Birthday /112

Advertisements /114

Time management /115

Boating /116

Apps /117

Computers and internet /118

Teenagers /119

Pets and animals /120

Saving money /121

Science /122

Part 2 回答九大准则 /123

Part 2 练习方法 /124

Part 2 范例答案 /125

Part 3 回答七大准则 /193

Part 3 练习方法 /193

Part 3 范例答案 /194

Work, careers, companies /194

Family, friends, neighbours, roommates, socialising, teamwork /200

Transport, commuting /203

Countryside and cities, accommodation, buildings /204

Hobbies, relaxation, lifestyles, sports, travel /207

Entertainment, celebrities, role models /209

Internet, technology /211

Children, young people, old people /214

Food /218

Study, language, education, skills /220

Emotions, changes, experiences /223

Media, TV, news /225

第 1 章

雅思口语考试介绍

 雅思口语考试的时间和地点

◆ **时间**：现在的雅思考试有纸笔考试和机考两种选择。纸笔考试中的口语考试可能安排在笔试前一周至笔试后一周之间的任意一天，但会尽量安排在笔试当天下午或笔试次日全天。

虽然考生可以在网上预约自己想要的口语考试时间，但这不一定是实际的考试时间。建议大家在拿到准考证后，再次确认口试的日期和时间，以免耽误考试。

机考的口语考试通常可以选择在当天或临近的一天进行。

◆ **地点**：纸笔考试中的口语考试地点一般与笔试地点相同，但也可能不是一个地方。

比如笔试地点在首都经济与贸易大学，口语考试安排在中国农业大学。建议考生在拿到准考证后，再三确认笔试、口试地点。如果笔试当天看到考场桌角的标签上列出的口试地点、时间与准考证上不一致，请以考试当天的信息为准。

机考的口试地点就在机考考点进行，考生会被安排到一个口试房间，面对电脑，和电脑里的考官进行英语对话。

(((◀ 雅思口语考试的流程和内容

口语考试是时长为 12～16 分钟的一对一谈话，主要内容分为 Part 1、Part 2、Part 3。

◆ **先会面寒暄一番（1～2 分钟）：**

考官见到考生，问是否携带了电子产品（Do you have any electronic device/item with you?）；考官带考生进入考场房间、坐下；问考生姓名（Can you tell me your full name please?/What's your full name?）和家乡（Where are you from?/Where do you come from?）；要求考生出示身份证件，核对信息（Can I see your ID/identification please?）；告知考生考试过程将被录音（This test will be/is being recorded. Is that OK?）。

现在中国大陆口语考试均为机考，考官会出现在电脑屏幕上。身份确认的环节会在考官出现之前完成。

◆ **Part 1（4～5 分钟）：**

这个部分的题目都是关于考生的个人生活，考官和考生进行一问一答。考生一般会被问到三个话题左右，每个话题会延伸出三四个小问题。

Part 1 可能出现的话题有：work or studies, hometown, home, travelling, holiday, shopping, sports, reading, music, movies, television, news, magazines, weekend, friends, family, cooking, housework, teachers, daily routine, sleep, computer, internet, Apps, barbecues, sky and stars…（还有很多可能出现的其他话题，以当季度考试题库为准。）

◆ **Part 2（3～4 分钟）：**

考官给考生一个话题，话题是"描述一个经历、地点、人物、物品或其他"。题目中会有四个小点提示思路，比如 when、who、where、why、how you feel 等。例如：

> **Describe a teenager you know.**
>
> **You should say:**
>
>   **who this teenager is**
>
>   **how you know this teenager**
>
>   **what he or she likes to do**
>
> **and explain how you feel about this teenager.**

考生有一分钟的准备时间，可以用考官提供的纸（白板）和笔写下关键词。一分钟后，围绕话题，开始 1～2 分钟的不间断回答。在作答结束后，考官会再问一道小题，官方把它叫作 rounding off question。这个题目的问法会非常简单。以上面 Describe a teenager you know 的话题为例，考官可能会问的 rounding off questions 有：When was the last time you saw this teenager? How often do you spend time with this teenager? Do your friends also like this teenager?

针对 rounding off question，考生无须过多扩展自己的答案，只要快速直接给出一两句话的回答便可。例如：

Q **When was the last time you saw this teenager?**

A: Oh, it was yesterday. We met in the supermarket while we were both picking up some groceries.

◆ Part 3（4~5 分钟）：

考官会延续 Part 2 的话题，与考生深入讨论，通常会提出大众的、社会性的、抽象的问题。问题数量在五个左右，但有的考官可能喜欢问很多问题。什么样的考官都有，大家要做好遇到各种不同情况的准备。

Part 3 中可能出现的问题（同样以前文 Part 2 题目 Describe a teenager you know 为例）：Do you think teenagers are happier than older people? What are the advantages of being a teenager? How do teenagers in your country entertain themselves? Why are there generation gaps between people?

🎙 口语"变题季"是什么意思？

雅思口语 Part 1 话题一般稳定在 30 个左右，Part 2 稳定在 50 个左右，Part 3 也有题库，但是实际考试中的很多 Part 3 题目是考官根据考生的回答当场发挥提问的。雅思考试有"变题季"一说，是因为在每年的 1 月、5 月、9 月，雅思口语题目中大概一半的旧题会被替换。所以 1 月、5 月、9 月的前两场考试通常是一些新题出现的时候，考生有可能会遇到自己未曾见过的题目。在前两场考试结束，新题基本浮出水面后，我们会说当季（1 月—4 月、5 月—8 月、9 月—12 月）题库"稳定了"。

想要了解每一季的题库，可以下载"学为贵雅思"App，或者关注新浪微博 @ 学为贵。

🎙 如果对成绩不满意，可以申请复议吗？

可以，但要从成绩单打印日期起的 4 周内申请。在 IELTS 报名网站上申请复议一项或多项成绩，复议费用均是 1 400 元，复议时间通常是六周。任何一项复议成功，复议费将退回申请人账户；复议失败，费用不退还。复议的结果有两种：分数不变或分数提高。复议并不会降低分数。大家需要注意，申请复议的前提是你的实力够强、发挥不错，而不是看其他科目分数或各科分数差距如何。

复议写实说：

杨帅老师有过五次复议经历，成绩均得到提高，收回了复议费！

第一次是在 2016 年 9 月，杨帅老师口语考了 8.5 分，写作 7 分。口语和写作均申请了复议，口语提高 0.5 分，变成 9 分；写作分数没变，还是 7 分。钱收回！

第二次复议是在 2017 年 6 月，口语获得 7.5 分，写作 7 分。口语和写作申请了复议，口语提高 0.5 分，变成 8 分（杨帅老师至今还对这次考试分数耿耿于怀）；写作分数没变，还是 7 分。钱收回！

第三次复议是在 2018 年 3 月，口语获得 8 分，写作 7.5 分。口语和写作申请了复议，口语提高 1 分，变成 9 分；写作分数不变，还是 7.5 分。钱收回！

第四次复议是在 2018 年 6 月，这次口语直接考了 9 分，没有复议。本次考试听力和阅读也是 9 分，写作 6.5 分。写作申请了复议，提高 1 分，变成 7.5 分。钱收回！

第五次复议是在 2021 年 12 月，这次对写作和口语进行了复议。口语 8.5 分，成绩没变；写作从 7.5 分提高到了 8 分。钱收回！

杨帅老师考过五次雅思口语 9 分。（2019 年和 2023 年考试没有复议，口语直接是 9 分）

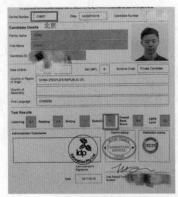
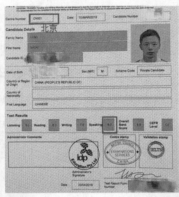
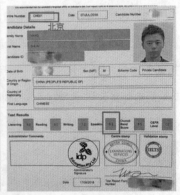

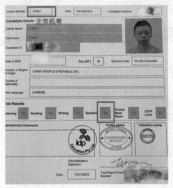

第2章

官方评分标准真经

2006 年，雅思考试官方向全球公布了口语评分细则，这些详尽的说明让一个依赖考官主观评分的过程趋于客观，让考官最终的评分**有理可依、有据可查**，保证了口语分数的**客观性和公平性**，也让雅思成绩更加为海外大学所**信赖**。

其实更重要的是，这个评分标准对所有雅思考生来说具有**最高指导意义**。事实上它已经指出了真正提高英语口语能力的**终南捷径**，它是雅思口语考试中的**最大金矿**！

雅思口语考试的四大官方评分标准是：*Fluency & Coherence*（流利度和连贯性）、*Lexical Resource*（词汇资源）、*Grammatical Range & Accuracy*（语法多样性和准确性）、*Pronunciation*（发音）。

即使你不考雅思，你也可以参考这四个标准，或者说朝着这四个方向来练习提升你的英语口语水平。有科学方向的指引，你的练习会更高效。

接下来，本书会深入讲解，在学为贵真经派，我们针对这四大评分标准设置的教学理念和目标，设计的配套练习和素材内容。

大部分考生的口语考试目标为 6 分以上。因此，本书侧重于应对 6 分和 7 分标准的相关技巧和练习。而且我们建议，**平时应该严格参照 7 分标准来练习和要求自己**，才能确保在考场上考出不低于 6 分的口语成绩。古语有云："谋其上，得其中；谋其中，得其下。"

如果你的目标是口语 9 分，欢迎拨打学为贵集团免费电话：4006236898。

(((▶ Fluency & Coherence 流利度和连贯性

关于 Fluency & Coherence（流利度和连贯性），我们先来了解 6 分和 7 分的官方评判标准。如下：

Band 6	● Is willing to speak at length, though may lose coherence at times due to occasional repetition, self-correction or hesitation. 虽然时有重复、自我更正、犹豫导致的连贯性缺失，但具备交流意识、愿意充分扩展。 ● Uses a range of connectives and discourse markers but not always appropriately. 能够使用一系列连接词和信号词，但有时使用不够准确。
Band 7	● Speaks at length without noticeable effort or loss of coherence. 轻松自如地充分扩展答案，语言连贯。 ● May demonstrate language related hesitation at times, or some repetition and/or self-correction. 偶尔会出现因思考语言导致的犹豫、重复、自我更正。 ● Uses a range of connectives and discourse markers with some flexibility. 灵活使用一系列连接词和信号词。

其实，口语的流利度和连贯性比起来，连贯性更基础，更容易上手提升。所以，我们先学如何提升连贯性。

🎤 连贯性

口语表达就像一条河流。从源头到大海，从开始到结束，这一路一直都在流淌。有时快、有时慢；有时激情、有时平静。但是它不会停止，一直前行。我们说话也是如此，从开始讲话到最终结束，中间应是自然流畅地向前推动。

为了做到这一点，就需要我们有很好的流利度和连贯性。我们先来聊聊连贯性。

简单地说，连贯性就是"层次结构、句句连接"；更简单地说，连贯性可以被理解成"逻辑"。

在一个较长的回答中（如口语 Part 2 答案），我们需要确定整体回答结构，而不是想到哪说哪，因为这样会导致逻辑混乱，说着说着就不知道自己在说什么了，最终影响自己对词汇、语法和思路的控制。确定了整体回答结构之后，还要确保说出来的每个段落或层次的开头是清晰的。

除了整体结构之外，在每个段落或层次中，如果不是只有一两个句子，那么几个句子之间需要有紧密的逻辑关系，这样就有了较好的连贯性。

连贯性是很多雅思口语考生，甚至雅思口语老师都忽略的一个评分标准，但是它非常重要。在很大程度上，更好的连贯性会带来更好的流利度，甚至带来更好的词汇和语法。

为什么？

1. 不少考生在口语考试中表达不够流利，并非因为自己英语很差，而是因为需要绞尽脑汁去思考一句话说完后，下一句话说什么。如果一个考生的连贯性不错，一句话结束后，立刻能够通过逻辑"推"出下一句，那就能减少思考时间，进而提高流利度。

2. 在口语考试中，词汇和语法的多样性很重要，但不少考生因为没有对一些回答进行扩展，而只是回答一点点内容，便失去了展现更多词汇和语法的机会。这导致他们在词汇和语法方面没有得到与自己水平相当的分数。

为了做到说话具有连贯性，我们需要学会如何通过逻辑对回答进行扩展，并适当使用一些连接词、信号词和连接方法。这些常用的连接方法也有利于我们更清晰、更有效地表达观点。

真经教学

> 学会拓展答案的技能，避免只用单词、短语、短句来回答考官问题，并展现更好的结构和流利度、更多样的词汇和语法。学会连接词、信号词、各种连接手段，有意识地运用在交流表达中。

先来学习连接词、信号词和连接方法。

🎤 因果连接

because = as = coz（口语中常见表达）因为（后面加句子）

due to sth. = because of sth. 因为，由于（后面加名词、代词、动名词）

so, therefore, as a result, as a consequence 所以，因此

in this case 这样的话

which means 这意味着

🎤 首先

first of all = for starters = first off = firstly 首先

one reason/problem/advantage/benefit is that... 一个原因 / 问题 / 优点 / 好处是……

🎤 其次

plus = also = besides = additionally = on top of that 另外

another reason/problem/advantage/benefit is that... 另一个原因 / 问题 / 优点 / 好处是……

Q **What are the benefits of travelling?**

A: Well, I think travelling has a multitude of benefits. <u>**For starters**</u>, it's a great way for people to unwind. Many people nowadays are under a great deal of pressure and they may even feel depressed because of it, so it's quite important for them to do something from time to time in order to relax. I believe travelling is one of the best things they can do. <u>**Another benefit of travelling is that**</u> it allows people to see different cultures, traditions and lifestyles. In fact, I just came back from New Zealand, and what I found there was that people in this country lived a very slow pace of life, which is really different from where I come from.

词汇 Key Words

a multitude of... 很多……

from time to time 偶尔

unwind [ʌn'waɪnd] *v.* 放松

allow sb. to do sth. 使某人能够做某事

be under a great deal of pressure 有很大压力

live a slow pace of life 生活节奏慢

depressed [dɪ'prest] *adj.* 抑郁的

比如和等等

for example = for instance 例如

let me give you an example 我给你举个例子

let me think of an example 让我找个例子

by way of an example 举例说明

such as = like 比如

and so on = and so forth 等等

具体化

to be specific, more specifically 具体说来，更具体地说

to be exact 确切地说，准确地说

especially = particularly 尤其

in particular 尤其，特别

e.g. The Forbidden City is hundreds of years old. <u>To be specific</u>, it was built in the 1400s, so that was 600 years ago.

e.g. After jogging for 5 months, I successfully got slimmer. <u>To be exact</u>, I lost 25 pounds.

词汇 Key Words

slim [slɪm] *adj.* 苗条的

使用"磅"这个计量单位，1 磅 = 0.454 千克）

lose...pounds 减掉……磅肉（在这里可以直接

Q How often do you go on a picnic?

A: I go on a picnic pretty frequently in the summer as the weather is usually ideal for it. <u>To be exact</u>, I go picnicking 2 or 3 times a month in July and August. My friends and I like to find some parks which aren't very crowded, <u>particularly</u> those with a lake, so that we can eat, drink and chat while enjoying the lake views.

词汇 Key Words

go on a picnic = go picnicking 去野餐

chat [tʃæt] *v.* 聊天

frequently ['fri:kwəntlɪ] *adv.* 频繁地，经常地

view [vju:] *n.* 风景

ideal [aɪ'di:əl] *adj.* 理想的

🎙️ 代词

人称代词：he, him, she, her, it, they, them

指示代词：this, that, these, those

注意：使用代词是一种高级的连接方式。很多考生代词使用较少，总是不断地重复名词，这样听起来很不自然。

🎙️ 定语从句

...who is...（当主句以某个人结尾的时候）

...which is...（当主句以某个物品、地点、事件等结尾的时候）

...where...（当主句以某个地点结尾的时候，从句可翻译成"在那里"）

Q **Who's your favourite celebrity?**

A: My favourite celebrity is Hebe, <u>who is</u> a really well-known singer in China. I like her because… um, just because she is so beautiful and has a wonderful voice. So I listen to her songs every day, no matter where I go.

词汇 Key Words

well-known [ˌwelˈnəʊn] *adj.* 著名的

Q **What outdoor activities do you like?**

A: Well, the outdoor activity that I enjoy the most is absolutely hiking, <u>which</u> I think <u>is</u> becoming more and more popular in China now. I like to go to the northeast of my hometown <u>where</u> I usually hike for three or four hours on the weekends, either alone or with some of my close friends, <u>which is</u> extremely enjoyable.

词汇 Key Words

enjoyable [ɪnˈdʒɔɪəb,l] *adj.* 令人愉快的，令人感到享受的

注意：使用从句不仅可以表达复杂思想，还能够起到连接的作用。考生如果对此理解不够，就无法地道地运用。

🎙️ 填充词

um, well, I mean, you know, like

填充词（fillers）是我们在思考的时候可以使用的词汇。思考和犹豫是无法避免的，在考试中一定会出现。当我们思考或犹豫的时候，不能完全不出声，也不能在考场上和考官大眼瞪小眼，而是

应该说一些填充词来过渡。填充词能帮助我们在思考的同时，保证自己的语流顺畅地进行下去，让交流过程没有断档和冷场。只要不是一直使用填充词，或者总使用一个相同的填充词，就没有问题。

注意：you know 在口语考试中完全可以使用，只要考生用正常的、思考的语气说出 you know，考官不会说 I don't know。有的考生用疑问语气说 you know 或 do you know，或者说 as you know，这些都是不对的，这时考官会说出 I don't know 就不足为奇了。

Q **Do you think you will live in your hometown forever?**

A: No, I don't suppose I will live in my hometown for the rest of my life, because…<u>um, you know</u>, I really want to move to a smaller city in the south of China at some point in my life, <u>like um</u>, Dali or Xiamen, and <u>I mean</u>, this is because in those places, the pace of life is much slower than that in my city…

词汇 Key Words

for the rest of my life 在我的余生里	pace of life 生活节奏
at some point in my life 在人生的某个时刻	

🎤 填充句

I'm not sure…

I don't really know, but…

Well, let me think about it…

Let me see…

Oh, that's a tough/tricky/difficult one…

Well, I'm not an expert on this, but…（an expert on sth. 对某个领域很了解的人）

I don't know much about this, but I guess…

I haven't thought about it before, because…

Hang on a second…（hang on 等一会儿）

What else can I say?

How can I put it?（put 说，表达）

Wait, I think I was wrong…

Oh, no, I thought I knew, but nothing comes to mind now…（come to mind 被想到）

God, I forgot the word. Um…

我们在和考官聊天的过程中可以自然地使用以上句子，帮助自己进行思考。灵活恰当地使用这些句子不会被扣分，反倒能帮助我们把英语说得更加流畅。

有的同学担心过多使用填充句会造成自己分数降低。不用纠结，说点什么一定比不说话分数高。当然最理想的状态是恰当使用。

Q What are the differences between the buildings in the north of China and those in the south of China?

A: <u>Um, god, that's a tough one. I'm not an expert on buildings</u>, so I don't suppose I can give you a good answer, but <u>um</u>, what I can only think of is that…<u>well</u>, since it's much colder in the winter in the north of China, the walls tend to be thicker than those in the south…

词汇 Key Words

tend to 往往会，常常会

thick [θɪk] *adj.* 厚的

Q What is the definition of happiness?

A: <u>Oh, my goodness, this is a really tricky question. Um, I haven't thought about it before</u>, but in fact, I was thinking before this test that if I could get a good score this time, I would definitely be super happy and celebrate it by inviting my friends to sing karaoke with me, haha. <u>So, the definition of happiness? Let me think…well</u>, I don't suppose I can give you a very good one, but I just think that happiness is the feeling you get when you have achieved something important or are doing something you enjoy.

词汇 Key Words

sing karaoke 唱卡拉 OK

Q Is there anything you don't like about your hometown?

A: Oh, yeah, it's the fact that there are so many people everywhere. You know, every morning, when I go to work, the bus is…<u>um, what's the word? Sorry, I was going to say a very good word, haha.</u> <u>Oh yeah,</u> jam-packed! Buses are usually jam-packed in my hometown, which makes my ride to work very uncomfortable.

词汇 Key Words

jam-packed [dʒæm'pækt] *adj.* 非常拥挤的

ride [raɪd] *n.*（乘车或骑车的）短途旅程

🎤 提出观点

I think…, what I think is that… 我认为……

I guess…, I suppose… 我觉得……

in my opinion, as far as I'm concerned, the way I see it 我的观点是……

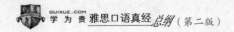

I believe..., I bet..., I'm convinced that... 我相信……

e.g. **What I think is that** cities will be less noisy in the future because factories are being moved out of cities and fewer and fewer drivers honk their horns on the roads.

词汇 Key Words

honk one's horn 鸣笛

e.g. **I bet** I'll live in my hometown for the rest of my life coz I'm so attached to it.

词汇 Key Words

be attached to sth. 喜欢……；对……有感情

🎤 表示时间

five years ago 五年前

last week 上周

when I was a child = when I was a kid = when I was growing up 在我小的时候

when my parents were young 在我父母年轻的时候

in the future 在未来

in the near future 在不远的未来

in the foreseeable future 在可预见到的未来

in 20 years 20 年后

50 years from now 50 年后

🎤 重复前文

as I said (before), as I mentioned earlier 如我（之前）所说，正如我之前提到的

在我们说话的过程中，很有可能在某一个点需要重复一下之前提到过的信息，这个时候，我们就可以使用以上几个表达。

🎤 对比

but, however, on the other hand, in/by contrast

e.g. Elderly people generally like to do tai chi, square dancing and just go for a walk in parks in their spare time. Young people, <u>on the other hand</u>, tend to go shopping a lot, and they also like to work out at the gym.

词汇 Key Words

elderly people 老人	go for a walk 散步
tai chi 太极拳	work out at the gym 在健身房健身
square dancing 广场舞	

e.g. Men usually talk a lot about sports, like basketball and soccer. <u>By contrast</u>, women are more fond of talking about friends, families and what kinds of clothes are in fashion.

词汇 Key Words

in fashion 流行

通常

generally speaking, generally, typically

e.g. <u>Generally speaking</u>, Chinese students are quite shy when it comes to giving a speech or presentation, so they absolutely have to work more on these.

e.g. Old people <u>generally</u> get up pretty early every day, around 6 o'clock or even earlier than that.

e.g. <u>Typically</u>, children in China are asked by their parents to learn a musical instrument when they're very small.

词汇 Key Words

when it comes to... 当谈到……时；就……而论	musical instrument 乐器

让步

having said that, that said 话虽如此

e.g. It takes years of hard work to learn a language well. <u>Having said that</u>, some people are very talented and perhaps they can master a foreign language within a short period of time.

e.g. What I enjoy doing in my spare time is staying home and doing some reading, which I think is quite relaxing. <u>That said</u>, I do feel a bit lonely from time to time, and in that case, I'll call some of my friends and we'll meet up.

词汇 Key Words

years of hard work 多年的刻苦学习	master ['mɑːstə(r)] *v.* 熟练掌握
talented ['tæləntɪd] *adj.* 有天赋的	within a short period of time 在很短的时间内

英文中常用的连接方法不止以上这些，大家可以在本书的其他例句和范例答案中学习到更多。

在上文，我们提到了想要连贯性强，逻辑扩展、一环扣一环地将答案说下去是至关重要的。逻辑能力的训练和提升，不仅提升连贯性，还能带来更好的流利度。所以关于逻辑扩展，我们主要在下面的"流利度"中进行讲解。

🎤 流利度

流利，是交流水平高的体现，包含了思维流利和表达流利，二者缺一不可。思维流利便是我们一直在强调的逻辑，表达流利是一个人语言硬实力的展现。

虽然看上去流利度的要求很高，但提高流利度，我们有真经。

🎤 提升语感

没有很好的语感，一个人讲话就会磕磕巴巴的，而不是自然流畅的。

短时间内提升语感的最好方法是多听、多读、多说、多背。大家可以将本书中给出的每个例句都反复听录音，然后朗读很多遍，直到能够熟练背诵。

这个过程会很无聊，纯体力活。就像在健身房健身举铁，练着练着，身材就变好了。坚持着坚持着，语感就有了。

🎤 省去翻译

很多考生会说自己做不到这一点，因为不想中文意思的话，他们根本不知道要如何造出正确的句子。但是，在脑海中不断翻译会降低我们说话的流利度。其实，我们可以通过如下方法解决"不断想翻译"的问题：

◆ **方法 1**：在朗读和背诵英文句子的时候，不去想中文翻译，而是去感受它的意思。可以先从单词开始，再到短语、短句，最后到长句。

◆ **方法 2**：练习"立刻张嘴说英语"。如果大家有语伴的话，这会比较方便。你们可以和语伴不断地练习用英文对话，逼着自己不要想太久就迅速地说出句子。如果你没有语伴，只是一个人练习英语，也可以选择"自言自语"的方法。不管想到什么或看到什么，都用英文表达出来（可以小点声，甚至戴上口罩，以免别人觉得你奇怪……）。"I'm going to a park now, and I need to take the bus to get there. Where is my bus stop? Oh, there it is. What? The bus is already there and it's leaving? No! I can't catch it now…" 这样的练习很容易，随时随地都能做，而且很有效。

◆ **方法 3**：沉浸在英语当中。大家可以每天尽量多地听英语新闻、看美剧英剧、看英语电影。让自己沉浸在一个英语的环境中可以帮助大家很快地培养英语思维习惯，跨越从中文翻译到英文的过程。省去这个时间，英语自然流利。

🎤 不要纠结语法错误

很多同学流利度不高，一个很大的原因是在说话时纠结语法，不断思考句型结构（先行词、后置定语、半倒装……）。这样的话，流利度自然会下降。还有的同学在听到问题后不立刻张嘴答题，明明题目很简单，却要一等再等，可能是在思考第三句话的语法结构……不要这样！立刻张嘴，开始展示你的英文。

其实，对于大部分中国考生来说，大家是可以犯一些语法错误的。

因为 6 分评分标准的语法部分提到"在使用复杂结构的时候可能会频繁出错，但这些错误很少会影响理解"。7 分评分标准的语法部分提到"频繁地说出没有错误的句子，但还是有一些语法错误存在"。绝大多数中国考生的口语目标分数是 6 或 6.5，有一小部分考生需要考到 7 分甚至更高。我们在平时练习口语的时候要尽量减少语法错误，因为过多的错误肯定会导致失分。但是在考试中应该以流利度为重，因为我们毕竟不需要做到语法完美。更重要的是，在口语表达中先要做到自然流畅地沟通，然后才能去思考语法是否完全无错。

🎤 不要纠结"加分词"

地道的、有亮点的词汇是可以给考生加分的，这一点我们在后文"词汇资源"部分会专门学习。但是，一些考生有"词汇至上"的想法，认为任何基本的、普通的、简单的词汇都需要进行替换，变成有亮点的加分词汇。这种想法很危险。

首先，考生无须把每个词都换成所谓的"加分词"，因为只要在考试中给出一些亮点词汇，向考官证明自己有很不错的词汇水平，就可以获得加分了。

另外，当考生想将一个普通词汇换成加分词汇时，如果对该加分词汇不够熟悉，则很有可能导致口语流利度的下降，因为考生需要更多时间思考。

所以建议大家，在不能自然快速地使用某个加分词的时候，使用普通词汇就好了。

不能为了给考官展示词汇而牺牲口语交流的流利度。

为了让自己放心地在大部分地方使用普通词汇，大家可以先把书翻到第 29～30 页，阅读一下词汇 6 分和 7 分的评分标准。我们可以看出，得到 6 分（大部分考生需要的口语分数）并不要求我们使用所谓的亮点词汇。7 分才有这样的要求。但是，你是不是应该先获得 6 分，然后再去冲击 7 分呢？

🎤 逻辑为王

考生在雅思口语考试中不是每道题只说一句话就够了，而是应该"能扩展则充分扩展（不能扩展则自信停下，但不能大部分都不扩展）"，这样考生才能在有限的 12～16 分钟内向考官充分证明自己的口语水平，能扩展答案而不去做就等于在浪费机会。

在这种情况下，想要保证流利度，就需要考生在说完一句话后，立刻想到下一句话说什么，再下一句话说什么。这需要很好的逻辑能力作为支撑，用之前学过的内容来说，就是连贯性要好！

来学习真经派的逻辑训练！

提高雅思口语的逻辑能力并不难，我们在下面会学习一些扩展方法，教会大家如何从前一句话"推"到后一句话。我们先来看一段回答：

Q **Can you tell me something about your hometown?**

A: Yes, sure. My hometown is Beijing and it has a long history. I mean, it's over 3,000 years old and because of that, there are many places of historical importance here, like the Great Wall, the Summer Palace, the Forbidden City and so on. Out of these places, the most famous one is absolutely the Great Wall because people from all around the world know it and also if you go to the Great Wall, you will see that it's usually very crowded…

词汇 Key Words

place of historical importance 古迹；具有历史
   重要性的地方

out of… 在……当中

all around the world 全世界

crowded ['kraʊdɪd] *adj.* 拥挤的

我们现在来分析一下这个相对较长的答案是如何扩展下去的：

long history ⟶ 多长？3,000 years ⟶ 表现？many places of historical importance ⟶ 哪些？the Great Wall, the Summer Palace, the Forbidden City… ⟶ 最有名？the Great Wall ⟶ 怎么证明？people from all around the world + crowded

通过这个答案，我们大致可以了解什么叫"一句推一句"了。

到底怎么"推"？剑桥雅思官方建议考生在回答问题时，通过"原因""举例""对比""个人经历"等扩展自己的回答。我们根据官方的指导总结出了如下简单高效的逻辑扩展。

🎙 我们推荐：少说原因

这可能会让很多考生感觉困惑，毕竟说 "because…" 基本上是一种下意识的反应了——任何一道题的第二句都是以 because 开头的。其实，我的意思并不是不能说原因，而是建议大家不要永远都让自己给出原因，因为这是一种较为抽象的思维方式，在答题时需要更多的思考，随之而来的便是流利度的降低。如：

回答 "What colour is your favourite?" 这道题时，如果我说 "I like purple the most"，然后添加更为具体化的扩展 "I have quite a lot of clothes that are purple, like the T-shirt I'm wearing now, a hoodie that I bought last weekend and so on." 就较为简单；但如果我的扩展是 "because…"，答案便相对较难想到，流利度也会下降。

所以，不是完全不说原因。当你立刻想到一个 reason 的时候，完全可以快速添加，但不要在这里纠缠太久，尽量快速进入具体化扩展的部分。或者，可以直接略过原因，在表达观点后立刻进入更为具体、细节的内容。

🎙 最为简单、直接、有效的扩展——宽泛到具体

My hometown is Beijing and it has a long history. I mean, it's over 3,000 years old and because of that, there are many places of historical importance here, like the Great Wall, the Summer Palace, the Forbidden City and so on. Out of these places, the most famous one is absolutely the Great Wall because people from all around the world know it and also if you go to the Great Wall, you will see that it's usually very crowded…

在这段回答中，便有不少"具体"。3,000 years old 是相对于 a long history 的具体；the Great Wall, the Summer Palace, the Forbidden City and so on 是相对于 many places of historical importance 的具体；the most famous one 是对前面三个列举出来的地方的更具体扩展。

若想口语水平快速提高，掌握"宽泛到具体"的方法最为重要！

如何将宽泛的内容变成具体的内容呢？我们通过一些句子来进行分析：

e.g. **taking photos of picturesque scenery is my favourite**

宽泛：picturesque scenery

具体：the sunset, flowers in the countryside and some lakes in my hometown

更具体：flowers in the countryside

更更具体：chrysanthemums

更更更具体：some chrysanthemums near my grandparents' house

串联成一个段落：Taking photos of picturesque scenery is my favourite. Um, I take photos of the sunset, flowers in the countryside and some lakes in my hometown. I think I particularly like those flowers in the country, especially all the chrysanthemums, which are so beautiful and…whenever I go and visit my grandparents, and see some chrysanthemums near their house, I snap dozens of pictures of them.

词汇 Key Words

picturesque [ˌpɪktʃə'resk] *adj.* 风景如画的	in the countryside = in the country 在乡下
take photos = snap pictures 拍照	chrysanthemum [krɪ'sænθəməm] *n.* 菊花
sunset ['sʌnset] *n.* 日落	dozens of… 几十个……

这是一个经过充分扩展的段落，方法只用了"宽泛到具体"。至于它可以应对什么题目，其实并不重要。不少同学将题目作为自己口语备考的核心，这是错误的。题目并不重要，我们能够说出

什么样的英文最为重要。提升自己的能力，去应对各种题目。比如，上面这个段落中的内容（无须完整内容）其实可以用来回答很多问题：

Do you like taking photos?

What do you often do to relax?

How do you spend your weekend?

Do you like the city or the countryside?

What do you like to do during public holidays?

除了口语 Part 1 题目，相同的方法也照样可以用到 Part 2 和 Part 3 的回答中。唯一的区别是，上面这个段落的内容是在聊个人生活，它适用于 Part 1 和 Part 2，不太适用于 Part 3，因为这个部分需要考生谈论整体性、社会化、抽象的内容。

e.g. **I spend an hour listening to music every day**

宽泛：every day

具体：in the morning

更具体：on my way to work

宽泛：music

具体：hip-hop, R&B and Jazz

更具体：Lee Hom（R&B singer）

更更具体：《龙的传人》（a Chinese song, translated as *Descendants of the Dragon*）

串联成一个段落：I spend an hour listening to music every day and it usually happens in the morning…
on my way to work, actually, coz it takes me about an hour to get to work by subway
and that's a perfect time to listen to some music, like hip-hop, R&B and Jazz. Oh, the
singer I like the most is Lee Hom, who is an R&B musician and his song《龙的传人》…
Descendants of the Dragon, I think, is what I have to listen to every day…

词汇 **Key Words**

R&B 节奏布鲁斯，蓝调音乐	musician [mjʊˈzɪʃn] *n.* 音乐人，音乐家
Jazz [dʒæz] *n.* 爵士乐	descendant [dɪˈsendənt] *n.* 后代，子孙，传人

注意：我们现在是在练习"宽泛到具体"的扩展能力，而不是要求大家一定要在一个回答中完整说出这一大段内容。这个段落可以被拆分、组合为多个 Part 1 答案或 Part 2 答案中的某一个部分。

e.g. **I use social media on a daily basis**

宽泛：social media

具体：Weibo, WeChat, Douyin and so forth

宽泛：on a daily basis

具体：every night, before going to bed

更具体：scroll through Douyin videos

更更具体：videos that teach English

更更更具体：videos by 帅哥（哎，帅哥现在不在抖音发展了……）

更更更具体：帅哥's videos that help students improve their pronunciation

更更更更具体：还没完没了了？！

串联成一个段落：I use social media on a daily basis. There are a few sites and Apps that I really like, including Weibo, WeChat, Douyin and so forth. Every night, for example, I use Douyin for a while before going to bed, um…to scroll through some videos, especially those that teach English. My favourite teacher on Douyin is 帅哥, who always shares some tips on how to improve pronunciation…

词汇 Key Words

on a daily basis 每天	scroll through videos 刷视频
site [saɪt] *n.* 网站（＝website）	tip [tɪp] *n.* 窍门，指点
App [æp] *abbr.* 应用程序	

e.g. **coffee is part and parcel of my life**

宽泛：coffee

具体：black coffee

宽泛：life

具体：every day

更具体：every morning

更更具体：get up at 6:30

串联成一个段落：Coffee is part and parcel of my life and I definitely have it every single day. I usually get up at 6:30 in the morning and the first thing I do is go to the kitchen and brew a cup of coffee…black coffee, most of the time, coz it's the best in terms of helping me wake up.

词汇 Key Words

part and parcel of sth. ……的重要部分	in terms of sth. 在……方面，就……而言
brew [bru:] *v.* 沏（茶），冲（咖啡）	wake up 醒来

e.g. **parks are places where people go to do exercise**

宽泛：parks

具体：a park close to my home

更具体：300 metres away

宽泛：people

具体：middle-aged and elderly people

更具体：my grandparents

宽泛：exercise

具体：take a walk, do tai chi, play badminton and so on

更具体：tai chi is something that my grandpa has done for 20 years

串联成一个段落：Parks are places where people go to do exercise, particularly middle-aged and elderly people, I would say. They often go to parks to take a walk, do tai chi, play badminton and so on. For instance, my grandparents go to the park close to our home on a regular basis, and my grandma takes a stroll there, and my grandpa does tai chi, which has been one of his passions for at least 20 years.

词汇 Key Words

middle-aged ['mɪdleɪdʒd] *adj.* 中年的	(be) close to... 离……很近
elderly ['eldəlɪ] *adj.* 老年的	on a regular basis 定期，经常
take a walk = take a stroll 遛弯	passion ['pæʃn] *n.* 热衷的爱好，酷爱的事物

以上的段落都并非单个题目的答案，但方法和理念却可以用到雅思口语任何一个部分及题目中。

主动添加信息——时间、地点、人物、事件、感受

先来看一道帅哥曾经在口语考试中遇到的题目：**How often do you do physical exercise?** 这道题问的是 "How often"（频率/时间），但在答题时，除了回答频率/时间，我们还可以添加 "在哪里、和谁、做什么、感受如何" 等信息。如：

A: I work out on a daily basis and most of the time, I like to run on the treadmill in my apartment, and sometimes, I might go jogging in the park with some of my friends. I think exercising daily is a good habit and it has helped me keep fit and stay in shape.

时间：on a daily basis

地点：in my apartment, in the park

人物：I, my friends

事件：running, jogging

感受：a good habit, keep fit and stay in shape

词汇 Key Words

treadmill ['tredmɪl] *n.* 跑步机

go jogging 去慢跑

keep fit 保持健康

stay in shape 保持身材

如果题目不是 "How often do you do physical exercise?"，而是 "**Where do you do physical exercise?**"，答案是否可以基本相同呢？

A: I like to work out in my apartment, or sometimes I go to the park. The form of exercise I often do is running, so I can run on the treadmill or in the park close to my apartment…alone or with some of my friends. I think exercising daily, wherever it is, is a good habit and it has helped me keep fit and stay in shape.

如果问题是 "**Who do you often do physical exercise with?**" 呢？

A: I like to do some exercise alone or with my friends. When I'm running on the treadmill in my apartment, I do it alone, of course. But sometimes, I also go jogging in the park with some of my closest friends. Whichever it is, exercising daily is a good habit and it has helped me keep fit and stay in shape.

如果问题不是关于 physical exercise 呢？

What do you like to do on the weekend?

How do you spend your morning time?

What's your favourite way to relax?

Are there any parks near your home?

…………

在回答这些问题时，我们都可以用到和前面答案类似的内容。需要注意的是，在口语考试中，题目并不是我们最应该关注的，自己能说出的英文才是我们最该关注的——扎根自身，辐射众多题目！

当然，我们无须在任何题目中都充分使用 "时间、地点、人物、事件、感受" 这五个元素。很多时候，我们只需要使用两个、三个、四个，并且，我们还可以随时把之前练习过的 "宽泛到具体" 添加到答案中。

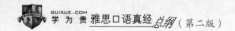

Q Which public holiday do you like most?

A: The one I like most is the National Day holiday when we all have seven days off, and I like to take advantage of that time to do some travelling, with my college classmates, most of the time. We particularly like to go to places off the beaten track and…it's a great time and opportunity for us to get away and relax.

时间：National Day holiday

地点：places off the beaten track

事件：do some travelling

人物：college classmates

感受：get away and relax

词汇 Key Words

National Day 国庆节

have…days off 休息……天

take advantage of sth. 利用……

places off the beaten track 人迹罕至的地方

get away 离开；外出度假

Q Did you learn anything about wild animals at school?

A: Yeah, I did. I remember when I was in primary school…I must have been a third grader, and in a PE class…um, it's interesting that I learned stuff about wild animals from a PE teacher…um, he talked about how cheetahs are the fastest animals on earth and I was really fascinated by what he said.

时间：primary school, when I was a third grader

地点：PE class

人物：PE teacher

事件：talked about cheetahs

感受：fascinated

词汇 Key Words

a third grader 一个三年级学生

cheetah ['tʃiːtə] *n.* 猎豹

fascinated ['fæsɪneɪtɪd] *adj.* 着迷的；极感兴趣的

Q Have you ever planted trees before?

A: Let me think…Yeah, I have. I remember when I was in primary school…I must have been a third grader, and one day, we were taken to a hill about 5 kilometres from our school and planted some trees together with some of our teachers. Although it was really tiring, I still had a blast that day.

时间：primary school, when I was a third grader, one day

地点：a hill

人物：some of our teachers

事件：planted some trees

感受：tiring, had a blast

> **词汇** Key Words
>
> tiring ['taɪərɪŋ] *adj.* 令人疲倦的　　　　　　have a blast 玩得开心

我们也可以在给出一些答案之后继续添加 "时间、地点、人物、事件、感受"，来证明之前所说内容的真实性。在这时，我们可以用 "过去" 来证明，也可以用 "将来" 来证明。如：

Q How often do you take a rest?

A: Well, I take a break from work every hour or so and usually, standing up and doing some stretches helps me recover and relax a bit.

Oh, this is what I did this morning. I was working on a report and trying to get it done before noon, coz I was coming here in the afternoon for the test. Um, after working for a little over an hour, I decided to take a breather and stretched my arms and back. I felt pretty good.

时间：this morning

人物：I

事件：working on a report, stretched my arms and back

感受：felt good

> **词汇** Key Words
>
> take a rest = take a break = take a breather 休息　　　do some stretches 做做拉伸运动
> 一下　　　　　　　　　　　　　　　　　　　　　　　　get it done 做完它
> every hour or so 每隔一小时左右

Q What is the most popular animal in China?

A: Oh, it has to be the dog, which is most people's favourite pet, and you can see folks walking dogs all the time.

I went to the park yesterday evening and while walking there, I guess I saw at least 20 dogs… different breeds, like Corgis and…I don't know the names of other breeds, sorry. But yeah, there were so many of them and that definitely shows how popular dogs are in China.

时间：yesterday evening

地点：park

事件：saw many dogs

词汇 Key Words

folks [fəʊks] *n.* 人们

Q **Do you like to read at home or in other places?**

A: My preference is to read in our school library. I just feel that when I'm surrounded by people who are also reading, that gives me motivation to keep going.

Speaking of this, I'm definitely going to that library again tomorrow morning to get started on a book I bought a couple of days ago. I will most likely go there alone coz I'll go pretty early. I hope I will enjoy this book and my time in the library tomorrow.

时间：tomorrow morning

地点：library

人物：I

事件：read a book

感受：I hope I will enjoy…

词汇 Key Words

preference ['prefrəns] *n.* 偏好，偏爱

be surrounded by... 被……围绕

motivation [ˌməʊtɪ'veɪʃn] *n.* 动力

a couple of 两个，两三个

most likely 很有可能

Q **Have you ever bought shoes online?**

A: No, I haven't. All of the shoes I've owned were bought in physical stores because I had to try them on before buying them.

Oh, this reminds me. I'm actually going to buy a pair of sneakers this weekend for gym, and there's no doubt that I'm going to a brick-and-mortar store, Nike or Adidas. Hopefully, I'll find a good pair.

时间：this weekend

地点：a brick-and-mortar store, Nike or Adidas

人物：I

事件：buy a pair of sneakers

感受：Hopefully, I'll find a good pair.

词汇 Key Words

physical store = brick-and-mortar store 实体店

try sth. on 试穿……

sneakers ['sniːkəz] *n.* 运动鞋

gym [dʒɪm] *n.* 体育活动；健身（这里不可数）

there's no doubt... 毋庸置疑……

hopefully ['həʊpfəlɪ] *adv.* 希望，但愿

对比

在扩展答案的过程中，我们也可以主动使用"对比"，使自己的回答扩展得更加充分，通过展示一些"比较"的语言，证明自己的高分语法水平。

常用词汇和句型：

but 但是

however 然而

whereas = while 然而

compared to... 与……相比

unlike... 不像……

by comparison = in comparison 相比之下

by contrast = in contrast 相比之下

A is much/far/a lot more...than B　A 比 B……得多

A is not as...as B　A 没有 B 那么……

通过对比进行扩展时，我们有多种方式可以使用。如：自己 vs. 别人，某个 vs. 其他，现在 vs. 过去，中国 vs. 外国……

Q　What do you like about your neighbourhood?

A: Well, off the top of my head, it should be the fact that there's a subway station only 300 metres away, which makes it super convenient for me to go anywhere by subway.

对比：One of my friends lives in the southwestern suburb of the city where there's no subway station at all. He always complains about the lack of public transportation in his neck of the woods. I think I'm much luckier.

词汇 Key Words

off the top of my head 我立刻想到的是

the lack of public transportation 没有公共交通

in his neck of the woods 在他所在的区域

Q What was your favourite subject in high school?

A: Well, it must have been Chinese. I guess it's because of my Chinese teacher, who was hilarious and knowledgeable and…most importantly, she was very good-looking, haha.

对比：By comparison, my math teacher was…what's the word? Um, his lessons were rather mind-numbing. He never told any jokes in class and so I don't think his class was as interesting as Chinese.

词汇 Key Words

hilarious [hɪ'leərɪəs] *adj.* 滑稽的；极有趣的

knowledgeable ['nɒlɪdʒəbl] *adj.* 知识丰富的

mind-numbing ['maɪndnʌmɪŋ] *adj.* 无聊的

Q How many hours do you sleep?

A: Oh, this is a sad question, because I'm only able to get 6 hours' sleep every day, which is far from enough. I've been very busy since the beginning of this semester and so I'm constantly sleep-deprived.

对比：I used to sleep much more in middle school. At that time, I went to bed every day around 10 o'clock at night and got up at 7 a.m., which was awesome! Compared to that time, my life is miserable now.

词汇 Key Words

far from enough 远远不够

constantly ['kɒnstəntlɪ] *adv.* 不断地；一直地

sleep-deprived [sli:pdɪ'praɪvd] *adj.* 缺乏睡眠的

awesome ['ɔ:səm] *adj.* 非常棒的

miserable ['mɪzrəbl] *adj.* 悲惨的

Q Do you like watching advertisements?

A: No, I'm not a fan of them at all. Most adverts are pretty annoying, especially when they appear all of a sudden while I'm watching a show that I really like.

对比：But, in fact, when I was a kid, I used to really like watching some commercials, coz I found many of them interesting.

词汇 Key Words

annoying [ə'nɔɪɪŋ] *adj.* 令人很烦的

all of a sudden 突然

commercial [kə'mɜ:ʃl] *n.* 电视广告

Q Do you have a pet?

A: No, I don't have a pet. I love small and adorable animals, but my apartment is rather cramped, and there's not enough room for me to keep a kitten or puppy.

对比：When I was a teenager, however, I had a dog. It was really cute, and I would feed it, play with it and walk it in the park every day. Sadly, it was run over by a car when I was 17.

词汇 Key Words

adorable [ə'dɔ:rəbl] *adj.* 可爱的（ = cute）	puppy ['pʌpɪ] *n.* 小狗
cramped [kræmpt] *adj.* 窄小的	feed [fi:d] *v.* 喂
kitten ['kɪtn] *n.* 小猫	

Q **What is the most popular extreme sport in your country?**

A: I'm not even sure if we have a popular extreme sport in China. Some people do go bungee-jumping, scuba-diving and surfing, but those people are few and far between—

对比：whereas these sports are far more popular in other countries like the US. I've seen quite a lot of shows that feature people engaging in extreme sports.

词汇 Key Words

bungee-jumping ['bʌndʒɪ'dʒʌmpɪŋ] *n.* 蹦极	few and far between 稀少的
scuba-diving ['skju:bə'daɪvɪŋ] *n.* 潜水	feature sth. 以……为主要内容，重点介绍……
surfing ['sɜ:fɪŋ] *n.* 冲浪	engage in sth. 参加……

🎙 虚拟语气

　　使用虚拟语气同样是一种实用的扩展方法，还可以向考官证明自己强大的语法能力。很多考生觉得虚拟语气是一个非常复杂的语法现象，不易学习、容易犯错。其实不然，只要大家掌握了基本的虚拟语气句型，就可以很好地应用它了。偶尔犯一些小错误，也没有太大关系，毕竟只有少数考生的目标分数是 8 分以上。

　　在雅思口语考试中，我们一般会对"现在"进行虚拟。基本句型如下：

　　If…were/was/could/did…, …would/could… 如果……，那么……

　　I wish I were/was/could/did…Then, I would/could… 我真的希望……。那样的话，我……

　　It would be fantastic if I were/was/could/did… 如果我……就太好了！

Q **Would you want to be a teacher?**

A: No, I don't think so, because I'm a rather short-tempered person.

虚拟：<u>If I were</u> a teacher and <u>had</u> to deal with kids every day, I guess <u>I would</u> lose my temper all the time. <u>That wouldn't</u> be good for the kids or for me.

词汇 Key Words

short-tempered [ɔ:t'tempəd] *adj.* 脾气不好的，易怒的	deal with kids 应对孩子们
	lose one's temper 发脾气

Q **Do you often wear jewellry?**

A: No, I don't. One major reason is that the pieces of jewellry that I really like are too pricey, and I can't afford them. What I can afford are low in quality and I don't want to wear them.

虚拟：If I were wealthier, I would buy many high-quality necklaces and bracelets and earrings. I would wear them every day. I believe others would envy me a lot. That would make me feel great!

词汇 Key Words

pricey ['praɪsɪ] *adj.* 昂贵的

can't afford 买不起

low in quality 质量差的

high-quality [haɪ'kwɒlətɪ] *adj.* 高质量的

necklace ['nekləs] *n.* 项链

bracelet ['breɪslət] *n.* 手镯；手链

earring ['ɪərɪŋ] *n.* 耳环

envy ['envɪ] *v.* 羡慕

Q **What's your favourite form of transport?**

A: Well, my favourite should be driving, but I don't drive very often, because I don't have a car now. I'm not a local and so I'm not allowed to buy a car. This is why I take the bus every day, which is super uncomfortable.

虚拟：I wish I could buy a car here. Then, I would drive it every day. It would be fantastic if I could sit in my car, listen to music and smoke a cigarette without having to fight for space on a crowded bus.

词汇 Key Words

a local 当地人

be allowed to do sth. 被允许做某事

Q **Is there anything you don't like about your hometown?**

A: Oh, off the top of my head, it must be the fact that it's a sleepy place. By that I mean, there's not much fun going on here. We don't have many malls, cinemas, karaoke bars…

对比/虚拟：You know, I wish my hometown were more vibrant and dynamic. I wish there were more malls here so that I could go shopping every weekend with my friends. We would have more things to do and enjoy our lives more.

词汇 Key Words

sleepy ['sliːpɪ] *adj.* 寂静的；死气沉沉的

go on 发生

vibrant and dynamic 充满生气的，活跃的

Q **How often do you spend time with your family?**

A: Oh, we don't spend time very often, because we live extremely far away from each other. We only see each other once or twice a year.

对比 / 虚拟：It would be fantastic if my parents agreed to move to where I'm living. Then, we would hang out every day, chat with each other, and play mahjong together. I could go shopping with my mom and she could help me pick out shoes. The problem is, they don't want to move.

以上便是在口语考试中最为常见及简单的扩展方法——宽泛到具体；时间、地点、人物、事件、感受；对比；虚拟。

同学们一定还见过其他各种扩展方法，但是上述的几种是最简单，也是在考试中最实用的。较为复杂的扩展方法需要考生在回答时投入更多思考时间，这势必会降低流利度，并占用考生思考词汇和语法的时间。

另外，一定要注意：大家在前面看到的范例答案都比较长（对于 Part 1 来说），因为这是在通过简单的题目学习和练习较为强大的扩展能力。在真正的口语考试中，大家也可以对一些 Part 1 题目给出较长的答案，即便被考官打断也没有关系（除非你的答案是提前背诵的）。不过，对于一些较难或不易扩展的题目，即使没有充分扩展答案，也没有关系。要秉承"能扩展则充分扩展，不能扩展则自信停下"的宗旨去应对 Part 1。

虽然前面的大部分例题都来自 Part 1，但这些方法同样适用于 Part 2 和 Part 3。

(((Lexical Resource 词汇资源

即使你是金山词霸，也不一定能在雅思口语考试中拿到高分。口语是语言的输出，是语言的运用。

所以，口语考试讲究的不是词汇量有多大，而是运用词汇的能力有多强，看谁把词汇用得好、用得妙、用得地道。我们重点讨论口语 6 分和 7 分所对应的词汇要求。

Band 6	• Has a wide enough vocabulary to discuss topics at length and make meaning clear in spite of inappropriateness. 有充足的词汇量来详细谈论不同话题；虽然有词汇使用不当的情况出现，但是可以保证表达清晰。 • Generally paraphrases successfully. 当表达较为复杂的概念的时候，通常可以使用较为简单的语言转述成功。

Band 7

- Uses vocabulary resource flexibly to discuss a variety of topics.

  能够灵活使用词汇资源来谈论多种不同话题。

- Uses some less common and idiomatic vocabulary and shows some awareness of style and collocation, with some inappropriate choices.

  能够使用一些非常见词汇及习语表达，并可以很好地使用词组搭配，有时会出现表达不恰当的情况。

- Uses paraphrase effectively.

  当表达较为复杂的概念的时候，可以很好地使用较为简单的语言转述。

真经教学

1. 考生需要具备一定的词汇量，能够谈论不同话题。尤其要专注雅思口语中的高频话题和当季热门考试话题的相关核心词汇。

2. 当考生发现自己无法表达某些复杂概念的时候，不应过于纠结，而是应当使用自己已有的词汇将该概念进行转述，把自己想表达的事情说清楚即可。过于纠结自己不熟悉的某个词汇会影响流利度。

3. 想考雅思口语高分的考生，应该在备考期间积累一些"非常见词汇"、"词组搭配"和"习语表达"；目标分数只是 6 分的考生，也可以尽可能积累这三类词汇，以保证自己的词汇分数。但是，当考生试图使用自己不熟悉的某个词汇而导致流利度下降的时候，应放弃使用该词汇来保证流利度。

注意：词汇 7 分评分标准中提到的 idiomatic vocabulary 不仅包含 idioms（习语），也包括其他很多地道的英文词汇，即对于母语者来说听起来非常自然的词汇表达。这种词汇很难进行归类，不少母语者也难以说清究竟哪些才算是 idiomatic vocabulary。所以，在本书中，我们只总结学习 idioms（习语）。同学们可以通过书中众多例句和范例答案学习更多的地道词汇。

对于"非常见词汇"、"词组搭配"和"习语表达"的积累，不应过于追求数量，因为背诵过多的东西可能导致的结果是无法熟练使用这些表达。所以，我们给大家总结了"三十组同义形容词"、"四十五个动词词组"和"四十二个习语"。大家把这些表达熟练背诵，反复朗读例句，并多思考如何将它们使用到雅思口语话题中。

在练习使用这些地道词汇的时候，大家可以使用一种"逆推"的方式，即在学习了一个词汇之后，立刻思考它可以被使用到哪些雅思口语话题中。确定了可以使用的话题或题目，就将词汇带入自己的回答中，做到脱口而出。这种输出的过程非常重要，因为只有对一个词汇真正使用过几次，才能在以后的口语表达中不经过任何思考就能用上它。

🎤 三十组同义形容词

雅思口语 7 分以上评分标准词汇部分提到考生应能使用非常见词汇（less common vocabulary），这有利于提高考生的词汇分数。什么是"非常见词汇"呢？其实就是那些我们非常了解的简单词汇的替换词汇。如，beautiful 是常见词汇，它可以被替换为非常见词汇 gorgeous、picturesque 等。大家不要把"非常见词汇"想得太难，认为它们就是我们看都看不懂、根本不认识的词汇。事实上，"非常见词汇"也可以很简单。

笔者建议：在雅思口语考试中，如果可以，尽量用不同的词汇表达相同的意思，这能够体现出大家的词汇多样性，避免用词重复，进而提高口语分数。但是，请注意，当你使用替换词汇时，如果思考的时间太久，影响你的流利度，请一定使用简单、普通的词汇。

再次强调，即便是简单、普通的词汇，也完全可以在考试中使用！我们可以对词汇进行替换，但大部分时候还是会使用那些常见词汇，这能保证我们沟通的自然和流畅。

下面，请大家学习英语中最常见的三十组同义形容词。

① 困难的

常见词汇：hard, difficult

非常见词汇：tough, tricky

e.g. Oh, um, this is indeed a very **tough** question and I've never thought about it before.（tough 难办的；难解决的）（当碰到一个很难的题目，需要思考一会儿的时候，可以用这句话来拖延时间。）

e.g. Parking can be **tricky** in my hometown as there are so many cars and so few parking spots.（tricky 难办的；棘手的）

词汇 Key Words

parking ['pɑːkɪŋ] *n.* 停车　　　　　　parking spot 停车位

② 简单的

常见词汇：easy

非常见词汇：effortless

e.g. I'm not sure about other people, but to me, learning how to ride a bike was **effortless**.（effortless 容易的；不费力的）

③ 富有的

常见词汇：rich, wealthy

非常见词汇：affluent, well-to-do

e.g. Chinese people are becoming more and more **affluent**, so an increasing number of people go travelling overseas now. (affluent 富裕的，富有的)

词汇 Key Words

an increasing number of 越来越多的 | travel overseas 出国旅游

e.g. I wasn't born into a **well-to-do** family, so my childhood was kind of hard. (well-to-do 富裕的，有钱的)

词汇 Key Words

be born into... 出生在……(的家庭) | kind of 有点

④ 好的

常见词汇：good

非常见词汇：awesome, superb, impressive

e.g. I watched the movie *Doctor Who* last weekend and it was **awesome**. (awesome 很好的)

e.g. George Clooney's movies are **superb**. I can't believe how talented he is. (superb 极佳的；卓越的)

词汇 Key Words

talented ['tæləntɪd] *adj.* 有才华的

e.g. The rice terraces in Yunnan are really **impressive**. (impressive 给人以深刻印象的；了不起的)

词汇 Key Words

rice terrace 梯田

⑤ 难以置信的

常见词汇：unbelievable

非常见词汇：incredible

e.g. He's gone skydiving a couple of times, which I think is truly **incredible**. (incredible 难以置信的；了不起的)

词汇 Key Words

skydiving ['skaɪdaɪvɪŋ] *n.* 高空跳伞

⑥ 坏的，不好的，糟糕的

常见词汇：bad

非常见词汇：awful, dreadful

e.g. The air quality in Beijing used to be **awful**.（awful 让人讨厌的；糟糕的）

e.g. The traffic is **dreadful** in my hometown. People are always stuck in the middle of a traffic jam for a long time.（dreadful 糟糕透顶的）

词汇 Key Words

be stuck in the middle of a traffic jam 被堵在路上

⑦ 好吃的

常见词汇：delicious, tasty

非常见词汇：scrumptious, palatable

e.g. The sushi I had last week was **scrumptious**.（scrumptious 美味的，可口的）

e.g. My favourite food is spaghetti. I think it's so **palatable**.（palatable 美味的，可口的）

词汇 Key Words

spaghetti [spə'getɪ] *n.* 意大利式细面条

⑧ 漂亮的，好看的

常见词汇：beautiful

非常见词汇：gorgeous, pretty, picturesque

e.g. I bought a really **gorgeous** dress yesterday and I love it a lot.［gorgeous 漂亮的（人或物）］

e.g. My niece is a **pretty** little girl and everyone likes her.［pretty 漂亮的，好看的（通常指人，尤其是女孩）］

e.g. Tibet is such a **picturesque** place and many people in China long to go there.（picturesque 风景如画的）

词汇 Key Words

long to do sth. 渴望做某事

⑨ 饥饿的

常见词汇：hungry

非常见词汇：starving, famished

e.g. We had been waiting for our food for half an hour and it still hadn't been served. We were **starving**.（starving 饿极了的）

e.g. I suffered from insomnia and I didn't fall asleep until 3:00 in the morning. Then, I felt **famished**, so I just got up and went to a KFC.（famished 饿极了的）

词汇 Key Words

suffer from insomnia 失眠　　　　　　　fall asleep 入睡

⑩ 口渴的

常见词汇：thirsty

非常见词汇：parched

e.g. I was so **parched** yesterday that I bought a Coke and drank it all in one minute.（parched 干渴的）

词汇 Key Words

a Coke 一瓶可乐

⑪ 高兴的

常见词汇：happy

非常见词汇：overjoyed, ecstatic

e.g. I was **overjoyed** when the girl I had a crush on said she loved me.（overjoyed 欣喜若狂的，万分高兴的）

词汇 Key Words

have a crush on sb. 暗中喜欢某人

e.g. I felt **ecstatic** when I found out that my boyfriend had booked two plane tickets for us to go to Sanya.（ecstatic 狂喜的，欣喜若狂的）

⑫ 沮丧的

常见词汇：upset

非常见词汇：deflated, despondent

e.g. I felt rather **deflated** when my mom said we wouldn't go anywhere during the holiday.（deflated 沮丧的；灰心的）

e.g. I found out that the girl I loved already had a boyfriend. I was **despondent** for a whole week.（despondent 沮丧的；失望的）

⑬ 长时间的

常见词汇：long

非常见词汇：lengthy

e.g. It was such a **lengthy** meeting that I almost fell asleep in the middle of it.（lengthy 漫长的；冗长的）

⑭ 困倦的

常见词汇：sleepy

非常见词汇：groggy, bleary-eyed

e.g. I felt **groggy** the whole morning. It was awful.［groggy（因疲劳）昏昏沉沉的；困倦的］

e.g. I was so **bleary-eyed** yesterday afternoon, so I bought a cup of coffee from the café downstairs.［bleary-eyed（因困倦）视线模糊的］

⑮ 生气的

常见词汇：angry

非常见词汇：mad, peeved

e.g. My neighbours kept making noise the entire day and that made me really **mad**.（mad 愤怒的，非常生气的）

e.g. We waited an hour for our food and I was **peeved** about it.（peeved 恼怒的，气恼的）

⑯ 安静的

常见词汇：quiet

非常见词汇：peaceful, tranquil, serene

e.g. Where I live is a **peaceful** part of town and this is the reason I chose this particular place.（peaceful 宁静的，平静的）

e.g. The park near my home is **tranquil** and beautiful.（tranquil 宁静的，安静的）

e.g. I was on holiday in Fiji for a week. I really loved the **serene** atmosphere there.（serene 宁静的，平静的）

词汇 Key Words

on holiday 度假

17 寒冷的

常见词汇：cold

非常见词汇：freezing (cold), bitterly cold

e.g. It was **freezing cold** in Harbin and so I put on six layers of clothes. [freezing (cold) 极冷的]

词汇 Key Words

layer ['leɪə(r)] *n.* 层

e.g. It's **bitterly cold** in my hometown in the winter and the temperature can be as low as minus 20 degrees.（bitterly cold 极冷的）

词汇 Key Words

minus ['maɪnəs] *adj.* 零下的

18 热的

常见词汇：hot

非常见词汇：scorching (hot)

e.g. I don't like the fact that it's **scorching hot** in the summer. I only want to be at home with the air conditioner on. [scorching (hot) 极热的]

词汇 Key Words

air conditioner 空调

19 重要的

常见词汇：important

非常见词汇：vital, crucial

e.g. Museums are absolutely **vital** in cities.（vital 必要的；至关重要的）

e.g. It's **crucial** that we take some time off once in a while to recharge our batteries.（crucial 至关重

要的）

词汇 Key Words

take some time off 休息一段时间

recharge one's batteries 放松；补充精力

20 有意思的，有吸引力的

常见词汇：interesting

非常见词汇：fascinating, captivating, gripping

e.g. My favourite teacher was Mr. Zhao, our history teacher. Whatever he said was really **fascinating**. （fascinating 迷人的，极有吸引力的）

e.g. My all-time favourite TV show is the *Ellen Show*, which is a **captivating** talk show.（captivating 迷人的，极有吸引力的）

词汇 Key Words

all-time favourite 一直以来最喜欢的

e.g. That book is so **gripping** that I just can't put it down.（gripping 迷人的，极有吸引力的）

词汇 Key Words

can't put it down（好看到）停不下来

21 大的

常见词汇：big

非常见词汇：gigantic, huge, spacious

e.g. The building we visited was **gigantic**.（gigantic 巨大的，庞大的）

e.g. My hometown has a **huge** population. If I'm not mistaken, there are about 10 million people here.（huge 巨大的，极大的）

e.g. The apartment I live in now is quite **spacious**. I mean, it's about 150 square metres in size. （spacious 广阔的，宽敞的）

22 小的

常见词汇：small

非常见词汇：tiny, cramped

e.g. I remember the gift I loved the most at that birthday party was a **tiny** bike which was given to me by my aunt.（tiny 非常小的）

e.g. My bedroom is pretty **cramped**, so I'm thinking of moving to a bigger place.（cramped 狭小的）

㉓ 有名的

常见词汇：famous, well-known

非常见词汇：renowned, celebrated

e.g. Jolin is a singer from Taiwan who is **renowned** for her great voice.（renowned 有名的；有声望的）

e.g. I idolise Jacky, a **celebrated** actor and martial artist. I really admire his tenacity and persistence.（celebrated 有名的；受人敬仰的）

词汇 Key Words

idolise ['aɪdəlaɪz] *v.* 把……当作偶像崇拜

martial artist 武术家

tenacity [tɪ'næsɪtɪ] *n.* 坚毅

persistence [pə'sɪstəns] *n.* 毅力；锲而不舍

㉔ 流行的

常见词汇：popular

非常见词汇：well-liked

e.g. Singing karaoke is a **well-liked** leisure activity in my country.（well-liked 流行的；深受喜欢的）

词汇 Key Words

sing karaoke 唱卡拉 OK

㉕ 知识丰富的

常见词汇：knowledgeable

非常见词汇：well-read

e.g. My dad is a **well-read** person. Every time I ask him a question, he knows the answer.［well-read 博览群书的；博学的（这里的 read 是过去分词，读音和 red 相同）］

㉖ 无聊的

常见词汇：boring

非常见词汇：dull, mind-numbing

e.g. I found math rather **dull**. No matter how hard I tried, I couldn't get into it.（dull 无聊的，枯燥无味的）

e.g. My history teacher was really **mind-numbing**. She was my least favourite teacher in high school.（mind-numbing 超级无聊的）

27 苗条的

常见词汇：thin

非常见词汇：slender, statuesque

e.g. Alice is a **slender** girl who is really well-liked in my class.（slender 苗条的）

e.g. She is a **statuesque** lady and looks attractive all the time.［statuesque（女性）高挑挺拔的］

28 肥胖的

常见词汇：fat

非常见词汇：chubby, pudgy

e.g. Junk food is extremely popular with kids and we can always see a lot of **chubby** children.（chubby 肥胖的；圆滚滚的）

e.g. My friends always teased me by saying I was **pudgy**, so I decided to lose weight.（pudgy 微胖的）

词汇 Key Words

tease sb. 取笑某人	lose weight 减肥

29 老的

常见词汇：old

非常见词汇：old-fashioned, run-down

e.g. While on holiday in Lijiang, we stayed in an **old-fashioned** inn, which I found to be quite interesting.（old-fashioned 老式的；不时髦的）

词汇 Key Words

inn [ɪn] n. 小客栈	find sth. (to be) 觉得……（怎么样）

e.g. I used to live in a **run-down** area when I was growing up.［run-down（建筑物、地区）破旧不堪的；失修的］

30 流行的

常见词汇：fashionable

非常见词汇：chic, trendy

e.g. My favourite piece of clothing is a dress which is **chic** and beautiful. [chic 时髦的（注意这个词的读音 [ʃiːk]）]

词汇 Key Words

a piece of clothing 一件衣服

e.g. There's a **trendy**-looking café quite close to my home and I go there pretty often.（trendy 时髦的，时尚的）

实战使用

不少同学碰到的一个问题是，明明背了一些替换词汇，但考试的时候第一反应还是那个最基本、简单的词。其实，我们在考试中不仅可以给出第一反应，也可以说出第二反应。

e.g. I've been to Harbin and it was so cold when I was there…absolutely **freezing**.

e.g. Her acting in the movie is really bad, I mean, it's just **awful**!

e.g. This is a hard question. Seriously, it's the **toughest** I've ever heard.

🎙 四十五个动词词组

动词词组（phrasal verbs）是英语词汇的重要组成部分，它也是一种 idiomatic vocabulary。很多英语母语者会通过一个英语学习者对动词词组的掌握程度来判断此人的英语水平。

一个动词词组通常由一个动词和一个副词或介词（后接宾语）组成，如：grow apart、pass away、come across sb./sth. 等。如果介词后面需要添加的宾语是代词，则通常将这个代词放到动词和介词中间，如：give it up、call it off。但这条规则对于某些动词词组不适用，如：come across him、take after her 等。大家在学习中应该反复朗读、背诵例句，提升语感，当说到某个地方时，才能自然正确地使用某一个动词词组。

下面我们学习四十五个在雅思口语考试中很常用的动词词组。

① back sb. up 支持某人

　　e.g. No matter what I do, my wife **backs** me **up**.

② bring sb. up 抚养某人长大

　　e.g. People have different opinions on whether it's harder or easier to **bring up** kids today.

③ call sth. off 取消某事

e.g. I was shocked when Judy told me that she had **called off** her wedding.

词汇 Key Words

shocked [ʃɒkt] *adj.* 震惊的

④ not care for sth. 不喜欢某事

e.g. I don't **care for** cooking coz I find it pretty time-consuming.

词汇 Key Words

time-consuming [taɪm kən'sjuːmɪŋ] *adj.* 耗费时间的

⑤ carry sth. out 执行……，实施……

e.g. Those who diligently **carry out** tasks over a long period of time are the ones that become successful.

词汇 Key Words

diligently ['dɪlɪdʒəntlɪ] *adv.* 辛勤地　　　　　　a period of time 一段时间

over ['əʊvə(r)] *prep.* 在……期间

⑥ catch up (with sb.) 了解某人近况，与某人叙旧

e.g. We hadn't seen each other in 10 years, so we spent 3 hours **catching up**.

⑦ catch up on sth. 补上……，赶上……

e.g. I had a day off yesterday, so I was finally able to **catch up on** some sleep and then（catch up on）some shows that I really like.

⑧ cheer (sb.) up（使某人）高兴起来

e.g. I like to listen to some rap music to **cheer** myself **up** when I'm feeling down.

词汇 Key Words

down [daʊn] *adj.* 沮丧的；消沉的

⑨ come across sb./sth. 偶然碰到 / 遇到……

e.g. I'm glad that I **came across** this book because it has absolutely changed my life.

⑩ come up with sth. 想出……，提出……

e.g. Hopefully, politicians can **come up with** a good plan to deal with population aging.

词汇 Key Words

politician [ˌpɒlə'tɪʃn] *n.* 政客，政治家   population aging 人口老龄化

11 cut down on sth. 减少……

e.g. I'd better **cut down on** my sugar intake since I've been gaining too much weight in the last two years.

词汇 Key Words

intake ['ɪnteɪk] *n.* 摄入（量）   gain weight 增肥；增重

12 do away with sth. 废除……；终止……

e.g. Corporal punishment has been largely **done away with** in Chinese schools.

词汇 Key Words

corporal punishment 体罚

13 eat out 外出就餐

e.g. My family **eats out** once a week, and that's usually my favourite day of the week.

14 end up 最终成为……；最终处于某种状态

e.g. No one ever thought that my nephew would **end up** being so successful academically. He was slacking off every day in school!

词汇 Key Words

academically [ˌækə'demɪklɪ] *adv.* 在学术方面   slack off 松懈；懈怠

15 fall out (with sb.)（与某人）闹翻

e.g. We used to be best friends. Nobody could foresee that we would **fall out** over the issue of artificial intelligence. It was stupid.

词汇 Key Words

foresee [fɔ:'si:] *v.* 预见；预料   artificial intelligence 人工智能

over sth. 由于……

16 figure sth. out 弄明白；想清楚

e.g. Tackling climate change requires global efforts, so governments have to **figure out** a way to cooperate with each other.

词汇 Key Words

tackle ['tækl] *v.* 应对；解决

climate change 气候变化

global ['gləʊbl] *adj.* 全球的

effort ['efət] *n.* 努力

17 find out 查明；弄清

e.g. I've been dating a girl for a while, but I don't want my parents to **find out**.

词汇 Key Words

date sb. 和某人谈恋爱

18 flick through sth. 浏览；草草翻阅

e.g. One of my favourite pastimes is **flicking through** magazines.

词汇 Key Words

pastime ['pɑ:staɪm] *n.* 消遣；娱乐

19 follow through (with sth.) 将……（已经开始的事）进行到底、完成

e.g. I'm not someone that quits easily, so I'll have to **follow through with** this project.

词汇 Key Words

quit [kwɪt] *v.* 停止；放弃

20 get along (with sb.) （和某人）相处得很好

e.g. My neighbours and I really **get along** and I love this sense of community.

21 get away 度假；休假

e.g. It feels so nice to **get away** from time to time. Nothing beats this feeling.

词汇 Key Words

from time to time 偶尔；有时

beat sth. 比……更好

22 get together 聚会，小聚

e.g. My high school classmates and I would **get together** at least twice a year in the first few years after graduation, but not anymore.

23 give (sth.) up 放弃（某事）

e.g. If you have your heart set on something, then no matter what happens, you should never **give up**.

词汇 Key Words

have one's heart set on sth. 渴望 / 一心想要……

24 **goof off** 混日子；偷懒

e.g. My teacher kept telling me to stop **goofing off**, but I never listened. I really regret it.

词汇 Key Words

regret sth. 后悔某事

25 **grow apart** 疏远

e.g. My cousins and I don't **have** much **in common**, so we've gradually **grown apart** over the years.

词汇 Key Words

have...in common 在……方面有共同点

26 **hang out** 待着；玩；做一些休闲的事（大部分中国考生认为这个词组是"闲逛"的意思，其实不然。它的英文解释是 to spend a lot of time in a place，也就是说，在家里也可以 hang out，而无须 go out）

e.g. What I like the most about my apartment is that we have a big balcony where I can **hang out** alone, or with my friends when we're not studying.

27 **keep up with sth.** 跟上……；与……保持同步

e.g. Social media can have negative effects, but it also allows me to **keep up with** what's going on in the world.

词汇 Key Words

what's going on 正在发生的事情

28 **let sb. down** 令某人失望

e.g. I promised my parents that I wouldn't **let** them **down**, so in the end, they said that they would support my decision to go and study in the UK.

29 **look back (on sth.)** 回首（往事）

e.g. I feel so nostalgic when I **look back** on my childhood days.

词汇 Key Words

nostalgic [nɒˈstældʒɪk] *adj.* 怀旧的

30 look forward to (doing) sth. 期待……

e.g. We're going to Fiji on holiday next month, and we're really **looking forward to** it.

31 look sth. up（在词典、书籍、网络等资源中……）查阅（事实或信息）

e.g. I couldn't remember when that event happened, so I tried to **look** it **up** on the internet.

32 look up to sb. 尊敬 / 敬仰某人

e.g. My granddad is someone that I really **look up to**. He's taught me a lot over the years.

33 make sth. up 编造某事

e.g. I didn't want to be told off, so I **made up** a story hoping my parents would believe me.

词汇 Key Words

tell off 责备；斥责

34 meet up (with sb.)（与某人）见面、会面（非正式）

e.g. I was supposed to **meet up** with a friend that evening, but she felt a little sick, so we called it off.

词汇 Key Words

be supposed to do sth. 应该做某事

35 pick sb. up（通常指开车）接某人

e.g. Most kids these days are **picked up** by their parents or grandparents after school, whereas back in the day, we would just walk or cycle home ourselves.

词汇 Key Words

these days 当今

back in the day 从前，过去

cycle ['saɪkl] *v.* 骑自行车

36 put sth. off 推迟某事

e.g. I'm a big procrastinator; I always **put off** doing my homework until the last minute.

词汇 Key Words

procrastinator [prəʊˌkræstɪˌneɪtə] *n.* 拖延者

37 put up with sb./sth. 容忍……；忍受……

e.g. It was impossible to **put up with** all the smoking at the party, so I just left.

38 **run out of sth.** 用完；耗尽

e.g. My mom told me that we were **running out of** time, so we had to hurry up.

词汇 Key Words

hurry up 抓紧；赶快

39 **set sth. up** 安排；建立，创立

e.g. Those that **set up** their own businesses and are successful must share some qualities that set them apart from others.

词汇 Key Words

quality ['kwɒlətɪ] *n.* 品质；特质   set sb. apart from sb. else 使某人与众不同

40 **show off** 炫耀

e.g. Some people like to **show off** their possessions—watches, cars, luxury bags and so on. I can't be friends with them.

词汇 Key Words

possession [pə'zeʃn] *n.* 所有物；财产   luxury ['lʌkʃərɪ] *adj.* 奢侈的；奢华的

41 **take after sb.** （长相、性格等）像某人

e.g. I **take after** my mom in so many ways. For example, we're both very optimistic people.

词汇 Key Words

in...ways 在……方面   optimistic [ˌɒptɪ'mɪstɪk] *adj.* 积极的；乐观的

42 **take up** 占（时间、空间……）

e.g. Reading **takes up** about 50% of my leisure time; it's my favourite pastime.

43 **think sth. over** 仔细思考；认真考虑

e.g. I got a job offer from an electronics company last week, but I'm not sure if I'll take it. I'll have to **think** it **over**.

词汇 Key Words

job offer 工作机会；工作邀请   electronics company 电子产品公司

44 **wear off** 逐渐消失 / 停止；消逝

e.g. Running that race was so exhausting, but my fatigue soon **wore off**.

词汇 Key Words

race [reɪs] *n.* 赛跑

fatigue [fə'tiːg] *n.* 疲惫感

exhausting [ɪg'zɔːstɪŋ] *adj.* 令人筋疲力尽的

45 **work out** 健身；锻炼身体

e.g. In order to live a healthy life, we need to **work out** regularly and eat a balanced diet.

词汇 Key Words

regularly ['regjələlɪ] *adv.* 定期地

a balanced diet 均衡的饮食

注意：英文中的动词词组数量很多，除了上述四十五个需要我们着重练习之外，希望考生们在平时的阅读、听力练习中，在看剧、看电影时，也随时积累更多词组，扩大自己的词汇储备，并主动运用在自己的口语表达中。

🎙 四十二个习语

在英语中，有一种词汇表达叫作习语。乍一看，很难理解这些表达的意思，如 a walk in the park，在公园里走路？是什么意思？其实这是"简单"的意思。我们可以讲：Cooking is a walk in the park to me. 再如 in the pink，在粉色中？这个表达的意思是"身体健康"。我们中文也有类似表达："你看这小脸儿，红扑扑、粉嫩嫩的。"

习语就好像我们中文的成语一样，在一个人说话自然流畅的前提下，偶尔使用一两个习语，会给人一种用词非常地道、语言水平很高的感觉。但是，不要故意添加太多习语，因为那样会很不自然，就好像很少有哪个中国人每说一句话都加一个成语。另外，习语这种高级词汇的使用前提是你已经可以在整体沟通中保持大致的流畅度。如果你连英文都说不利索，却说出好几个习语表达，考官立刻知道你的备考方法有问题，英语水平其实不太行。

还需注意的是，总会有一些母语者说"我们平时不这么说，我们根本不用这个或那个习语"，但这并不能代表所有人。每个人、每个地区、每个阶层、每个年龄段的人说话风格和用词习惯可能都不尽相同，所以不用纠结于一些母语者所说的话。

在下文中，我们将学习一些在雅思口语考试中非常实用的习语。

1 **recharge one's batteries** 放松；养精蓄锐

e.g. I like to go travelling once in a while to **recharge my batteries**.

词汇 Key Words

once in a while 偶尔，有时

② **a walk in the park** 非常简单的事

e.g. I thought drawing was **a walk in the park** when I was a kid, but now I just feel that I can't draw at all.

③ **no picnic** 很难

e.g. Painting is **no picnic** to me. I can never do it well.

④ **on the ball** 敏锐的；注意力集中的；能够快速采取行动的

e.g. Driving at night is dangerous, so my uncle was trying his best to stay **on the ball**.

⑤ **can't wrap my head around sth.** 不理解……

e.g. This car is both expensive and loud. I still **can't wrap my head around** why it's popular in China.

⑥ **once in a blue moon** 难得一见，千载难逢

e.g. I take the bus **once in a blue moon** coz it's always crowded.

⑦ **out of the blue** 突然地；出乎意料地

e.g. My sister had decided to go to a Japanese restaurant. Then **out of the blue**, she changed her mind.

词汇 Key Words

change one's mind 改变主意

⑧ **a drop in the ocean/bucket** 九牛一毛，沧海一粟

e.g. The country needs a lot of funds to improve its education. This amount is just **a drop in the ocean**.

词汇 Key Words

funds [fʌndz] *n.* 资金；款项

⑨ **on cloud nine** 超级开心的（ = in seventh heaven）

e.g. When my dad told me that he would take me to Disneyland, I was **on cloud nine**.

⑩ **have a blast** 玩得开心（ = have a ball = have a whale of a time）

e.g. I threw a party at home last Sunday and **had a blast/had a ball/had a whale of a time** with my friends.

⑪ **bread and butter** 主要收入来源

e.g. I major in interior design now, so I guess designing houses will be my **bread and butter** in the future.

词汇 Key Words

interior design 室内设计

⑫ **rat race** 大城市里（为财富、权力等）的疯狂竞争

e.g. Living in a large city is really stressful, so I want to move to a smaller city to get out of the **rat race**.

词汇 Key Words

stressful ['stresfl] *adj.* 给人很大压力的

⑬ **shoot the breeze** 闲谈

e.g. I often **shoot the breeze** with my parents during and after dinner.

⑭ **hit the sack/hay** 上床睡觉

e.g. I like to do some reading before **hitting the sack**, which helps me fall asleep faster.

⑮ **on the same wavelength** 志趣相投；观点一致

e.g. My parents and I are **on the same wavelength**, so we find it pretty enjoyable talking with each other about different things.

⑯ **see eye to eye** 观点一致

e.g. He and I **see eye to eye** on almost everything.

⑰ **be in/of two minds about sth.** 犹豫不决，拿不定主意

e.g. I was **in two minds about** the book, so I decided not to buy it.

⑱ **have mixed feelings about sth.** 对……有复杂的感情

e.g. I **have mixed feelings about** my hometown. On the one hand, it's where my family and friends are, but on the other, it's crowded and expensive.

⑲ **a chip off the old block** 很像妈妈 / 爸爸

e.g. I think I'm **a chip off the old block**. My dad and I are equally shy.

词汇 Key Words

equally ['i:kwəlɪ] *adv.* 同样地；相等地

⑳ **run in the family** 为一家人所共有

e.g. My dad is a hard-working man. I think it **runs in the family** coz I also consider diligence to be a very important quality.

词汇 Key Words

diligence ['dɪlɪdʒəns] *n.* 勤奋   quality ['kwɒlətɪ] *n.* 品质

㉑ **follow in sb.'s footsteps/follow in the footsteps of sb.** 仿效某人；追随某人的脚步

e.g. I think I'm gonna **follow in my dad's footsteps** and become a director too.

词汇 Key Words

gonna = going to

㉒ **be in the same boat** 处于同样的困境

e.g. Countries around the world **are all in the same boat** when it comes to climate change. We have to take action together!

词汇 Key Words

take action 采取行动

㉓ **have a lot on one's plate** 有很多事情要做

e.g. I've been **having a lot on my plate** recently, so I haven't had much time to read.

㉔ **work like a beaver** 工作很忙（**as busy as a beaver** 非常忙）

e.g. I've been **working like a beaver** lately and I really need a vacation.

㉕ **give it my best shot** 尽我最大努力

e.g. It was one of my neighbours who encouraged me to **give it my best shot** to improve my English.

㉖ **as healthy as a horse** 非常健康

e.g. I go to the gym on a regular basis and this is why I'm **as healthy as a horse**.

㉗ **under the weather** 身体有点不舒服

e.g. I'm feeling a little **under the weather** today, so I'm sorry if I don't seem to be very enthusiastic about our conversation.

㉘ **around the corner** 即将到来

e.g. Hanson's concert is **around the corner** and I'm super excited about it.

㉙ **all the rage** 非常流行

e.g. This social media App is **all the rage** now.

㉚ **a household name** 一个家喻户晓的名字

e.g. My favourite singer is Jessie, **a household name** in China.

㉛ **second to none** 最棒的；无出其右的

e.g. Even though many Chinese people have never heard of the country, Palau, its scenery is absolutely **second to none**.

词汇 Key Words

Palau [pə'lau] *n.* 帕劳

㉜ **run of the mill** 普通的；乏味的

e.g. Although everybody said that he was the best math teacher in our city, I just thought his classes were **run of the mill**.

㉝ cost a fortune 花一大笔钱（ = cost an arm and a leg）

e.g. This coffeemaker **cost me a fortune**, so I'm not going to splash out on anything expensive anytime soon.

词汇 Key Words

coffeemaker ['kɒfɪ,meɪkə] *n.* 咖啡机

splash out on sth. 花大笔钱买……

anytime soon（用于否定句和疑问句）即将；马上

㉞ be up to speed on sth. 了解关于某事的最新消息

e.g. I like to read news online and it allows me to **be up to speed on** what's going on in the world.

词汇 Key Words

what's going on 正在发生的事情

㉟ drive sb. up the wall 令某人不爽，令某人心烦

e.g. My neighbours always make a lot of noise and that **drives me up the wall**.

㊱ a pain in the neck 令人很烦的人 / 东西 / 事

e.g. There's a lot of construction going on near my home and that's **a real pain in the neck**.

㊲ under the gun 承受很大压力

e.g. Being a successful businessperson, she is **under the gun** all the time.

㊳ throw in the towel 认输；放弃努力

e.g. I was so determined to get up at 5:30 every day, but I **threw in the towel** after only three days.

词汇 Key Words

determined [dɪ'tɜːmɪnd] *adj.* 下定决心的；坚定的

㊴ take one's breath away 令人惊叹

e.g. The beauty of that place **took my breath away** and I took hundreds of photos there.

㊵ pick one's brains 向某人请教 / 讨教

e.g. I enjoy hanging out with my grandpa because I can always **pick his brains** on some issues.

㊶ be set in one's ways 习惯难改；固执已见

e.g. My grandparents **were set in their ways** and didn't want to come to live with us in the city.

㊷ if memory serves/if my memory serves me correctly 如果我没记错的话

e.g. If memory serves, I was 12 years old when I first heard of this book.

(((▶ Grammatical Range & Accuracy 语法多样性和准确性

口语就是口头造句。而造句，就要遵守构建句子的规则，这就是语法。

雅思考试和国内的英语考试不同，没有专门的语法题，而是把语法考查融入写作和口语之中。

在学为贵真经派，语法的学习分成两个层次：一是语法知识的掌握，二是语法的恰当、灵活、地道的运用。

先看雅思官方关于语法 6 分和 7 分的评分标准：

Band 6	● Uses a mix of simple and complex structures, but with limited flexibility. 能够混合使用简单和复杂的结构，但缺乏灵活性。 ● May make frequent mistakes with complex structures, though these rarely cause comprehension problems. 在使用复杂结构的时候可能会频繁出错，但这些错误很少会影响理解。
Band 7	● Uses a range of complex structures with some flexibility. 能够有一定灵活度地使用一系列复杂结构。 ● Frequently produces error-free sentences, though some grammatical mistakes persist. 频繁地说出没有错误的句子，但还是有一些语法错误存在。

真经教学

　　雅思口语语法 6 分以上评分标准中，所谓的"复杂结构"并不复杂。比如，大家总说的"I think…"就能引出一个宾语从句；"If you…"是一个条件状语从句；"When I was a child…"是时间状语从句。

　　有很多考生认为以上三个从句过于简单，不会让考官认为考生具备很高的语法水平。事实上，口语中的语法本身就不是特别复杂，英语母语者根本不会在说话的时候说出很多既长又难的句子。

　　那么，我们如何在雅思口语备考期间提升自己对"复杂结构"的使用水平呢？真经派的教学理念是——靠句型。

　　让你背四十九个句型，和让你学一本四十九个章节的语法书相比，哪个更简单呢？

　　你背了四十九个句型之后，我们能担保你的口语表达有了多样性、复杂性，而且句型有准确性。但你把语法书学完后，我们不能保证你自己会用，且造句准确。

　　四十九个句型可以给大家的口语表达提供足够的多样性和复杂性，而且七乘七等于四十九，七在雅思考试中是很吉利的数字，希望各位考生都能获得口语 7+！

注意：大家不仅要学习句型，也要将所有句子熟练背诵下来。在这个过程中，你的语感会快速提升，这也会有效地帮助你在口语表达中减少语法错误。另外一个减少小错误的方法是在练习答题时给自己录音，然后听自己的英文表达，这可以让处在旁观者位置的你更容易、清晰地发现自己的问题。确认自己的一些问题后再次录音，这次尽量保证不要犯刚才的错误。每次练习都要耐心，可以多次录、多次听，这个方法能帮助大家很快意识到自己会犯错或正在犯错，也就可以更好地避免错误。

🎙 四十九个语法功能句型

①　**I find sth. +** *adj.* 我觉得……

I find the work I do quite stressful.

I found the new *Fast and Furious* movie pretty boring.

词汇 Key Words

stressful ['stresfl] *adj.* 令人紧张的；给人很大压力的

②　**What I think is that...** 我认为……，我的想法是……

What I think is that newspapers will most likely be gone in the future.

What I think is that being likeable is the most important quality in a teacher. Students won't learn if they don't like their teacher.

词汇 Key Words

most likely 很有可能

be gone 消失

likeable ['laɪkəbl] *adj.* 讨人喜欢的

quality ['kwɒlətɪ] *n.* 品质

③　**What I like (the most) about sth. is that...** 关于某事/物，我（最）喜欢的是……

What I like the most about my major *is that* not a lot of people study it, which means I will have less competition when I try to find a job.

What I like the most about music *is that* it can always cheer me up after I've been sad or depressed.

词汇 Key Words

competition [ˌkɒmpə'tɪʃn] *n.* 竞争

cheer me up 令我高兴起来，令我心情变好

depressed [dɪ'prest] *adj.* 沮丧的；抑郁的

④ What's great about sth. is that... 某事/物的一个好处是⋯⋯

What's great about my hometown *is that* there are many shopping malls here, which is fantastic for me, coz I'm a shopaholic.

What's great about playing computer games *is that* not only can it help me relax, I can learn some English at the same time.

词汇 Key Words

shopaholic [ˌʃɒpəˈhɒlɪk] *n.* 购物狂

⑤ The reason why...is that.../The reason...is because... ⋯⋯的原因是⋯⋯

The reason why I like reading so much *is that* it equips me with so much information and knowledge that I can share with others.

The reason why I chose to live here *is that* it's close to many good amenities.

The reason we have to work hard at school *is because* this is how we can have a promising future.

The reason some people can get up so early *is because* they have those genes.

词汇 Key Words

equip sb. with sth. 给某人提供所需的设备、工具等；令某人有（某种能力）	promising [ˈprɒmɪsɪŋ] *adj.* 有前途的；前景很好的
amenity [əˈmiːnəti] *n.* 生活福利设施；便利设施	gene [dʒiːn] *n.* 基因

⑥ ...and this is why... 这就是⋯⋯的原因

Coffee is so important to me *and this is why* I invested in a good coffeemaker recently.

People are living longer and longer *and this is why* some politicians are proposing later retirement ages.

词汇 Key Words

invest in sth. 买进；投资	propose sth. 提议；建议
coffeemaker [ˈkɒfɪˌmeɪkə] *n.* 咖啡机	retirement [rɪˈtaɪəmənt] *n.* 退休
politician [ˌpɒləˈtɪʃn] *n.* 政客；政治家	

⑦ There's no doubt that... 毋庸置疑

There's no doubt that more and more Chinese people like travelling.

There's no doubt that being bilingual and even multilingual can make us more competitive when we enter the job market.

词汇 Key Words

multilingual [ˌmʌltɪˈlɪŋgwəl] *adj.* 使用多种语言 的；会说多种语言的

competitive [kəmˈpetətɪv] *adj.* 有竞争力的

enter the job market 进入就业市场

8 It goes without saying that… 无须赘言

It goes without saying that everybody wants to live in a big house. The majority of people just can't.

It goes without saying that those who are friendly can get ahead professionally more easily.

词汇 Key Words

majority [məˈdʒɒrətɪ] *n.* 大多数

get ahead 获得成功

professionally [prəˈfeʃənəlɪ] *adv.* 在职业领域

9 No one can deny the fact that… 没人可以否认……

No one can deny the fact that parks are extremely important for a city.

No one can deny the fact that the main reason why people eat out more and more is that they're becoming increasingly busy.

词汇 Key Words

eat out 出去吃饭

10 Despite the fact that… 尽管 / 虽然……

Despite the fact that a big proportion of our goals are usually not achieved, we should still set clear aims for the future.

Despite the fact that our flight was an hour late, we still got there on time.

词汇 Key Words

a big proportion of… 很大比例的……

set aims 设定目标（＝set goals）

on time 准时

11 All I want to do is… 我只想……（后面可以直接加动词原形）

Whenever the weekend rolls around, *all I want to do is* sleep in.

When I'm not studying, *all I want to do is* cook and eat my own food.

词汇 Key Words

roll around 到来

sleep in 睡懒觉

12 **..., which I think is...** 我觉得这件事……

I snack on some chocolate from time to time, *which I think is* great. It puts me in a better mood.

I often do some reading for an hour or so in my downtime, *which I think is* pretty relaxing.

词汇 Key Words

snack on 吃……（零食）

an hour or so 一小时左右

downtime ['daʊntaɪm] *n.* 不工作的时间

13 **..., which means that...** 这意味着……

The word "success" always puts us under pressure, *which means that* if we're more laid-back, we can be happier.

If a teacher has a good sense of humour, the class will be more fun, *which means that* students will pay more attention.

词汇 Key Words

put sb. under pressure 给某人很大压力

laid-back [,leɪd'bæk] *adj.* 悠然自得的；放松随
　和的

a good sense of humour 良好的幽默感

fun [fʌn] *adj.* 有趣的；有意思的

pay attention 集中注意力

14 **those who...** 那些……的人

Those who have supportive parents tend to be more confident.

Those who visit my country all want to see the Great Wall.

词汇 Key Words

supportive [sə'pɔːtɪv] *adj.* 给予帮助的，支持的

tend to 通常，往往

15 **...where...** （在那里）

I like to go to the park near my home *where* my son can ride his scooter and play football.

I know there's a famous zoo in Chengdu *where* you can see those adorable pandas.

词汇 Key Words

scooter ['skuːtə(r)] *n.* （儿童）滑板车

adorable [ə'dɔːrəbl] *adj.* 可爱的

16 **Wherever.../No matter where...** 无论在哪里，无论去哪里

Wherever you go, there are so many vehicles on the roads and people are always caught up in traffic.

Wherever I go, I wear a hat. It's been my habit for years and I don't think I'll ever change it.

No matter where you go, you see ads—in subway stations, in shopping malls, and even in public bathrooms.

No matter where I go, I take a book with me. I like to read on the subway or on the bus.

词汇 Key Words

vehicle ['viːɪkl] *n.* 车辆	for years 好几年，多年
be caught up in traffic 被堵在路上	ad [æd] *abbr.* 广告 (= advert = advertisement)
it's been = it has been	

17 **Whenever…/No matter when… 无论何时**

Whenever I hang out with my parents, I just feel that time passes pretty quickly.

Whenever you go to a movie theatre, you'll see that it's usually overcrowded because seeing movies is one of our favourite pastimes in China.

No matter when you go to the beach, you'll find that it's overrun with tourists. I'm actually one of those people who often hit the beach.

No matter when you go to a park, you can see a lot of people, especially elderly people, dancing in big groups there.

词汇 Key Words

movie theatre 电影院	be overrun with tourists 充满游客
overcrowded [ˌəʊvəˈkraʊdɪd] *adj.* 非常拥挤的	hit the beach 去海边
pastime ['pɑːstaɪm] *n.* 消遣，休闲活动	elderly people 老年人

18 **Every time I… 每当我……**

Every time I give my girlfriend a bunch of roses, she seems extremely happy, so this is why I always do it.

Every time I take the bus, I find that there are way too many people on it, which makes it very uncomfortable.

词汇 Key Words

a bunch of roses 一束玫瑰	way too 特别，非常

19 **It is/was…that/who… 强调句式**

It was my uncle *who* bought me my first ever watch.

It's my English teacher *who*'s had the greatest influence on my life.

It was last week *that* I realised that I needed to buy a car of my own.

20 **It's important/necessary/difficult/convenient...for sb. to...** 对某人来说，……是重要/必需/困难/方便的

It's important for overweight people *to* cut back on junk food and begin to eat healthy diets.

I believe *it's necessary for* us *to* go out and soak up the sunshine.

My school was about 10 kilometres from my home and *it was* only *convenient for* me *to* go in my dad's car.

I have unusually small feet, so *it's difficult for* me *to* buy shoes that fit me.

词汇 Key Words

overweight [ˌəʊvə'weɪt] *adj.* 肥胖的；超重的	healthy diet 健康的饮食
cut back on 减少	soak up the sunshine 吸收阳光

21 **It's important/essential/necessary/crucial/vital that...** ……是很重要/必要/必需/关键/至关重要的

It's extremely *important that* we try to be polite all the time.

It's necessary that we're updated on what's happening around the world.

It's vital that children have hobbies that they can resort to when they're tired or stressed.

词汇 Key Words

be updated on... 了解……的最新消息	be stressed (out) 感到有压力的
resort to 诉诸	

22 **It's not uncommon for sb. to do sth.** 表示普遍

It's not uncommon for Chinese people *to* buy luxury cars now.

It's not uncommon for young people *to* go to the movie theatre every weekend in order to relax.

23 **be becoming/has become increasingly/more and more...** 变得越来越……

My hometown *is becoming increasingly* congested.

Julie *is becoming more and more* stylish now because she's going out with a fashion designer.

I tend to believe that our society *is becoming increasingly* selfish.

词汇 Key Words

congested [kən'dʒestɪd] *adj.* 拥堵的	fashion designer 时装设计师
stylish ['staɪlɪʃ] *adj.* 时尚的；有格调的	selfish ['selfɪʃ] *adj.* 自私的
go out with... 和……在一起；和……约会	

㉔ have/has…over the last…years/decades 在过去的……(十)年间

I've bought three cameras and taken roughly 100, 000 photos *over the last* three *years*.

I've been to 7 countries *over the last* 5 *years*.

The kind of gifts we buy for our family and friends *has* changed a lot *over the last* two *decades*.

The way Chinese people relax *has* changed dramatically *over the last* 30 *years*.

词汇 Key Words

roughly ['rʌflɪ] *adj.* 粗略的，大概的 | change dramatically 发生很大的改变

㉕ …used to… 过去，曾经(常常)

I *used to* be told by my parents that only they could make decisions for me.

We *used to* be a predominantly tea-drinking nation, but nowadays coffee is getting more and more popular.

词汇 Key Words

predominantly [prɪ'dɒmɪnəntlɪ] *adv.* 占主导地位地 | nation ['neɪʃn] *n.* 国家

㉖ I would…every…/…times a… (过去、曾经)每隔……我会……

I would (always)… (过去、曾经)我(总)会……

I would draw *every* single day when I was a kid, and that gave me a lot of pleasure.

I would take swimming lessons *twice* a week and I even thought I might become a professional swimmer.

I would always tell my friends that I would be a well-known director when I grew up.

词汇 Key Words

pleasure ['pleʒə(r)] *n.* 快乐，愉快 | well-known [ˌwel'nəʊn] *adj.* 有名的

㉗ I remember (clearly/vividly/distinctly) that… 我(清楚地)记得……

I remember clearly that the shoes I wore as a child only cost about 50 or 60 yuan, far cheaper than the shoes now.

I remember vividly that I used to be told off by my parents for having bad handwriting.

I remember distinctly that I was super nervous when I was about to tell that boy that I liked him.

词汇 Key Words

as a child 在小的时候 | handwriting ['hændraɪtɪŋ] *n.* 笔迹；字迹
be told off 被斥责 | be about to 刚要；即将

28 **I was doing sth. when...** 我当时正在……，然后……

I was doing my homework *when* a bolt of lightning flashed across the sky.

I was walking in the mall and *chatting* with two of my friends *when* I suddenly heard a familiar song.

词汇 Key Words

a bolt of lightning 一道闪电

flash [flæʃ] *v.* 闪耀；闪光

chat [tʃæt] *v.* 聊天

familiar [fə'mɪliə(r)] *adj.* 熟悉的

29 **The last/first time...was...** 上一次／第一次……是在……

The last time my family went on a road trip *was* two months ago when we drove to Dalian.

The first time my brother talked with a foreigner *was* when he was only 7. That Canadian lady was impressed by my brother's English.

词汇 Key Words

go on a road trip 去自驾游

be impressed by sth. 对……印象深刻／深感钦佩

30 **It's been years/ages/forever since...** 自从……已经很久了

It's been years since I did my last science experiment. I don't remember how it felt anymore.

It's been ages since my sister had her last burger. It used to be her favourite.

It's been forever since the last time I chatted with someone on QQ.

词汇 Key Words

experiment [ɪk'sperɪmənt] *n.* 实验

31 **...will be able to...** ……将能够……

Students who take time to learn more skills *will be able to* find better jobs after they graduate.

I've heard that if you meditate for 5 minutes a day, you *will be able to* focus better and have more willpower.

词汇 Key Words

graduate ['grædʒueɪt] *v.* 毕业

meditate ['medɪteɪt] *v.* 冥想

willpower ['wɪlpaʊə(r)] *n.* 意志力；毅力

32 **It's highly likely that...** 很可能……

It's highly likely that television will be a thing of the past in a few decades.

It's highly likely that kids today won't know how to use printed maps in the future.

词汇 Key Words

a thing of the past 过去的事物；陈年往事　　　　printed map 纸质地图

33 **There will definitely/probably be... 肯定 / 很可能会……**

With robots taking more and more of our jobs, *there will probably be* more emphasis on art subjects on the school curriculum in the future.

There will definitely be fewer and fewer people who regard newspapers as their main source of information.

词汇 Key Words

emphasis on... 对……的强调　　　　　　　　regard sth. as... 把……看作……

art subjects 艺术学科　　　　　　　　　　　main source of information 主要信息来源

curriculum [kə'rɪkjələm] *n.*（学校里的）全部课程

34 **It takes/took...to do sth. 花费多长时间做……**

It only *takes* 20 minutes *to get* to the nearest department store, so that's where I like to hang out with friends on the weekend.

It took us 10 hours *to fly* to Australia only to see some koalas. These little animals didn't let us down.

词汇 Key Words

department store 百货商店　　　　　　　　　let sb. down 令某人失望

koala [kəʊ'ɑːlə] *n.* 考拉

35 **I wish...were/had/could... 我希望……（注意虚拟语气）**

I wish I *had* different neighbours. The people living next door always make a lot of noise, which is a pain in the neck.

I wish I *were* a better singer. I've never been able to sing well.

词汇 Key Words

live next door 住在隔壁

36 **It would be great if...were/had/could... 如果……，那就太好了（注意虚拟语气）**

It would be great if my apartment *were* bigger. The one I'm currently living in is way too cramped.

It would be great if I *were* richer. That way, I would be able to buy better cameras.

词汇 Key Words

currently ['kʌrəntlɪ] *adv.* 目前，当下	that way 那样的话
way too... 特别，非常	

③⑦ If I had to..., I would say... 如果我必须……，那么……（一般用在从一些选项中挑选一个的时候）

If I had to pick one, *I would say* Saipan is my favourite place to visit. It's gorgeous and the people are really hospitable.

If I had to choose, *I would say* Jackson is better because he has some singing skills that other singers don't possess.

词汇 Key Words

Saipan [saɪˈpɑːn] *n.* 塞班岛	hospitable [hɒˈspɪtəbl] *adj.* 热情好客的
gorgeous [ˈgɔːdʒəs] *adj.* 非常美丽的	possess [pəˈzes] *v.* 具有；拥有

③⑧ whether (...) or not 是否

One of my roommates asked me *whether or not* I would like to try scuba-diving, and I said "Yeah!"

It's not a question of *whether* we should relax *or not*; it should be how we relax.

Some people have been asking the question of *whether* we should celebrate foreign festivals *or not*.

词汇 Key Words

scuba-diving [ˈskjuːbəˈdaɪvɪŋ] *n.* 潜水

③⑨ so that.../in order to... 为了；以便

I dragged myself out of bed extremely early *so that* I could catch the early train.

My sister and her fiancé prepared a small cake for every guest *so that* everyone had something to eat before the wedding ceremony.

I would like to take a Spanish course *in order to* prepare myself for opening a diner in Spain.

I used to sing a lot in front of my classmates *in order to* impress the girl I had a crush on. It didn't work.

词汇 Key Words

drag oneself out of bed 挣扎着起床	impress sb. 给……留下深刻印象
fiancé [fɪˈɒnseɪ] *n.* 未婚夫	have a crush on sb. 暗中喜欢某人
prepare sth. for sb. 为某人准备某物	it didn't work 这没有成功
diner [ˈdaɪnə(r)] *n.* 小餐馆	

40 **provided that... 如果，在……条件下**

Parents should take their kids to parks as often as possible *provided that* there's one close to their home.

Provided that I'm free on the weekend, I go back to my parents' place. That's my safe haven.

词汇 Key Words

as often as possible 尽可能经常地 | safe haven 避风港

41 **as long as... 只要……**

I believe *as long as* we work hard, we can learn a foreign language well.

As long as the weather's good and I don't have anything more important to do, I go cycling, either alone or with my friends.

词汇 Key Words

go cycling 去骑单车

42 **given the fact that... 鉴于；考虑到……**

Given the fact that it was usually pretty polluted in my hometown, we could barely see any stars at night. It's changed a lot now.

Given the fact that kids are too young to make informed decisions, they have to consult their parents first.

词汇 Key Words

barely ['beəlɪ] *adv.* 几乎不；几乎没有 | 的，经过深思熟虑的
it's changed = it has changed | consult sb. 咨询 / 请教某人
informed [ɪn'fɔːmd] *adj.* (猜测或决策) 明智 |

43 **unless... 除非……**

Normally, I don't eat any chocolate—*unless* I feel despondent. Chocolate makes me happier.

I never wear anything pink or red *unless* my girlfriend makes me.

词汇 Key Words

despondent [dɪ'spɒndənt] *adj.* 苦恼的；沮丧的 | make [meɪk] *v.* 强迫

44 **Unlike... 不像……**

Unlike youngsters, middle-aged and old people are typically more interested in the news.

Unlike our parents' generation, we generally like to do some adventurous activities like bungee-jumping and paragliding.

词汇 Key Words

middle-aged ['mɪdleɪdʒd] *adj.* 中年的

typically ['tɪpɪklɪ] *adv.* 通常；一般地（＝generally）

adventurous [əd'ventʃərəs] *adj.* 冒险的；敢于

冒险的

bungee-jumping ['bʌndʒɪ'dʒʌmpɪŋ] *n.* 蹦极

paragliding ['pærəglaɪdɪŋ] *n.* 滑翔伞运动

45 …much/a lot/far + 比较级 + than………比……（形容词）得多

Roses are *much* more expensive on Valentine's Day *than* the rest of the year.

There are *a lot* more reality shows on TV *than* other types of programmes.

The effects of climate change could be *far* more serious *than* we can imagine.

词汇 Key Words

Valentine's Day 情人节

rest [rest] *n.* 剩余部分

reality show 真人秀

effect [ɪ'fekt] *n.* 影响；效果

climate change 气候变化

46 …is not as…as… ……没有……那么……

Some people say that living in the city *is not as* comfortable *as* living in the countryside. I don't agree.

Being able to read a map *is not as* important *as* in the past as our GPS on the phone is so easy to use.

47 …one of the most… 最……的……之一

That article was *one of the most* misleading news articles I've ever read.

I saw *one of the most* imposing buildings while I was sightseeing in Bangkok.

词汇 Key Words

misleading [ˌmɪs'liːdɪŋ] *adj.* 误导性的；迷惑性的

imposing [ɪm'pəʊzɪŋ] *adj.* 壮观的

Bangkok [bæn'kɒk] *n.* 曼谷

48 …, whereas… ……，然而，……

When it comes to food, Chinese people have so much variety to choose from now, *whereas* it was even hard to have eggs every day 50 years ago.

I'm a huge fan of Western food, *whereas* my parents only like traditional Chinese food.

词汇 Key Words

when it comes to sth. 关于……；在……方面

variety [və'raɪətɪ] *n.* 变化；多样化

choose from sth. 从……中选择

I'm a huge fan of… 我非常喜欢……

49 be regarded as/be considered (as)/be seen as... 被看作······

Our home *is regarded as* a refuge from the outside world.

Wallets *were considered* a necessity before, whereas now we don't need them anymore.

She *is seen* by many *as* an up-and-coming pop star.

词汇 Key Words

refuge ['refjuːdʒ] *n.* 避难所；慰藉

necessity [nə'sesətɪ] *n.* 必需品

up-and-coming [ˌʌpənd'kʌmɪŋ] *adj.* 有前途的；有希望的

(((▶ Pronunciation 发音

我们都知道，陌生人见面，第一印象很重要。在雅思口语考场上，考官对你口语水平的第一印象，其实就是你的发音。如果在刚开始短短半分钟的礼貌寒暄问候中，你展现出标准地道的发音，考官心中会想："这是自己人啊，很地道啊，有语言天赋，估计 7 分以上。"反之，两句英语对话之后，考官心中想："哎哟，你这个英语我听不懂啊！"你最后的口语分数一定会"扎心了，老铁！"。

最后说一句：发音好会激发你一生学习英语的兴趣，就像音色好的人爱唱卡拉 OK 一样。认真练好英语发音，你会受益终生。

请学习关于发音的评分标准：

Band 6	• Uses a range of pronunciation features with mixed control. 能够运用一系列发音现象，掌控程度不一。 • Shows some effective use of features but this is not sustained. 对发音现象有效运用，但无法一直维持这种水平。 • Can generally be understood throughout, though mispronunciation of individual words or sounds reduces clarity at times. 整体可以被听懂，偶尔会出现单个词或音发错的情况。
Band 8	• Uses a wide range of pronunciation features. 能够充分大量地运用发音现象。 • Sustains flexible use of features, with only occasional lapses. 持续不断并灵活运用发音现象，偶尔会有疏忽。 • Is easy to understand throughout; L1 accent has minimal effect on intelligibility. 容易被听懂；第一语言的口音对考生英语发音有很小的影响。

注意： 我们并没有写出 7 分的发音评分标准，因为 7 分的要求是 "能够做到所有 6 分要求和一些 8 分要求"。

真经教学

> 单个音、单个词要发音准确；了解并练习英文中重要的发音现象：重读、弱读、略读、连读等，有意识地运用到口语中，不断提升地道性；反复模仿标准地道发音，固化下来，积累起来。

我们将在后文将发音讲解分成如下几类：

1. 单个音

2. 连读（普通连读）

3. 失去爆破（特殊连读）

4. 重读和弱读

注意： 我们不会讲解所有单个音及发音现象，而是对大部分中国考生的主要问题进行针对性讲解。除了研习下面的发音讲解，考生们还需要对英语句子、段落等进行更多的跟读模仿，不断提升发音！

🎤 单个音

关于单个音，我们主要强调几个中国考生最容易出错的发音：/iː/、/ɪ/、/uː/、/ʊ/、/æ/、/e/、/aɪ/、/aʊ/、/ɒ/、/ɔː/、/n/、/l/、/θ/、/ð/。

🎤 /iː/ vs. /ɪ/

长元音 /iː/ 这个音很简单，和我们中文中 "一" 的发音很类似。不要只是单纯觉得 /iː/ 的发音应该延长，更重要的是，发这个音的时候嘴唇是紧张的、用力的（请听录音）。

练习

beat, eat, stream, heat, jeep, real, she, keys, deed, feet, feel, mean, heal, neat

想发出 /ɪ/ 这个音，大家微微张开嘴，嘴型不要做出变化，完全放松、不要用力，去说 "一"，你就会发出 /ɪ/ 这个音（请听录音）。

练习

it, bit, kiss, chick, did, fill, fit, hit, hill, bill, kit, tip, kick

对比 练习

sheep vs. ship

feel vs. fill

seat vs. sit

beach vs. bitch

sheet vs. shit

feet vs. fit

sleep vs. slip

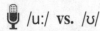 /u:/ vs. /ʊ/

/u:/ 和 /i:/ 相同，都是长元音，但更重要的是发音时嘴都要紧张用力。/u:/ 要噘嘴。

练习

move, soon, tool, school, clue, flu, rule, cool, groom, bloom, fruit

/ʊ/ 和 /ɪ/ 相同，都是短元音，但更重要的是发音时嘴要放松、不用力。/ʊ/ 不要噘嘴或微微噘嘴。

练习

took, wood, put, look, foot, good, would, should, could

对比 练习

food vs. foot

Luke vs. look

pool vs. pull

shoot vs. should

tool vs. took

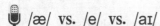 /æ/ vs. /e/ vs. /aɪ/

这三个音是令很多中国考生痛苦的音，因为在普通话中没有 /æ/ 和 /e/ 这两个音。大部分中国学生可以发出 /aɪ/ 这个音，因为它和标准普通话中 "我爱你" 的 "爱" 的发音是基本相同的。/aɪ/ 可以被理解成 /ɑ:/→/ɪ/。

练习

like, my, slight, fly, flight, pie, kite, slice, China, why, migrate, bite, cry, sign, mile, hide, white

那 /æ/ 和 /e/ 怎么发音呢？

我们先来看 /e/。想发好这个音，其实不难。大家把嘴微微张开（注意是 "微微" 张开，一点儿就可以了），然后嘴型不要（这里很重要）做出任何变化，去说 "爱"，就是 /e/ 这个音了（请听录音）。

练习

bet, dead, kettle, met, desk, felt, slept, gesture, medicine, pet, petty, internet, get, digest

想发出 /æ/ 这个音，我们可以使用一个非常有意思的技巧 —— 先发 /e/，再发 /ɑ:/，把两个音连到一起（请听录音）。

这是一种比较夸张的美音的读法，英音没有这么夸张。大家可以通过这个方法先读对这个音，然后再稍微放松一些，就能达到英音的效果（请听录音）。

练习

back, black, pat, cat, fat, gas, catch, lack, pal, sand, shallow, that, had, value, hat

对比 练习

dad vs. dead vs. died

cat vs. kettle vs. kite

lash vs. less vs. lice

math vs. meth vs. mice

flat vs. flesh vs. flight

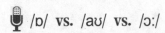 /ɒ/ vs. /aʊ/ vs. /ɔː/

很多考生经常把 /ɒ/ 和 /aʊ/ 两个音弄混，因为我们在中文中，不会区别对待这两个音。在英文中，/aʊ/ 叫作双元音，即在发音过程中，嘴型有变化。/aʊ/ 可以有两种读法，现在最流行的一种读音是从 /æ/ 过渡到 /ʊ/，大家也可以从 /ɑː/ 过渡到 /ʊ/（请听录音）。

练习

now, about, slouch, allow, south, crowded, cow, down, found, town, pout, wow, towel, power

/ɒ/ 是单元音，即张开嘴后，嘴型没有变化，只停留在一个位置（请听录音）。

练习

not, possible, pot, modern, fog, bomb, college, popular, hobby, hot, dot, mock, shop, stock

注意：/ɒ/ 这个音在美音中类似 /ɑː/。

对比 练习

now vs. not

pout vs. pot

foul vs. fog

cow vs. cot

house vs. hobby

down vs. dot

mouse vs. mock

/ɔː/ 的发音有点像 "沃"，保留 "沃" 后半部分的发音就可以了（请听录音）。

练习

for, horse, more, short, store, four, court, course, mourn, warm, quarter, small, wall, tall, hall, ball

比较特别的是，如果 /ɔː/ 在单词的字母组合的最后有 r，美国人通常会卷舌，读成 /ɔːr/（请听录音），比如 for、horse、more、short 等。如果元音组合里没有 r，美国人读音类似 /ɑ:/，和上面 /ɒ/ 的美音读法是一样的，比如 talk、walk、bought、thought 等。

🎤 /n/ vs. /l/

/n/ 和 /l/ 这两个音出现在一个单词末尾时，很多考生总是不发音，这是不对的。其实，正确地发出这两个音，在很多时候可以帮助我们自动产生连读。如：This notion~is(nis) good. This is a can~of(nof) soup. I feel~it(lit). You sell~a(la) lot of clothes.

那么，该如何正确发出这两个音呢？

首先，发 /n/ 时，你的舌尖一定要顶到上齿龈，练习的时候可以夸张点，以"呢"结尾。真正说的时候放松，不用说"呢"，但舌尖还是要顶上去（请听录音）。

练习

notion, fashion, animation, question, can, begin, in, on, been, town, station, intonation

接下来，我们一起来看 /l/ 如何发音。练习时，不要单独读 /l/，在前面加上一个 /ə/，读成 /əl/。同时，在后面再加上一个 /ə/，读出"了"的感觉。这时你就肯定发出了 /l/ 的音。真正说的时候，把最后的 /ə/ 去掉（请听录音）。

练习

bill, fill, feel, full, beautiful, fool, pool, school, sell, bell, deal, reveal, thrill, film, field, fall

🎤 /θ/ vs. /ð/

/θ/ 是清辅音，/ð/ 是浊辅音，但它们的字母组合通常都是 th。究竟什么时候发 /θ/，什么时候发 /ð/，需要查字典，没有一以贯之的辨别方法。比如，"呼吸"的名词形式 breath 中的 th 发 /θ/ 的音，而动词形式 breathe 中的 th 发 /ð/ 的音。

很多考生的一大问题是，发 /θ/ 和 /ð/ 时，不吐舌头，读成了 /s/ 和 /z/。要想快速解决这个问题，我们在练习时，要用力吐舌头，舌头越往外吐越好。通过这种夸张的练习让自己的嘴和舌头快速记住这两个音的发音方法，这样，当我们自然说话时，不经过思考，也可以发出正确的音（请听录音）。

练习

think, thought, thick, thin, thanks, three, thirty, teeth, mouth

注意，/θ/ 和 /s/ 是不一样的，发 /s/ 不需要咬舌（请听录音）。

对比 练习

think vs. sink

thought vs. sought

thick vs. sick

mouth vs. mouse

练习

that, this, those, these, though, thus, there, their

/ð/ 和 /z/ 的发音是不一样的，发 /z/ 的音不需要吐舌（请听录音）。clothes 这个单词比较特殊，/kləʊz/ 和 /kləʊðz/ 都是正确的读音。

🎤 连读（普通连读）

当一个单词以辅音结尾、下一个单词以元音开头时，两个单词之间要连读（请听录音）。

my name is = my namis

pick up a language = piku pa language

speak up = speakup

eat it = eatit

work out = workout

move away = movaway

the notion is = thenotionis

from America = fromamerica

have a cup of tea = hava cu pof tea

speak English well = speakEnglish well

make it easy = makiteasy

this App is good = thisAppis good

part of the room = par tof the room

再来看一组句子中的连读现象：

My name^is …

His music^is very catchy and^the words^are romantic.

I want^to speak^English like^a native speaker.

In^order to succeed, she works hard^every day.

We should^never give^up.

People^often say, "Time^is money".

I bought^it and^then^I lost^it.

上面的句子中也出现了下面要讲的特殊连读现象。

🎤 失去爆破（特殊连读）

爆破音（p、b、t、d、k、g）与大部分辅音相邻，前面的爆破音留住位置，但不读出声音（失去爆破）——急刹车的感觉。

September, postcard, goodbye, blackboard, grandmother, atmosphere, admit, investment, advice, absolutely, definitely

我们看一组句子中的失去爆破和连读现象，做综合练习。

Good^morning. Good^afternoon. Good^evening. Good^night.

Most^people like^to go travelling in the summer.

I use^email to communicate^with my teacher about^my essays.

My mom took^great^care^of me when^I was^a child.

I'm not^crazy about^shopping coz^I find^it^really tiring.

🎤 重读和弱读

重读和弱读在英文中非常重要，但在中文里却不是很明显，所以不少中国考生在讲英文时语调太平，不具备英文特点，可能会被扣分。更大的问题是，语调很平会让人觉得没有感情，如果考生还说得较为流利的话，考官很可能会认为考生在背答案。这样的话，分数也肯定高不了了。

重读就是读某个词的时候声音稍微大一些、音调稍微高一些、时间稍微长一些。弱读则完全相反——声音稍微小一些、音调稍微低一些、时间稍微短一些。重读词通常由实义词（名词、动词、形容词、副词）构成。刚开始练习的时候要足够夸张，高的地方使劲高上去，声音更大、同时延长，低的地方努力降下来，同时声音要小、并很快过去。

练习

I can make it.

He likes to grab a coffee after work.

I never go to museums.

It's a wonderful day for a walk in the park.

The traffic in my hometown is quite bad.

Jimmy told me that he would come.

还有几点需要注意：

🎤 在实义词中，名词的发音会更重一些

练习

Jimmy likes the snow.

Lily is going to Japan.

Tom likes this bike.

The boy comes from China.

Adam lives in Fiji.

Joe wants a soccer ball.

John washes clothes.

Children love ice cream.

My friends often go shopping.

Mia goes to the pool every week.

在实义词的修饰性搭配中，被修饰的词发音会更重一些

练习

It's a good book.

What a small room.

She is a lovely girl.

It's a gorgeous park.

Beijing is a modern city.

The book is really good.

The room is pretty small.

This park is very beautiful.

The soup is quite cold.

Math is really hard.

中国考生常见错误：重读代词

读一读以下句子：

I like it.

He saw me.

They have it.

He buys them.

It's not very important to me.

It's nice of him to do it.

I need something.

We need to go somewhere to relax.（somewhere 是副词，但是类似上面的代词，不该强调）

🎤 复合名词中，一般是前重后轻

一个复合名词中包括两个单词（有时甚至更多），这两个单词既可以写到一起也可以分开，但它们组成了一个名词（名词词组）。对比以下四组词：

a white house vs. the White House 一幢白色的房子 vs. 白宫	a hot girl vs. a hot dog 一个性感的女孩 vs. 一个热狗
a beautiful station vs. a subway station 一个美丽的车站 vs. 一个地铁站	a new ball vs. a football 一个新的球 vs. 一个足球

练习

bus stop, newspaper, television, airport, passport, coffee shop, girlfriend, boyfriend, parking lot, washroom, bedroom, living room, greenhouse, haircut, Superman, grownup, overcoat, classroom, supermarket, goldfish

🎤 名词性物主代词通常会重读，因为它们被当作名词看待

名词性物主代词有：mine, yours, his, hers, ours, yours, theirs

练习

That ticket is mine.

This is yours.

We bought ours yesterday.

My notebook is red. Hers is yellow.

🎤 can't 通常会重读

练习

I can't go to the party tomorrow.

He can't make it on time.

My mother tells me I can't be late for school.

对比

I can go to the party tomorrow.

I can make it on time.

🎤 语意上强调的词要重读

练习

I'm not going to school today.（正常语调）

I'm not going to school today.（强调今天不去）

I'm not going to school today.（强调不去）

She cooked this fish.（强调鱼是她做的）

She cooked this fish.（强调鱼是她自己做的，而不是买的或别人给的）

She cooked this fish.（强调她做的是这条鱼）

She cooked this fish.（强调她做的是鱼，而不是别的东西）

学习完重读的部分，我们再来看看哪些词需要弱读和略读。

通过刚才的学习，我们掌握了实义词要重读的规律。除实义词（名词、动词、形容词、副词）之外的所有词，都叫作功能词。它们通常会被弱读。很多弱读的功能词中的元音会被略读，读成 /ə/。那么，哪些词可能会被略读呢？

以 can 为例，它在略读的时候读作 /kən/。

练习

I can wait.

I can play basketball.

We can go shopping during public holidays.

注意：在一些情况下，功能词要读它本来的音。

1. 当这些功能词在语意上被强调的时候。

Yes, I can make it. It's not that I can't.

This gift is for John. It's not from him.

2. 当它后面没有其他词时。

Yes, I think I can.

I don't think I should do that, but I would.

我们总结了一些常见的略读词：

can, at, as, are, or, for, your, was, will, that（连词）, to, and, of, have（助动词）, has（助动词）, had（助动词）

练习

- **can** /kən/ (strong form /kæn/)

  can run, can cook, can win

  I can run fast.

  She can cook.

  Everyone says I can win.

  I can't promise anything, but I will do what I can.（读本来音）

- **as** /əz/ (strong form /æz/)

  as soon as, as much as, as easy as

  I'll try to do that as soon as possible.

  I don't work out as much as before.

  Life will never be as easy as it is now.

- **are** /ə(r)/ (strong form /ɑː(r)/)

  are pretty boring, are really nice, are gorgeous

  Some newspapers are pretty boring.

  Chinese people are really nice.

  The views are gorgeous there.

  Yes, they are.（读本来音）

- **for** /fə(r)/ (strong form /fɔː(r)/)

  for me, for fun, for 20 years

  When my uncle told me the toy was for me, I was really happy.

  I ride a bike every day for fun.

  I've been living here for 20 years.

  There was a big table in the room. I didn't know what that was for.（读本来音）

- **will** /wəl/ (strong form /wɪl/)

  I will never, I will go, we will live

  I will never move to another city.

  I guess I will go to parks more often in the future.

We will live here for the rest of our lives.

Yes, I will.（读本来音）

- **to** /tə/（后面的词以辅音字母开头时）

to learn, to study, to jump, to school

English is easy to learn.

I'm going to study overseas.

I had no choice but to jump.

I'm not going to school today.

I want to eat it.（这里的 to 不略读，因为后面的词 eat 以元音字母开头，而非辅音字母）

- **and** /ənd//ən/ (strong form /ænd/)

nice and easy, you and I

rock 'n' roll, hot and cold

fish and chips, bread and butter

happy and proud, noodles and dumplings

I feel extremely happy and proud of myself.

I really like eating noodles and dumplings.

- **of** /əv/ (strong form /ɒv/)

a lot of water, out of date, nice of him

There was a lot of water in the room.

Nokia is out of date.

It was very nice of him.

- **have** /əv/ (strong form /hæv/)

would have done

should have done

must have done

I would have done it if I were you.

You should have come earlier.

They must have lived in America before.

当 have 作助动词的时候，通常可以略读为 /həv/，我们在上面主要学习了 would/should/must have done 这种形式。

第 **3** 章

口语素材大全

 Part 1 回答五大准则

◆ **准则 1**：能扩展则充分扩展，不能扩展则自信停下。很多考生担心自己在 Part 1 说得太多，被考官打断，会影响分数。其实不会的。你的分数和是否被打断没有关系。所以我们建议考生碰到可以充分发挥的题目，就充分扩展答案，证明自己的口语实力。但是，如果偶尔碰到实在不知道说什么的题目，也可以回答一两句话之后自信停下。有长有短的回答，才会更加自然可信。

◆ **准则 2**：扩展答案的时候可以采取在说出答案之后再给出原因的方式，也可以给出与答案有关的更多细节，如说完 I'm quite into music 之后可以说自己为什么喜欢 music，也可以说自己喜欢什么类型的 music、最喜欢的歌手是谁、多久听一次 music 等。给出原因和细节的方法可以搭配在一起使用，但是我们更建议多聊细节、少扩展原因。具体扩展答案的方法见第 2 章 "官方评分标准真经" 的 "流利度和连贯性" 部分。

◆ **准则 3**：回答时要给出完整的句子，而不是蹦词。如，问题是：How long have you lived in your hometown? 只回答 Twenty years 就不太好，最好说：Well, I've lived here for 20 years, ever since I was born.

◆ **准则 4**：Part 1 是考生与考官的一问一答，有一点 conversation（对话）的感觉，所以我们建议考生在沟通中一定要自然、轻松，就像在酒吧和朋友聊天一样。可以偶尔使用填充词 um、well、you know、I mean 等，也可以偶尔向考官承认自己没有想法、需要一点时间思考。比如：Um, well, I have no idea what to say. This is a little embarrassing. 或者：I haven't thought about it before. Let me see. 还可以说：Why do I like shopping? Um, well, I guess it's because…

◆ **准则 5**：尽量使用口语化、生活化的语言，少用大词难词。

Part 1 练习方法

◆ **方法 1**：熟练掌握"流利度和连贯性"部分的逻辑扩展方法。

◆ **方法 2**：学习本章 Part 1 例题的范例答案，积累词汇、句型、连接性表达。

◆ **方法 3**：听范例答案录音，改善发音；反复朗读范例答案，提高语感，并在此过程中掌握 Part 1 回答逻辑。

◆ **方法 4**：在"学为贵雅思" App 找到当季的 Part 1 题库，按照题库练习答题。

◆ **方法 5**：自己练习 Part 1 题目时均以录音的方式进行——给自己的回答录音，答完一遍之后，听自己的回答，把听到的词汇、语法、逻辑、发音等方面的问题记下来，并思考可以把哪些词汇和句型替换成更地道的语言。再录一遍、再听、再录、再听。每道题至少录音回答三次。

◆ **方法 6**：找一个同样在准备雅思考试或英语口语较好的同学协助自己练习。让这位同学充当雅思考官的角色，提出问题，模拟雅思考试现场。

注意：我们不建议大家完全背诵范例答案。范例答案是为了帮助各位考生积累语言储备、学习逻辑思路。大家应尽量说出自己的回答。

Part 1 范例答案

🎤 Work or study

Q *Are you a student or do you have a job?*

A1: I have a job and I've been working as an accountant for five years.

A2: I'm a university student and I study accounting. I've been studying it for three years and I'm going to graduate next year.

真经点评：在回答完自己在学习或在工作后，可以用现在完成进行时（I've been working…/I've been studying…）继续扩展、给出细节，展现更高水平的英文。

Q *Do you like your job?*

A: Well, not really. I can't say I'm a fan of my job because it's super stressful. I always have to work overtime on weekdays and there's even work to do on the weekend from time to time. More importantly, the pay isn't that satisfying. The reason I'm taking this test is because I want to study overseas so that I can be more competitive in the job market and find a better-paying job.

Q **Why did you choose this job?**

A: I chose this job as a Chinese teacher mainly because I had always been crazy about Chinese literature. Reading was my only pastime when I was growing up, so studying Chinese literature and then becoming a Chinese teacher seemed like a natural option.

Q **Do you plan to change jobs in the future?**

A: Yes, I do, and this is partly why I'm sitting here today taking this test. What I'm doing isn't exactly my dream job—I'm doing this only because I believed it would have good job security. But after several years of being in this field, I've realised that I really have to pursue my dream, which is to become a fashion designer, and this is why I'm going to further my studies in the UK.

真经点评："…this is partly why I'm sitting here today taking this test…" 这里可以让考官觉得考生在很自然地进行沟通、聊天。你聊天越自然，越可能让考官觉得你的口语水平很不错。

Q **Why did you choose this major?**

A: I chose to study advertising because…um…in fact, it's not because I'm passionate about this field or anything; it's just when I was choosing what to study, I thought it would be fun designing stuff and trying to be creative and imaginative all the time. The thing is, I'm not that creative, so I'm doing pretty badly in this major.

Q **What are you going to do after you finish your studies?**

A: Well, I'm not quite sure. You know, with my major, Korean, I can do basically anything and it also means nothing. By anything, I mean, no matter what it is, as long as it's somewhat related to this language, I can do it. But it also means that I don't have any competitive edge over other job applicants when it comes to applying for a job that calls for further expertise.

词汇 Key Words

work as… 做……的工作	satisfying ['sætɪsfaɪɪŋ] *adj.* 令人满意的
stressful ['stresfl] *adj.* 给人很大压力的	study overseas 出国学习
work overtime 加班	competitive [kəm'petətɪv] *adj.* 有竞争力的
the pay 工资	a natural option 一个很自然的选择

dream job 梦想的工作

good job security 好的工作保障

creative [krɪˈeɪtɪv] *adj.* 有创造力的

imaginative [ɪˈmædʒɪnətɪv] *adj.* 有想象力的

do badly 做得不好

somewhat [ˈsʌmwɒt] *adv.* 有点

be related to sth. 和……有关系

competitive edge 竞争优势

job applicant 工作申请者

call for 需要

expertise [ˌekspɜːˈtiːz] *n.* 专业技能

🎤 Hometown

Q *Tell me something about your hometown.*

A: My hometown is Xi'an, which is a city with a lot of history. If I'm not mistaken, we have a history of over 3,000 years, and because of this, you can see myriad places of historical importance here, like Emperor Qin's Mausoleum—this is where the Terracotta Warriors are. We also have quite a few other places that are very popular with visitors. At the same time, my hometown is pretty modern as well. I mean, we see a lot of high-rises springing up every year…

真经点评：3,000 years、Emperor Qin's Mausoleum、high-rises，这些内容都是很好的扩展，将前面有些宽泛、抽象的内容具体化，以此来展现更多的层次、词汇和语法。

Q *Is that a big city or a small place?*

A: Well, I'd say that my hometown is pretty big, it's large actually, because it takes several hours for people to drive from one side to another. In fact, I've done it before. One time, I drove from the northeast of my hometown to the southwest and it took me five hours, which can definitely prove how big it is.

Q *What do you like most about your hometown?*

A: Oh, as a matter of fact, there are tons of things that I like about where I live, but if I had to pick a favourite, I'd say it would be the food, which is really good. In my opinion, Xi'an food is the best nationwide. In particular, I'm a huge fan of 肉夹馍, which can be seen as our own style of hamburgers. I think it's incredibly palatable.

Q *Is there anything you dislike about it?*

A: Well, I suppose the traffic is a big problem—it's bumper-to-bumper every day. This is because, first of all, we have a huge population and therefore there's a large number of vehicles on the roads. Plus, some people, not many, um, don't follow traffic regulations, which creates chaos sometimes. So yeah, I do think that the local government should come up with ways to tackle the problem.

Q *Do you think you will continue living there for a long time?*

A: Um, I'm not sure. You know, I've never thought about this before. I'm going to study in Australia and I will be there for three years. What will I do afterwards? I can't be certain now. I mean, perhaps I'll just stay there and find a job, or maybe I'll come home. There's plenty of time for me to make a decision.

真经点评："What will I do afterwards?" 这种一边思考一边说话的方法非常好，因为考生虽然有犹豫，却还在展现自己的英文，没有影响流利度。

词汇 Key Words

a city with a lot of history 一个有悠久历史的
　城市

myriad ['mɪrɪəd] *adj.* 很多

mausoleum [ˌmɔːsəˈliːəm] *n.* 陵墓

be popular with sb. 在……中间很流行

high-rise ['haɪ'raɪz] *n.* 高楼大厦

spring up 迅速出现

as a matter of fact 事实上

if I had to pick a favourite, I'd say… 如果我必
　须得选一个最喜欢的话，我觉得……

nationwide [ˌneɪʃn'waɪd] *adv.* 在全国范围内

be seen as 被当作，被看作

incredibly [ɪn'kredəblɪ] *adv.* 非常地

palatable ['pælətəbl] *adj.* 好吃的，美味的

bumper-to-bumper ['bʌmpətə'bʌmpə] *adj.* （交
　通）很拥堵的

a huge population 很大的人口数量

traffic regulations 交通规则

chaos ['keɪɒs] *n.* 混乱

come up with 想出

tackle the problem 解决问题

certain ['sɜːtn] *adj.* 确定的

🎤 Home/Accommodation

Q *Do you live in a house or a(n) flat/apartment?*

A: I live in an apartment and I've been living there for three years.

Q *Can you tell me something about your flat/apartment?*

A: Um, sure. My apartment is not very big coz housing prices are sky-high in my hometown and I can't afford to buy a huge apartment. Some apartments cost 5 or even 6 million RMB! There are two bedrooms, a small living room, a kitchen and a balcony where I like to do some reading or listen to music.

Q *Which part of your home do you like the most?*

A: Well, I guess it would be the balcony coz, like I said, I do some fun and relaxing things there. But another place that I also dig is the kitchen because I'm a cooking expert, haha. I'm particularly good at making Japanese food. So if I'm not very busy, I might just be in the kitchen cooking something.

Q *Do you plan to live there for a long time?*

A: Yeah, I think so. I've only lived there for three years, which is a very short amount of time. I'm convinced that I will live there for many years to come. Plus, it's pretty convenient around there—the subway station is within walking distance; there are three supermarkets nearby; there's a kindergarten only 300 metres away, for my future kid, of course. So yeah, I don't see any reason why I should move.

真经点评：聊到 convenient，立刻对它进行了扩展——subway station、supermarkets、kindergarten。

词汇 Key Words

in an apartment 在一间公寓里（注意冠词用 an）

housing prices are sky-high 房价极高

can't afford to do sth. 负担不起……

relaxing [rɪˈlæksɪŋ] *adj.* 令人放松的

dig [dɪg] *v.* 喜欢

expert [ˈekspɜːt] *n.* 专家

a short amount of time 很短的时间

I'm convinced that 我确定……

for many years to come 在未来很多年

I don't see any reason why... 我想不到任何……的原因

🎤 Fruits

Q *What kind of fruit do you like?*

A: Well, I like various kinds of fruit like durians, pomelos, tangerines and so forth. But I suppose my favourite would be tangerines coz they're not only luscious, but also easy to peel and eat.

Q *Did you like to eat fruit when you were a child?*

A: Yes, I did. I was crazy about eating fruit. In fact, I've loved eating fruit all my life. When I was growing up, I would eat some cherries or kiwi fruit or grapes every day during or after dinner. When I was watching television with my parents, I would be snacking on something too. I guess fruit has always been part and parcel of my life.

真经点评：虽然问题只是关于"过去"，但不同时态交叉使用，展现了语法多样性。

Q *Is it important to eat fruit?*

A: Yeah, without a doubt. I believe it's of great importance to eat fruit on a regular basis, or even on a daily basis, because they're beneficial to people's health. Fruits are rich in vitamins and other nutrients that I don't know. In fact, I've even read an article that said that those people who eat a big amount of fruit tend to live longer lives than those who don't. So, yeah, fruits are vital for people.

词汇 Key Words

durian ['dʊərɪən] *n.* 榴梿

luscious ['lʌʃəs] *adj.* 美味的，可口的

peel [piːl] *v.* 剥皮

when I was growing up 在我小的时候

snack on something 吃些零食

be part and parcel of my life ……是我生活中非常重要的一部分

be rich in... 富含……

vitamins ['vaɪtəmɪnz] *n.* 维生素

nutrient ['njuːtrɪənt] *n.* 营养物质

vital ['vaɪtl] *adj.* 非常重要的

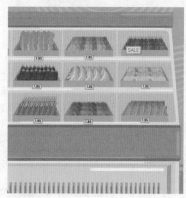

🎤 Transportation

Q *How did you come here today and why did you choose that?*

A: Well, I just took the subway here coz it's the most reliable form of transportation, I think. I knew exactly what time I would get here. However, if I had taken a bus or taxi, I wouldn't have known that because there could have been a traffic jam and I could have gotten caught up in it.

真经点评：使用对比进行扩展。

Q *What forms of transport/transportation do you usually use?*

A: Um, the subway actually. Not only did I take it today, I take it every day. Every morning I take it to work and it's a 40-minute ride—not too bad. And then, after work, I take it back home. The subway is an important part of my life.

Q *Is it convenient to take a bus in your city?*

A: Um, I think so. In my opinion, it's pretty convenient because there are bus stations everywhere and you can take the bus to every corner of the city. For instance, there's a station within walking distance of my home and roughly 15 buses come here and go to different parts of the city every day. So yeah, I'd say it's generally pretty good.

真经点评：用 for instance 进行举例，将答案具体化，更加充分扩展，展现了更多层次及词汇、语法。

Q *Is driving popular in your country?*

A: Yeah, it sure is. Driving is extremely popular in China because people's living standards are getting higher and higher, and more and more people want to go to different places in a more comfortable way, so an increasing number of people are buying cars. As a result, there are so many cars on the streets every day, which means the traffic is awful in many cities.

词汇 Key Words

reliable [rɪ'laɪəbl] *adj.* 可靠的

take a taxi 乘坐出租车

not too bad 还不错

an important part of my life 我生活中重要的一部分

roughly ['rʌflɪ] *adv.* 差不多；大致

popular ['pɒpjələ(r)] *adj.* 流行的

living standard 生活水平

awful ['ɔːfl] *adj.* 糟糕的

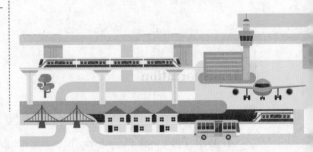

🎤 **Bus or taxi**

Q *How often do you take the bus?*

A: Well, I don't really take the bus very often, so I guess perhaps once in a few months, because most of the time I commute by subway. This is the most reliable form of transport I think coz there's no traffic underground, right? And also, although it's jam-packed all the time, I know when I can get to my destination, whereas if I take the bus, I might just be caught up in traffic.

Q *When was the last time you took a taxi?*

A: Um, it was last Saturday. My girlfriend and I went to the aquarium and since it's a little far from our university and we didn't want to take the bus or subway, we just hailed a cab. The cab driver was pretty nice and the ride was quite comfy.

Q *What are the advantages of taking a taxi compared to taking the bus?*

A: Off the top of my head, it's more comfortable, for sure. When you're taking the bus, you're usually surrounded by tons of people and you can seldom get a seat, which means you might have to stand for a long time, whereas in a taxi…um, it's just comfy, right? Another difference is that you have privacy coz you're alone, with a taxi driver, of course. In comparison, on a bus, whatever you do, other people are watching you.

词汇 Key Words

once a in a few months 几个月一次

most of the time 大部分时间

commute [kə'mjuːt] *v.* 通勤

no traffic 没有堵车

aquarium [ə'kweərɪəm] *n.* 水族馆

since [sɪns] *conj.* 由于

hail a cab 打手势叫出租车

privacy ['prɪvəsɪ] *n.* 隐私

🎤 Music

Q *When do you listen to music?*

A: I listen to music all the time because I am crazy about it. I have to say music is an essential part of my life, so no matter what I do, no matter where I go, I have my earphones on. For example, every morning, on my way to school, I listen to some R&B or hip-hop songs to pass the time.

Q *How much time do you spend listening to music every day?*

A: I guess if I add everything up, I probably spend about two hours or even three hours listening to music every day.

Q *What kinds of music do you listen to?*

A: I am a huge fan of music so I listen to all kinds of it, including hip-hop, R&B, rock and roll, country music and so on. I also listen to some classical music from time to time, but if I had to pick a favourite, I suppose it would be country music. When I feel a little down in the dumps, I just listen to some country songs, especially Taylor Swift's songs. Her music is pretty therapeutic.

真经点评：列举一些音乐类型后挑出一个继续进行扩展，这是很好的扩展方法。

Q *Have you ever been to a concert before?*

A: Yes, I've been to tons of concerts and the last time I went to one was three or four months ago. I went to Jolin's concert in Shanghai. Jolin is a household name in China and I adore her, so I went there with my mom who likes her as well and we had the time of our lives that day.

真经点评：在谈论一次经历时添加时间、地点、人物、事件、感受这几大要素。

词汇 Key Words

music

an essential part of my life 我生活中不可缺少
　的一部分

have my earphones on 戴着耳机

pass the time 打发时间

add sth. up 把……相加

I'm a huge fan of 我非常喜欢……

down in the dumps 沮丧的；伤心的

therapeutic [ˌθerə'pjuːtɪk] *adj.* 治愈的

tons of 很多

a household name 一个家喻户晓的人

have the time of one's life 玩得很开心

🎤 Sports

Q *What kinds of physical exercise do you like?*

A: I really enjoy working out, so in fact, I like many sports, including playing badminton, riding the exercise bike, hitting the gym to lift weights, swimming and so on. As a matter of fact, before coming here, I rode the exercise bike at home for about thirty minutes and it helped me work up a sweat. That made me feel really good.

Q *Do you think children should do sports regularly?*

A: Absolutely. There is no doubt that sport should play a vital role in children's lives. In fact, what I think is that it's not just about children; everybody should do the same. Um, regular exercise is important for children in so many ways. For starters, it allows them to lead a healthy life. Nobody should ever lead a sedentary life, so if they do sports on a regular basis, they can be healthier. Another reason is that a lot of sports are team sports, so by participating in them, children can learn how to work with others on a team, how to cooperate and stuff like that, which will be very important when they grow up.

Q *What was your favourite sport when you were young?*

A: When I was growing up, I think my favourite sport was playing badminton and I would do it on a daily basis with my parents. Every day after dinner, we would just go to the park near our home and play badminton for about forty or fifty minutes. It was a good opportunity for us to bond and it also helped me live a healthier life.

Q *What kinds of sports are popular in China?*

A: Many sports are well-liked here, like swimming and jogging. Perhaps swimming is the most popular sport, because every time you go to a public swimming pool, especially in the summer, you will see it's jam-packed with people. In one lane, there are usually dozens of people, so sometimes it makes it a little hard for people to swim.

词汇 Key Words

work out 运动

hit the gym 在健身房运动

work up a sweat 大汗淋漓，汗流浃背

there is no doubt 毋庸置疑

play a vital role in... 在……中扮演重要角色

lead/live a...life 过一种……的生活

on a regular basis 经常；定期

participate in sth. 参加……

on a daily basis 每天

a good opportunity to bond 一个培养感情的好机会

jam-packed [dʒæm'pækt] *adj.* 很拥挤的

lane [leɪn] *n.* 泳道

🎤 Relaxation

Q *What do you like to do to relax?*

A: There are several things I like to do on a regular basis to help me unwind, like reading, watching YouTube videos, working out at the gym and so on. I've only started working out at a gym close to my apartment recently, and I feel that whenever I'm running on the treadmill or lifting weights, it's super relaxing.

真经点评：从宽泛（several things）到具体（reading, watching videos and working out）再到更具体（working out）。

Q *Do you think vacation time is a good time for you to relax?*

A: Without a doubt. This is actually something that I forgot to mention just now, because going on vacation is one of my favourite things in life. Whenever I have about 7 days or 10 days off, or a little bit longer than that, I just want to go on a vacation somewhere—to the seaside, to the desert, to cities with a lot of history and so on. That's one of the most enjoyable things to do, and it's a wonderful opportunity for me to let off steam.

Q *Do you think students need more relaxing time?*

A: There's no question about that. Well, especially in China…I'm not sure about other countries, but in China, students have to study around the clock, but actually that's not good for their academic performance. If they could rest more, relax more and sleep more, they could do better at school.

词汇 Key Words

on a regular basis 经常；定期

unwind = relax = let off steam 放松

work out at the gym 在健身房健身

close to = near 离……很近

treadmill ['tredmɪl] *n.* 跑步机

lift weights 做力量训练；举重

relaxing [rɪ'læksɪŋ] *adj.* 令人放松的

without a doubt 毋庸置疑

mention ['menʃn] *v.* 提及

go on vacation = go on a vacation 去度假

have…days off 休息……天

a little bit longer than that（时间）比那稍微长一些

seaside ['siːsaɪd] *n.* 海边

desert ['dezət] *n.* 沙漠

cities with a lot of history 有很多历史的城市

enjoyable [ɪn'dʒɔɪəbl] *adj.* 令人享受的，令人愉快的

there's no question about that 毫无疑问

work/study around the clock 一刻不停地工作/学习

academic performance 学习/学术表现

🎤 **Family**

Q *How often do you meet your family?*

A: Well, since I go to university in another city, I can't see my folks very often. I only go back to my parents' during the summer holiday and winter holiday. When I do see them, we just hang out all the time, if they're not super busy, of course. We gab about everything—my studies, my boyfriend, their life, my plans for the future and so on. I really treasure the time I spend with my parents.

真经点评：对 hang out 进行具体扩展，然后对 gab（chat, talk）进行具体扩展。

Q *How do you spend time with your family?*

上个问题的答案可以回答这道题。

Q *Do you want to live with your family in the future?*

A： I do, but I don't think it's possible. I'll have to move out of my parents' place sooner or later because I'll get hitched and start my own family. I don't have a boyfriend yet, so it won't happen anytime soon, but it will happen.

Q *How has your family influenced you?*

A： Well, my family has influenced me in various ways. The first thing that comes to mind is that I'm a positive person because of my dad. He has a positive outlook on life and nothing ever bothers him, so over the years, I've learned from him to take it easy. Additionally, I'm a pretty good cook and I should give a shout-out to my mom. She began teaching me cooking when I was still a teenager and now I can cook a variety of dishes, which I think is a great skill.

词汇 Key Words

my folks 我的家人

my parents' 我父母家

hang out 待着；玩

gab [gæb] *v.* 闲聊

treasure ['treʒə(r)] *v.* 珍惜

sooner or later 迟早

get hitched 结婚

anytime soon 在不久的将来

in various ways 在很多方面

the first…that comes to mind 第一个出现在我
   脑海中的……

have a positive outlook on life 有一个积极的人
   生态度

bother sb. 使某人烦恼

over the years, I have… 这么多年来，我……

take it easy 放松；从容

give a shout-out to sb. 向某人表示感谢

🎙 Friends

Q *Do you have many friends?*

A: Yes, I think so. I'm a people person and I love to go out to meet new people and make friends. Every weekend, I meet up with some of my friends in a bar or someplace else and we have fun together. I also like to throw parties in my apartment and invite friends over to cook, eat, drink and play games together. I'm someone that can't live without friends.

Q *Do you remember your friends in primary school?*

A: Um…primary school, well, it's been so long—it's been about 20 years now, so honestly I don't remember all of my friends from back then. There are only a few of them that I'm still in touch with. Not only are we in touch, but we're still very close and we often hang out together now. When we meet up with each other, sometimes we reminisce about some fond memories we had before.

Q *How do you make friends?*

A: Um, I make friends in various ways. For example, I often go to parties or throw parties myself where I can meet new people and I really enjoy striking up conversations with them. It's very easy for me to make new friends this way. Plus, I'm a member of a local book club. You know, I'm a bookworm and being part of a book club is something amazing to me. This is where I often see some new faces and they become my friends soon after we meet.

Q *Do you like chatting with friends online?*

A: No, I'm not really a huge fan of that because um…I feel that chatting with people online with only words and emojis is way too impersonal. I prefer to meet friends in the flesh and talk with them with more emotion. I think this is much better communication.

词汇 Key Words

a people person 一个喜欢社交的人

meet up with sb. 和某人见面聊天

throw a party 举行派对

can't live without… 不能没有……

it's been so long 已经好久了

back then 那个时候

be in touch with sb. 和某人保持联系

hang out together 一起玩；一起待着

reminisce about sth. 回忆……

fond memories 美好的回忆

a bookworm 一个喜欢读书的人

soon after... 在……不久之后

emoji [ɪˈməʊdʒɪ] *n.* 表情符号（网络）

impersonal [ɪmˈpɜːsənl] *adj.* 缺乏人情味的

in the flesh 当面

🎤 Teachers

Q *What kind of teachers do you like best?*

A: Well, off the top of my head, I'd say good-looking teachers, haha. I say it for a good reason. You know, teachers who are handsome or beautiful can attract students to pay more attention in class, which leads to better academic performances, I think. Another quality that I think teachers should have is a sense of humour coz everybody likes those who are hilarious. My middle school history teacher was hysterical and he was always able to crack us up. Most of my classmates liked his lessons.

真经点评：通过中学历史老师的例子证明幽默感的重要性。

Q *Who was your favourite teacher when you were young?*

A: Um, I suppose it must have been my high school Chinese teacher, Mr. Li, who was extremely knowledgeable. He was a walking encyclopedia and whenever we had any questions, no matter what it was about, he would know the answer. I really looked up to him.

真经点评：不仅抽象地提到这位老师非常博学，也给出具体表现。

Q *Would you want to be a teacher in the future?*

A: No, I don't think so. Being a teacher is too much responsibility and I don't suppose I would want so heavy a burden on me. Plus, I'm neither good-looking, funny, or well-read, so I don't think I'm capable of being a teacher.

Q *Have you ever had bad teachers before?*

A: Oh, yeah, tons of them. Perhaps it's an exaggeration to say tons, but I've really had a few. When I was in primary school, my math teacher was extremely dull, but more importantly, whenever I made a mistake or anything, he would use a stick to hit me in the butt. I hated him.

词汇 Key Words

good-looking [gʊd'lʊkɪŋ] *adj.* 长得好看的

attract [ə'trækt] *v.* 吸引

pay attention 集中注意力

lead to 造成；引起

academic performance 学习成绩；学术成就

a sense of humour 幽默感

crack sb. up 令某人发笑

knowledgeable ['nɒlɪdʒəbl] *adj.* 知识丰富的

a walking encyclopedia 无所不知的人（行走的
百科全书）

look up to sb. 尊敬某人

doing sth. is too much responsibility 做……责
任重大

so heavy a burden on me 对我来说是很重
大的责任

be capable of doing sth. 有能力做某事

an exaggeration 夸张；言过其实

a few 一些

dull [dʌl] *adj.* 无聊的

hit me in the butt 打我屁股

🎤 Festivals

Q *How do you celebrate festivals in your country?*

A: We have tons of festivals in China because we have a long history and a rich culture. The most important is by far the Spring Festival. Everybody goes back to their hometown and we get together with members of our family. We eat, chat, play games, set off fireworks and firecrackers, and visit our relatives and friends. Yeah, we do all sorts of things during this festival.

Q *What special foods and activities do you have for these festivals?*

A: Off the top of my head, dumplings. Everybody knows dumplings, which are really popular in China, especially in the north of China. I'm from the north, so dumplings are my favourite food and we eat them a lot during the Spring Festival celebration and on some other occasions too. But in the south…for example, where my girlfriend comes from…she comes from Yunnan Province and her family doesn't have the habit or tradition of eating dumplings. They just eat a variety of other things. As for activities…I can think of dragon dance, lion dance, setting off fireworks and firecrackers, which I was a huge fan of when I was a kid. I don't do that a lot nowadays.

Q *How do you celebrate the Spring Festival?*

Q *What is your favourite festival?*

上面的内容完全可以回答这两道题。

词汇 Key Words

tons of... 很多……

a long history 悠久的历史

a rich culture 丰富的文化

by far 大大地（表示某事物比其他同类别的事
　物好、大、厉害……得多）

get together 聚在一起

set off fireworks/firecrackers 放烟花 / 鞭炮

on some other occasions 在一些其他场合

province ['prɒvɪns] *n.* 省

the habit/tradition of... ……的习惯 / 传统

as for... 至于 / 关于……

dragon/lion dance 舞龙 / 狮

a huge fan of sth. 非常喜欢……的人

Flowers

Q *What kinds of flowers do you know?*

A: My first reaction was to say that I know many kinds of flowers, but on second thought, I know some flowers like roses, carnations, sunflowers, and...what else? Haha, I actually don't really know that much about the names of different flowers.

Q *Are there any flowers that have special meanings in China?*

A: Yeah, there are. I can think of peonies right now, which are our national flower, if I'm not mistaken, and they represent prosperity, wealth and richness. Everybody wants to prosper in life, so peonies have a great meaning.

Q *Have you planted any flowers before?*

A: I don't suppose I have. Maybe I will do it in the future, but I'm not sure.

真经点评：能扩展则充分扩展，不能扩展则自信停下。

Q *Have you given flowers to anyone?*

A: Absolutely. I've given some carnations to my mom on several occasions, especially on Mother's Day. And also, I have a girlfriend and I give her some roses from time to time. She feels really happy when I'm standing in front of her and holding some roses in my hands.

词汇 Key Words

reaction [rɪ'ækʃn] *n.* 反应

on second thought 转念一想

rose [rəʊz] *n.* 玫瑰

carnation [kɑ:'neɪʃn] *n.* 康乃馨

sunflower ['sʌnflaʊə(r)] *n.* 向日葵

think of sth. 想到……

peony ['pi:əni] *n.* 牡丹

our national flower 我们的国花

if I'm not mistaken 如果我没说错的话

represent sth. 代表……

prosperity [prɒ'sperəti] *n.* 兴旺，繁荣

wealth and richness 富裕，富有

prosper ['prɒspə(r)] *v.* 兴旺，繁荣

absolutely ['æbsəlu:tlɪ] *adv.* 当然，肯定

on several occasions 几次

from time to time 偶尔，有时

🎤 Sunshine

Q *Do you like sunny days?*

A: Yeah, I do. Sunny weather is my favourite. In fact, I believe most people like sunny days, right? Whenever it's beautiful out there, I just naturally feel delighted.

Q *Do you want to go to a place with a lot of sunshine in the future?*

A: Yeah, sure. Like I said, I'm crazy about sunny days and it's natural that I adore places with a lot of sunshine too. I've always longed to go to Florida where it's sunny most of the time. I believe I'll be on cloud nine when I finally get a chance to go.

真经点评：喜欢 places with a lot of sunshine，所以进一步拿 Florida 举例。很简单的扩展方法，我们一提再提，就是因为它最为实用！

Q *Are there any technologies with sun nowadays?*

A: Yes, I'm sure there are many. Solar energy is cheap and sustainable, and so a lot of major tech companies are seeking to invent things with the help of it. I'm not certain if I'm correct, but I think many companies around the world are trying to create solar energy vehicles. People can just drive their cars and if it's sunny, the cars get more and more energy. It would be fantastic if I had a car like that.

词汇 Key Words

sunny days 晴天

delighted [dɪ'laɪtɪd] *adj.* 开心的

long to do sth. 渴望做某事

on cloud nine 超级开心的

solar energy 太阳能

sustainable [sə'steɪnəbl] *adj.* 可持续的

major tech company 大科技公司

seek to do sth. 试图做某事

Rainy days

Q *Does it rain much in China?*

A: Well, it rains very often in summertime. In July and August, it pours quite frequently and sometimes, if it doesn't rain heavily, it spits. All in all, we do get a lot of rain in the summer.

Q *Is there any part of China where it doesn't rain much?*

A: Yeah, it doesn't rain much in Inner Mongolia. I lived there for several months a few years ago and it hardly ever rained that summer. In Beijing, where I come from, it rains quite a lot in the summer and we even have downpours occasionally. Compared with Beijing, Inner Mongolia is a rather dry place.

真经点评：拿 Beijing 和 Inner Mongolia 进行对比，扩展答案，并进一步证明 Inner Mongolia 的干燥。

Q *In what month does it rain most in your hometown?*

上个问题的答案可以回答这道题。

Q *Can you remember any time when it rained particularly heavily in your hometown?*

A: Yeah, for sure. It was several years ago, on July 21st, if I remember correctly. It was the heaviest rainfall I've ever seen. It rained for about 5 hours nonstop and in the end, the whole city was flooded. I saw on the news that some people even drowned in the rain. It was a nightmare.

词汇 Key Words

frequently ['friːkwəntlɪ] *adv.* 频繁地

rain heavily 下大雨

it spits 下小雨

all in all 总而言之

occasionally [əˈkeɪʒnəlɪ] adv. 偶尔

if I remember correctly 如果我没记错的话

nonstop [nɒnˈstɒp] adv. 不停地

be flooded 被淹没

drown [draʊn] v. 淹死

a nightmare 一场噩梦

🎤 Sky and stars

Q *Do you like to look at the sky?*

A: I think I do. Whenever there's no pollution, when it's really beautiful up there, I might stop and look at the sky. I think it's gorgeous. It's peaceful and really enjoyable.

Q *Would you like to live on other planets?*

A: Yeah, I would definitely like that. It would be really cool and amazing to be one of the first human beings to live on another planet.

Q *Do you prefer the sky in the morning or at night?*

A: I seldom do any stargazing, so I don't always look at the sky at night. The sky in the morning… I think it's beautiful, but this is not to say night-time sky isn't pretty…I just don't have a preference between the two.

Q *Is there a good place to look at the sky where you live?*

A: I'm sure there are some really good places, like some tall mountains in the north of the city. I haven't been there before, so I'm not very sure whether they are the most optimal places to look at the sky, but they should be good.

词汇 Key Words

gorgeous [ˈɡɔːdʒəs] adj. 非常美丽的

peaceful [ˈpiːsfl] adj. 宁静的；安详的

enjoyable [ɪnˈdʒɔɪəbl] adj. 令人愉快的；令人
　享受的

amazing [əˈmeɪzɪŋ] adj. 非常棒的；令人称奇的

one of the first human beings 最早的一批人之一

stargazing [ˈstɑːɡeɪzɪŋ] n. 观星

I don't have a preference between the two
　我对这两者没有任何偏好

tall mountain 高山

optimal [ˈɒptɪməl] adj. 最优的；适宜的

🎤 Colours

Q *What's your favourite colour?*

A: Well, I would say it's blue. Actually, when I was a kid, I used to think that my favourite colour was red, and I still have a lot of red pieces of clothing. But now I prefer the colour blue because I just feel that it represents my personality more. I'm a thinker, and blue stands for deep thinking, I think.

真经点评：题目并没有问到曾经喜欢的颜色，但是考生可以在答案中主动添加。

Q *What colour do you dislike?*

A: It's really hard to think of one…um, pink comes to mind because that's a really feminine colour, and I'm a man; I want to be seen as masculine. But when I see something pink, I think it's beautiful too. Sorry, there's no colour that I dislike.

真经点评：即便这个答案前后似乎有些矛盾，也没有关系。只要我们用英文把这种矛盾表达清楚了，就没问题。

Q *What colours do your friends like most?*

A: Oh, my goodness, I have tons of friends, and they all have their own favourite colours, I suppose. If I asked them what their favourite colours were and each of them gave me an answer, we would be able to make a rainbow.

Q *What colour makes you uncomfortable in your room?*

A: If my bedroom were completely dark, like black or brown, I would feel in a terrible mood. That would make me really depressed and anxious every single day.

词汇 Key Words

a piece of clothing 一件衣服

sth. comes/came to mind… 想到……

feminine ['femənɪn] *adj.* 女性化的

be seen as… 被看作……

masculine ['mæskjələn] *adj.* 男性化的；有男子气概的

tons of… 非常多……

if I asked…, …gave…, …would…; if my bedroom were…, …would… 这两个句子都使用了虚拟语气（if…were… 是标准语法，但很多人也会说 if…was…）

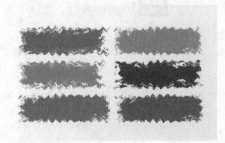

in a terrible mood 心情很糟糕

depressed [dɪ'prest] *adj.* 抑郁的

anxious ['æŋkʃəs] *adj.* 焦虑的

🎤 Politeness

Q *Who taught you to be polite?*

A: Oh, um, there must have been a lot of people who taught me how to be polite when I was growing up. If memory serves, when I was 4 or 5 years old, my mom told me that whenever we were having a meal, we shouldn't start eating until the elderly people began to eat. I'm sorry, it's been a long time, so my memory's pretty vague now.

真经点评： 从宽泛（a lot of people）到具体（my mom）；最后一句 "I'm sorry…" 是很好、很自然的聊天、沟通状态。

Q *How do Chinese people show politeness?*

A: Well, we show our politeness in myriad ways, including saying "thank you" to others, giving seats to the elderly on the subway or the bus, saying 您 instead of 你 when we say "you" in Chinese. In fact, this is particularly important where I come from. I remember being told off by my mom after not saying 您 to one of my uncles.

Q *What rules of politeness have changed in China?*

A: Um, that's a tricky one. It's really tough to think of something in a fraction of the time. Well, um, sorry, really nothing comes to mind. I suppose most of the things have just remained more or less the same today compared to what they were like in the past.

真经点评： 这个回应没有给出答案，但是考生一直在进行沟通，一边思考一边说。只要语言表达不错，就可以获得理想的分数，无须百分百回应题目。

词汇 Key Words

polite [pə'laɪt] *adj.* 礼貌的

if memory serves 如果没记错的话

it's been a long time 已经很长时间了

my memory's pretty vague 我的记忆相当模糊了

particularly important 尤其重要

tell sb. off 呵斥 / 斥责某人（尤其是孩子）

tricky ['trɪkɪ] *adj.* 困难的

in a fraction of the time 在很短的时间内

come to mind 被想到

more or less 差不多

in the past 在过去

🎙 Concentration

Q *Is it difficult for you to stay focused on something?*

A: It's really tough to stay focused nowadays, because there are so many distractions around us. Like there's social media, right? Sometimes when I'm studying or when I'm reading a book, or when I'm chatting with my friends or family, if I get a notification from Weibo, which is the Chinese Twitter, I will have this impulse to go and check Weibo, which isn't good. But I just can't help it.

Q *When do you need to be focused?*

A: I need to be focused in various situations—when I'm reading a book, when I'm studying for final exams and when I'm chatting with other people, particularly those that are really close to me. These are some situations where I have to stay focused on whatever I'm doing.

Q *What do you do to help you concentrate?*

A: Honestly, I don't do anything. If I did know what I can do to help me concentrate, I wouldn't lose focus so easily.

真经点评：没有答案也是一种答案。

词汇 Key Words

tough = hard = difficult 困难的

distraction [dɪ'stræk∫n] *n.* 分散注意力的事；
　　使人分心的事

get a notification 收到 (手机) 通知

impulse ['ɪmpʌls] *n.* 冲动；一时兴起的念头

check Weibo 去看微博

I can't help it 我忍不住；我情不自禁

in various situations 在各种不同的情况下

final exam 期末考试

particularly [pə'tɪkjələlɪ] *adv.* 尤其

a situation where… **situation** 后面通常用 where

honestly ['ɒnɪstlɪ] *adv.* 说实话；老实说

if I did know…, I wouldn't… 虚拟语气 (我不
　　知道做什么可以帮助自己 concentrate，但
　　是如果知道的话……所以这是虚拟语气)

lose focus 失去注意力；分散注意力

🎤 Mirrors

Q *How often do you look in the mirror every day?*

A: Well, I do it multiple times. Every morning and every evening, when I wash my face and brush my teeth, I'm standing in front of a mirror, that's for sure. And also, during the day, every once in a while, I pull out my small mirror and see if I look good.

Q *Have you ever bought mirrors?*

A: Yeah, I have. In fact, the last time I bought a mirror was just last week. My mom and I went to IKEA to buy a mirror and other pieces of furniture to refurbish our apartment. The mirror we bought was dirt-cheap. It only cost us 80 yuan or something.

Q *Would you use mirrors to decorate rooms?*

A: Um, I'm not sure what you mean…If there's a mirror that looks good and suits my room, it can absolutely be seen as a decoration. But I don't suppose I would put several or even many mirrors in a place just to make it look better.

词汇 Key Words

multiple ['mʌltɪpl] *adj.* 很多的

for sure 肯定；毫无疑问地

(every) once in a while 偶尔

pull out 掏出来

IKEA 宜家

a piece of furniture 一件家具

refurbish [ˌriːˈfɜːbɪʃ] *v.* 重新装修

dirt-cheap ['dɜːtˈtʃiːp] *adj.* 非常便宜的

suit sth. 适合……

be seen as 被看作，被当作

🎤 News

Q *Do you like reading newspapers?*

A: It's hard to say. I'm not sure if the BBC is considered a newspaper but I do like to read it on a daily basis. It's my main source of information.

Q *Do you like to get news from the internet or from newspapers?*

A: I always read the BBC, which I think is kind of like the internet, but what I do actually is that I have installed an App on my phone, the BBC App. I use it to read news pretty much every day and that allows me to get updated on what's going on in the world. I hardly ever read printed newspapers.

Q *What kind of news do you like to read or watch?*

A: My preference is to read entertainment and sports news, because they appeal to me more. They are lighthearted, not very serious. They are not like political or scientific news, which require that I read those articles really carefully to understand what's really going on. When I read a news article about an actor, a singer or a soccer star, I just feel that it's a good way for me to unwind.

Q *Do you like domestic news or international news?*

A: I read both. Maybe domestic news attracts me more because it's more relevant. I get a better understanding of what is happening around me. For example, perhaps the news says that housing prices have soared recently and I know it's not the time for me to buy an apartment. Oh, as a matter of fact, even if the prices were not sky-high, I still couldn't afford to buy an apartment.

词汇 Key Words

be considered (to be) 被认为是……

on a daily basis 每天

my main source of information 我的主要信息
　来源

install an App 安装一个应用

allow me to do sth. 使我能够做某事

get updated on sth. 了解……的最新消息

what is going on in the world 世界上正在发生
　的事情

preference ['prefrəns] *n.* 偏好，偏爱

appeal to me 吸引我

lighthearted ['laɪt'hɑːtɪd] *adj.* 轻松的，不严
　肃的

unwind [,ʌn'waɪnd] *v.* 放松

relevant ['reləvənt] *adj.* 相关的

soar [sɔː(r)] *v.* 高涨

sky-high ['skaɪ'haɪ] *adj.* 极高的

🎤 Letters or emails

Q *Do you write many letters or emails? Do you prefer to write letters by hand or using a computer?*

A: Well, I like writing emails better because obviously, it's much faster and a lot more convenient. I don't have to buy any envelopes or stamps and then run to a post office to mail anything. From time to time, I write an email to one of my teachers about my homework and then the teacher writes back to me. I think it's very convenient.

Q *Who do you usually write to?*

A: Well, like I said, I write emails to my teachers every once in a while, but in addition to that, I sometimes write to an American friend of mine who has been helping me with my English. In fact, we have Skype lessons on a weekly basis and because of that, we need to email each other from time to time to set times for our lessons.

真经点评："Like/As I said" 是很实用的表达，因为我们在沟通时，有可能会聊到前面提到的事，这时我们完全可以告诉考官 "我刚刚说过……"。不过，尽量在后面进行更多扩展，不要只是重复前文。

Q *What are the differences between writing a letter and writing an email?*

A: There should be tons of differences, but the only one I can think of now is that emails are much faster than letters. If you want to write a letter to a friend in another part of the country or even the world, it takes days for the letter to arrive, or even a month sometimes. However, if you write an email, after writing everything, you just click "Send", and the person you're writing to can receive this email instantly, which is very fast and convenient.

词汇 Key Words

much faster 快得多

a lot more convenient 方便很多

envelope ['envələup] *n.* 信封

stamp [stæmp] *n.* 邮票

from time to time = (every) once in a while 偶尔，
有时

write back to me 给我回信

in addition to 除了……之外

set times 定时间

instantly ['ɪnstəntlɪ] *adv.* 立即，即刻

🎤 Magazines

Q *Do you read magazines?*

A: Um, well, I hardly ever read magazines because I mainly get information on social media, Weibo, in particular, which is the Chinese equivalent of Twitter. This is my main source of information because it's much easier and way more convenient to learn what's going on in the world on it. Plus, it's free of charge.

Q *Did you read magazines when you were young?*

A: Yeah, I did. Before the advent of social media, I was a huge fan of magazines, particularly one called *Reader*. This used to be very popular with teenagers and young adults about 10 years ago. I would go to the newsstand near my home and buy it every week because it was issued weekly. I really liked this magazine back then because there were so many kinds of articles in it, not just about sports, but also entertainment, politics and so on. I could read anything in this one single magazine.

Q *Do younger people or older people prefer to read magazines?*

A: I want to say neither of them like to read magazines now because as for young people, we prefer to read things on social media and elderly people are more into reading newspapers. I honestly have no idea why, but it just seems like every time you see an old person reading something, they're very likely to be reading a newspaper.

Q *What kinds of magazines are popular in your country?*

A: Um, I don't suppose magazines are any different from newspapers. The most popular kinds of magazines should be about entertainment, sports, and current affairs. Out of these, perhaps the most well-liked type is entertainment coz everybody likes to read about celebrities and later gossip about them with friends.

词汇 Key Words

hardly ever 很少

social media 社交媒体

learn what's going on in the world 了解世界上
　　正在发生的事情

free of charge 免费的

particularly [pə'tɪkjələlɪ] *adv.* 尤其

be popular with... 在……中很流行

popular = well-liked 流行的

newsstand ['njuːzstænd] *n.* 报刊亭

be issued（报纸、杂志）出版，发行

weekly ['wiːklɪ] *adv.* 每周一次

be into sth. 喜欢……

have no idea 不知道；不了解

an old person...they 通常在不知道或没有
　　明确表达性别的情况下，一个人也可以
　　被称作 they

be likely to do sth. 可能做某事

current affairs 时事

celebrity [sə'lebrətɪ] *n.* 名人

gossip about sb. 聊某人的八卦

🎤 Sleep

Q *How many hours do you sleep every day?*

A: Most of the time, I hit the sack around 11:30 and um, I am a morning person, so usually I just get out of bed at 6:30. That makes it seven hours every day.

Q *Is it necessary to take a nap every day?*

A: It really depends on the person. For me, I don't suppose it is that necessary because I tend to be a rather energetic person and I have a lot of energy every single day. I hardly ever have any shut-eye after lunch. But I know that a lot of other people are completely different. If they don't take a power nap at noon, they just find it really hard to function in the afternoon…they just feel really groggy. For those people, it's pretty important.

Q *Do old people sleep a lot?*

A: Off the top of my head, I'd say that they do. They go to bed really early every night and they take some naps during the day, two or even three hours. So when everything is added up, I believe old people do sleep a lot.

Q *Do you always have a good sleep?*

A: I always have a very good sleep. When I sleep, I sleep like a baby. I never toss and turn and I never have a nightmare. I do feel I'm pretty fortunate.

词汇 Key Words

hit the sack 上床睡觉

a morning person 一个喜欢早起的人

get out of bed = get up 起床

necessary ['nesəsərɪ] *adj.* 非常重要的，必要的

energetic [ˌenə'dʒetɪk] *adj.* 精力充沛的

take a nap 小憩一会，小睡一会

groggy ['grɒgɪ] *adj.* 困倦的

sleep like a baby 睡得很好

toss and turn 辗转反侧

nightmare ['naɪtˌmeə] *n.* 噩梦

fortunate ['fɔːtʃənət] *adj.* 幸运的

🎤 Cooperation

Q *Do you prefer to study alone or with others?*

A: I think I generally like to study alone. When I'm studying with other people, it's okay. We can brainstorm ideas together, and they can help me with my work. But in general, I just feel that I can concentrate better on my project when I'm just completely by myself. When I'm surrounded by others, they always prove to be a distraction.

Q *What activities require cooperation?*

A: Tons of activities require cooperation. I'm trying to think of a few examples. Sorry, let me think about it. Well, nothing comes to mind…The only thing I can think of right now is actually a game—Tug-of-War. I think it's an activity, right? When you're doing Tug-of-War, you're cooperating with a bunch of people on your side, and you're competing with those on the other side. Cooperation is really important in this game.

Q *Do you remember a time when you needed to cooperate with others?*

A: Back in college, there were some presentations that we needed to do. For some of those presentations, I had to work together with a couple of others on the same team. For example, I remember doing a presentation about the history of America, and I cooperated with two of my classmates.

词汇 Key Words

generally = in general 总的来说

brainstorm ['breɪnstɔːm] *v.* 头脑风暴

concentrate on sth. 集中注意力于……

project ['prɒdʒekt] *n.* 研究项目；课题

be surrounded by… 被……环绕

prove to be… 被证明是……

distraction 令人分心的人、事、物

tons of… 很多

think of sth. 想出……

nothing comes to mind 想不到任何东西

tug-of-war [ˌtʌg əv ˈwɔː(r)] *n.* 拔河

cooperate with sb. 与某人合作

compete with sb. 与某人竞争

back in college 在大学的时候

presentation [ˌpreznˈteɪʃn] *n.* 展示；陈述；演讲

🎙 Maps

Q *Do you often use maps?*

A: Yeah, I do. I don't have a good sense of direction so I always have to find my bearings. For instance, whenever I go abroad, I have to hire a car, and because I might have never been there before, I usually have to try to find my way, and then, I will have to use a map.

Q *Who taught you to use a map?*

A: We had geography class in middle school. I vaguely remember that our geography teacher taught us something about using maps. It's been so long and my memory is a little sketchy.

真经点评：在谈论过去的事时，如果事情发生的时间较为久远，我们完全可以说 "It's been so long and my memory is a little sketchy." 或类似的话。

Q *Have you asked someone for directions?*

A: All the time. When I lose my way, I just try to find my bearings on a map on my phone. Sometimes, if there is someone near me, I will just go up to them and ask them how I can get to my destination. I've done that multiple times.

Q *When was the first time you used a map?*

A: I don't remember. Your questions are all about my past. It must have been 10 or 15 years ago. I don't know, I'm so sorry.

词汇 Key Words

a good sense of direction 好的方向感

find one's bearings 找到自己的位置

go abroad 出国

find one's way 找到路

I vaguely remember 我模糊地记得

it's been so long 已经很久了

my memory is a little sketchy 我的记忆有点模

糊了

multiple ['mʌltɪpl] *adj.* 很多的

🎤 Shoes

Q *Do you like buying shoes?*

A: I don't like buying shoes. I guess I only buy a pair of new shoes every year, because most of the shoes I buy are really durable and they can last a long time. For example, the shoes I'm wearing right now…I actually bought them 2 years ago, if I remember correctly.

Q *Have you ever bought shoes online?*

A: No, I don't think it's a good idea to buy shoes and clothing on the internet, because these are the things that you have to try on yourself to see if they fit. That's why whenever I want to buy some new shoes, I just go to a shoe store, find a pair, try it on and see if I want to buy that pair.

Q *Which do you prefer, fashionable shoes or comfortable shoes?*

A: I guess I would say that my preference is to buy comfortable shoes. They have to be comfortable, but it wouldn't hurt if they were fashionable and good-looking at the same time, right?

词汇 Key Words

a pair of shoes 一双鞋

durable ['djʊərəbl] *adj.* 耐用的，持久的

last a long time 持续很长时间

if I remember correctly 如果我没记错的话

a good idea 一个好主意

try sth. on 试穿……

fit [fɪt] *v.* 合身

my preference 我的偏好

it wouldn't hurt if they were… 如果它们……

肯定没什么不好(注意此处使用了虚拟语气)

good-looking [gʊd 'lʊkɪŋ] *adj.* 好看的

🎤 Jewellry

Q *How often do you wear jewellry?*

A: Well, I guess the only piece of jewellry on me is a ring that my boyfriend gave me on my last birthday. It's not a wedding or engagement ring or anything…and I wear it every day, wherever I go.

Q *What's your attitude towards jewellry?*

A: Um, my attitude towards jewellry? Well, I don't know where to begin…As for me, I don't suppose I'm the type of person that will wear a lot of jewellry coz, for one, it's heavy, right? Haha. Another reason is my preference is to have a minimalist look, you know, the simpler, the better. Honestly, I don't see it as beautiful when someone wears too much jewellry.

Q *What kind of jewellry do you like to buy?*

这个答案和上面的答案正好相反。

A: Oh, I'm into quite a few things actually, including pendants, studs, rings and so on. I have a lot of rings in my home. In fact, whenever I go to a new place, I like to see if they have some specially-designed rings there.

Q *Why do so many people choose to buy expensive jewellry?*

A: Well, the only reason that comes to mind is that it's a way for them to show off their social status or wealth. In fact, it's not just expensive jewellry, but anything that costs a lot of dough, from cars, bags, to pricey clothing. There's a friend of mine who wears a lot of jewellry and she goes around telling people where she got them and how much she paid for them. As a matter of fact, I don't really think what she wears are pretty at all, but she takes a lot of pride in them.

词汇 **Key Words**

jewellry ['dʒuːəlrɪ] *n.* 珠宝；首饰（不可数名词）

a piece of jewellry 一件首饰

ring [rɪŋ] *n.* 戒指

wedding ring 结婚戒指

engagement ring 订婚戒指

for one 首先，第一

preference ['prefrəns] *n.* 偏好，喜好

minimalist ['mɪnɪməlɪst] *adj.* 简约的

see sth. as… 把……看作……

I'm into 我喜欢

pendant ['pendənt] *n.* 项链坠饰

stud [stʌd] *n.* 耳钉

specially-designed ['speʃəlɪ dɪ'zaɪnd] *adj.* 特别
    设计的

show off 炫耀

social status 社会地位

expensive [ɪk'spensɪv] *adj.* 昂贵的

pretty ['prɪtɪ] *adj.* 漂亮的

take a lot of pride in sth. 为……感到很骄傲

🎤 Housework

Q *Do you do housework?*

A: Yes, I do. In fact, I have no choice but to do housework coz I live alone—there's no one to help me with all the chores. Um, I take out the trash every morning and do the dishes in the evening. I also sweep and vacuum the floor roughly three times a week. I'm not a fan of doing household chores, but I still have to do them.

Q *What kinds of housework do you dislike doing?*

A: Well, I dislike everything because it's both physically demanding and time-consuming. I suppose what I don't like the most would be washing the clothes. I don't really enjoy it when I dip my hands in cold water, and then have to rinse off all the soap.

Q *Did you help your parents do housework when you were young?*

A: Um, yeah I did. As a matter of fact, I was really into doing it when I was growing up coz my parents would pay me for the things I did. For example, if I swept the floor, they would give me 1 yuan and if I did the dishes for the whole family, I would earn 3 yuan, which was a big sum of money for me. I would then run off to buy my favourite snacks.

Q *Do you think men and women should share housework?*

A: Yeah, totally. I believe it's extremely important that men and women share household chores because this is good for their relationship, I think. When they're doing housework, it's some quality time that they spend together. Personally, I share everything with my wife. She cooks and I do the dishes; she sweeps the floor and I take out the trash. So we've never gotten in a big fight before over housework and this really helps our relationship.

词汇 Key Words

do housework 做家务

take out the trash 倒垃圾

do the dishes 刷盘洗碗

sweep the floor 扫地

vacuum the floor 用吸尘器清扫地面

I'm not a fan of sth. 我不喜欢……

physically demanding 耗费体力的

time-consuming [taɪm kən'sjuːmɪn] *adj.* 耗费时间的

dip my hands into cold water 把手浸在冷水里

rinse off the soap 冲洗掉香皂 / 肥皂沫

as a matter of fact 事实上

pay me 付给我钱

a big sum of money 很大一笔钱

totally ['təʊtəlɪ] *adv.* 完全地

extremely important 非常重要的

quality time 宝贵时光

get in a big fight (和某人) 吵架

🎤 History

Q *Do you like history?*

A: Yeah, I have a penchant for learning history. I often go to the library and check out some history books and then read them in the café near my dorm, which I think is super enjoyable.

Q *Do you think history is important?*

A: Yeah, absolutely. Learning history is of great importance. For starters, it allows people to become more intelligent because we can learn lessons from the past. You know, history always repeats itself, so whatever happened before might also happen tomorrow and learning history helps us better solve future problems. On top of that, it provides people with good talking points coz history is full of stories, right? If you like to learn history, you can talk about whatever you've learned with your friends or colleagues and this helps with your conversations.

Q *Do you like to watch programmes on TV about history?*

A: No, I'm not a fan of that coz I believe that the history I learn in books is more credible. Things on TV are usually tweaked in order to be more entertaining so that more people will watch them.

Q *What historical event do you find most interesting?*

A: Oh, my god, this is really tough for me in English. Off the top of my head, I like to read about the Renaissance because there were so many talented people back then—writers, artists, musicians, scientists and so forth. If I could, I would like to travel back in time to that period to meet those people.

词汇 Key Words

have a penchant for 非常喜欢

check out some history books 去图书馆借些历史书

enjoyable [ɪn'dʒɔɪəbl] *adj.* 令人愉快的，令人享受的

be of great importance 非常重要的

it allows sb. to do sth. 使某人能够做某事

intelligent [ɪn'telɪdʒənt] *adj.* 聪明的

learn lessons from the past 从过去学习、汲取知识

provide sb. with sth. 给某人提供某物（注意用 with）

talking points 谈资

be full of 充满……

credible ['kredəbl] *adj.* 可信的

tweak sth. 稍微调整……

in order to 为了

entertaining [ˌentə'teɪnɪŋ] *adj.* 有娱乐性的

so that 以便

the Renaissance 文艺复兴

talented ['tæləntɪd] *adj.* 有才华的

travel back in time 时光穿梭

🎤 Daily routine

Q *What time of the day do you like most?*

A: Um, I suppose it would be the morning, I mean between 6 and 7. I always drag myself out of bed at 6 and then go to nuke my breakfast and make myself a cup of coffee. Coffee is my favourite drink—it's a great pick-me-up and I suppose I like the morning partly because of coffee. Another reason is that it's very peaceful in the morning when everyone else is still asleep. There's no distraction and I can always get a lot of things done in an efficient way.

Q *What's your favourite daily routine?*

A: Well, um, this is hard to describe…Well, I like to get up early so that my day is prolonged, I mean, longer than others' days. During the day…well, I just do whatever I'm supposed to do—study and eat and hang out with friends. I really enjoy it when I can spend my evenings doing some reading coz it's a great stress-buster and I get to better myself in this way.

Q *What's the busiest part of the day for you?*

A: Well, it really depends. On most days, I don't usually feel very busy—I have very little on my plate. However, before mid-terms and finals, I can be swamped and have my hands full all day long.

Q *What's the difference between your daily routine now and when you were a teenager?*

A: Um, the only difference that comes to mind is that I hit the sack much earlier than when I was a teenager because I'm more health-conscious now and also I don't have as much homework as before.

When I was in high school, we got tons of homework to do every single day and I always had to burn the midnight oil.

词汇 Key Words

nuke sth. 用微波炉加热某物

make myself a cup of coffee 给自己做一杯咖啡

a great pick-me-up 一种很棒的提神的东西

peaceful ['pi:sfl] *adj.* 安静的

be asleep 睡着的

no distraction 没有干扰

get a lot of things done 做完很多事

efficient [ɪ'fɪʃnt] *adj.* 有效率的

in a...way 以一种……的方式

prolong sth. 延长……

be supposed to 应该

stress-buster 帮人减压的事物

get to do sth. 得以做某事，能够做某事

have very little on my plate 没什么事情做

mid-term [ˌmɪd'tɜ:m] *n.* 期中考试

final ['faɪn(ə)l] *n.* 期末考试

have one's hands full 很忙碌

all day long 一整天

the only...that comes to mind 唯一能想到的……

be health-conscious 注意健康的

burn the midnight oil 熬夜到很晚

🎙 **Birthday**

Q *How did you celebrate your last birthday?*

A: Um, let me think. Well, in fact, I just celebrated it with my girlfriend/boyfriend. We went out for dinner, a candle-lit dinner actually, so it was pretty romantic. And while we were eating, my girlfriend/boyfriend gave me a present, which was a 5,000-yuan watch/bag. I was taken aback because to us, that was a lot of money. But of course, I was overjoyed.

Q *Do you think it's important for people to celebrate birthdays?*

A: Yeah, definitely. In my opinion, it's extremely important for people to celebrate their birthdays because it's primarily a chance for them to get together with their family members and friends to have fun together. If you throw a birthday party, at home or in a restaurant, you will invite your friends and they will bring you presents. Then, at the party, you will enjoy a big meal together, chat and laugh with each other, which I think is pretty good. So yeah, like I said, celebrating a birthday is absolutely a good opportunity for people to have a great time.

Q *Do people in China do anything special to celebrate birthdays?*

A: Well, in fact, generally speaking, the way we celebrate birthdays now in most parts of China is pretty similar to any other country. I guess it's due to globalisation—invasion of Hollywood movies and western culture and stuff like that. But, something that only we do would be…um, some people still eat a bowl of longevity noodles on their birthdays to wish for a long life ahead. But I haven't done it in a long time.

Q *Are birthdays more important for children or for adults?*

A: Well, in my opinion, birthdays are absolutely more important for kids because I don't suppose I, as well as many of my friends, who are all adults, of course, look forward to birthdays as much as children. Perhaps it's because children all want to grow up, whereas we want to stay young. Well, of course, the key reason here is that kids look forward to presents much more than we do.

词汇 Key Words

go out for dinner 出去吃饭

candle-lit dinner 烛光晚餐

be taken aback 很惊讶

primarily [praɪ'merəlɪ] *adv.* 主要地；根本地

have fun 玩得开心

throw a birthday party 举办生日派对

chat [tʃæt] *v.* 闲聊

the way ……的方式

be pretty similar to sth. 和……很类似

due to 由于

globalisation [ˌgləʊbəlaɪ'zeɪʃn] *n.* 全球化

invasion [ɪn'veɪʒn] *n.* 入侵

longevity noodles 长寿面

look forward to sth. 期待，向往

stay young 保持年轻

key [ki:] *adj.* 关键的

🎙️ Advertisements

Q *Are there many advertisements in your country?*

A: Yes, absolutely. They're everywhere. I mean, we are just bombarded by different kinds of advertisements every day. No matter where you go in our country, you can see different ads. For instance, when you're on the internet and watching TV, you see tons of ads.

Q *Why do you think there are so many advertisements now?*

A: Well, it's just because every company needs to make profits and by putting ads everywhere, they can make more potential customers know the existence of their products or services and they're more likely to go and buy those things. Take Apple for example. Whenever a new iPhone comes out, you can see Apple ads in all sorts of places—on TV, on the internet, in shopping malls and so on. Apple is good at advertising and that's one reason why they're so successful now.

Q *How do you feel about advertisements?*

A: Well, of course, there are good points and bad points about them. As for the good points, some ads are really fascinating, especially some from the United States and Thailand. They can be touching, creative, imaginative and so on. On the other hand, a lot of adverts are incredibly annoying. They take up a lot of time while you're watching TV. You may be watching a captivating show, and then, all of a sudden, there is an ad, and that just really drives you up the wall.

词汇 Key Words

be bombarded by sth. 面对大量的……

advertisement [əd'vɜ:tɪsmənt] *n.* 广告

no matter where 无论何地

tons of... 很多……

make profits 盈利

potential customers 潜在的顾客

existence [ɪg'zɪstəns] *n.* 存在

come out 出版；发行；上市

be good at 擅长；非常了解

fascinating = captivating 精彩的，吸引人的

touching ['tʌtʃɪŋ] *adj.* 感人的

incredibly [ɪn'kredəblɪ] *adv.* 非常地

annoying [ə'nɔɪɪŋ] *adj.* 恼人的，讨厌的

take up a lot of time 占用很多时间

all of a sudden 突然

🎙 Time management

Q *How do you manage your time?*

A: Um, well, this question is tricky…In fact, I don't really manage it. I just do every single task that I'm given. Oh, I guess I should say the best way to manage time is just not to procrastinate. Whenever you have something to do, do it and then move on to the next task.

Q *Do you think young people manage their time in the same way as old people?*

A: Um, probably not. I believe young people generally use modern electronic devices to manage their time, like um…for example, they might make a to-do list on their phone or tablet and then constantly check that list to see what needs to be done and when. By comparison, elderly people might just write things down on paper or in a notebook simply because the majority of them are not quite familiar with modern technology. My granddad, for example, has never successfully learned how to use a smartphone. He has a small notebook within his reach all the time.

Q *Are you ever late for anything?*

A: Yeah, sure. By and large, I'm a very punctual person, which means I'm seldom late for things. But I can still remember a few times when I was late. For instance, last month, I was caught up in traffic one day and it took me much longer to get to work, so I was 15 minutes late.

Q *What excuses do you use when you are late?*

A: Excuses? Well, I don't really come up with any excuses. I mean, if I'm late, I just tell whoever I'm meeting the true reason why I'm late. I guess it's because I'm on time in most cases so that my colleagues and friends will usually forgive me when I'm a little late occasionally.

词汇 Key Words

tricky ['trɪkɪ] *adj.* 困难的

procrastinate [prəʊ'kræstɪneɪt] *v.* 拖延

move on to sth. 开始做另外一件事

generally ['dʒenrəlɪ] *adv.* 总的来说

electronic device 电子产品

a to-do list 待办事项列表

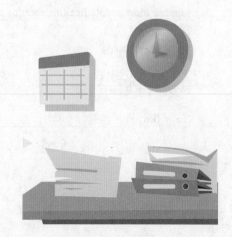

tablet ['tæblət] *n.* 平板电脑

constantly ['kɒnstəntlɪ] *adv.* 不断地

be familiar with 熟悉

within his reach 在他旁边 / 附近

punctual ['pʌŋktʃʊəl] *adj.* 准时的

be late for 迟到

excuse [ɪk'skju:s] *n.* 借口

come up with 想出

forgive me 原谅我

occasionally [ə'keɪʒnəlɪ] *adv.* 偶尔

🎤 Boating

Q *Have you ever travelled by boat?*

A: Yes, I have. Several years ago, in the summer actually, I went on a cruise trip along the Yangtze River with a few of my friends. The whole trip lasted about a week, and we had a great time.

Q *Do you like boating?*

A: Well, it's hard to say. Um, I don't have any special feelings for boating. It's indeed pretty relaxing and pleasurable when I row a boat on a lake with a few friends or with my folks, but I don't suppose boating is necessary in my life.

Q *Would you like to have your own boat?*

A: Yeah, it would be fantastic if I had a boat of my own. First of all, it would mean that I were rich and everybody wants to be wealthy, right? Plus, I could always go boating somewhere to relax and have fun. I believe it would be awesome.

Q *Are boat trips popular in your country?*

A: No, I don't think so, because boat trips are rather time-consuming. When we take a boat to go to another city or region, we usually need to be on it for quite a few days. So because of this, I don't suppose most people like this form of transport.

词汇 Key Words

go on a trip 去旅行

cruise [kru:z] *n.* 游轮

along the Yangtze River 沿着长江

a few of 一些

last [lɑ:st] *v.* 持续

my folks = my family members 我的家人

necessary ['nesəserɪ] *adj.* 必要的

it would…if I could/did/were… 虚拟语气

wealthy ['wel'θɪ] *adj.* 有钱的，富裕的

time-consuming 耗费时间的

form of transport 交通方式

🎤 Apps

Q *What Apps have you recently used?*

A: Actually, I haven't used any new Apps recently, but the few that I use on a daily basis are WeChat, Weibo and Douyin, which is the Chinese TikTok. I use these Apps to learn what my friends are up to, to learn what's going on in the world, and also to have fun by scrolling through some fun videos.

Q *What was the first App you used?*

A: I don't really remember because it was a long time ago. I think I was in middle school when I had my first smartphone and then I downloaded my first ever App. It might have been Weibo, but I can't remember.

Q *What kinds of Apps are you interested in?*

A: I guess I'm just interested in those social media Apps. Social media is something that everybody is on and I use it every single day. Like I said in my first answer, I use Weibo, WeChat and Douyin, which are social media Apps.

Q *What kinds of Apps would you like to use in the future?*

A: I've never thought about that before. I'm perfectly happy with the Apps that I have been using, and as for others…I don't know…I really can't predict what Apps will emerge in the future and what Apps I will like in the future.

词汇 **Key Words**

on a daily basis 每天

learn what my friends are up to 了解朋友近况

learn what's going on in the world 了解世界上
发生的事情

scroll through videos 刷视频，滚动浏览视频

fun [fʌn] *adj.* 有趣的

smartphone ['smɑːtfəʊn] *n.* 智能手机

my first ever... 我人生第一个……

it might have been Weibo 那可能是微博（对过去的虚拟）

be on social media 用社交媒体

I've never thought about that before 我从来没

有想过这个

I'm perfectly happy with... 我对……很满意

predict [prɪˈdɪkt] v. 预测

emerge [ɪˈmɜːdʒ] v. 出现；兴起

🎤 Computers and internet

Q *How often do you use the computer/internet? Do you use the internet very much?*

A: Yeah, I do. The internet is so important to me that I can't live without it. It's because I use it to do practically everything—working, relaxing and keeping in touch with friends. As for relaxing, I watch movies, stream music and play games online. So I'd say the internet is my main source of income and main form of relaxation. It's an indispensable part of my life.

Q *What kinds of computers are popular in China?*

A: What kinds of computers? Um, I'm not sure how to answer this question coz I feel like there's only one kind of computer, right? Oh, yeah, of course, there are desktop computers, laptop computers and also tablets, if they're regarded as computers too. These are all pretty popular.

Q *When was the first time you used the internet? Who taught you how to use a computer?*

A: Well, it must have been my dad when I was 7 or 8 years old. I remember one day, I saw that my dad was playing a game on his computer and I pestered him to teach me. He was pretty reluctant at first, but at last, he gave in and taught me. That game was good fun and um…yeah, that was the first time I used the internet.

Q *Do you think the computer has changed your life a lot?*

A: Yeah, absolutely. I mean, not only me, but everybody. The computer has shattered everybody's old life and created a whole new world for all of us. I think it's very obvious, right? Our lives depend on the computer and the internet now. I'm convinced that it will be even more so in the future.

Q *Is the internet very important to you? Do you think you could live without the internet?*

上述问题的答案可以回答这道题。

词汇 Key Words

practically ['præktɪklɪ] *adv.* 基本上

keep in touch with sb. 和某人保持联系

stream music 在网上听音乐

online [ɒn'laɪn] *adv.* 在线地

my main form of income 我的主要收入来源

desktop (computer) ['desktɒp] *n.* 台式电脑

laptop (computer) ['læptɒp] *n.* 笔记本电脑

tablet ['tæblət] *n.* 平板电脑

be regarded as 被看作

portable ['pɔːtəbl] *adj.* 便携的

on his computer 在他的电脑上（注意介词 on）

pester sb. to do sth. 缠着某人做某事

reluctant [rɪ'lʌktənt] *adj.* 不情愿的

give in 妥协

sth. is good fun 某事 / 物很有意思，很有趣

shatter sth. 打破……

depend on sth. 依赖……

I'm convinced that 我相信，我确定

even more so 更会是这样

🎤 Teenagers

Q *Do you like to spend time with teenagers?*

A: Yeah, I do. I have a 16-year-old brother and we hang out all the time. He's a big fan of video games and he teaches me how to play once in a while. I think it's a lot of fun spending time with him.

Q *Do you know anything about the kind of fashion that teenagers like?*

A: Well, the only thing that comes to mind is that a lot of teenagers are into baggy, loose-fitting clothing. I guess this is because hip-hop culture plays a big part in teenagers' lives and baggy clothing is an important part of this culture. My brother is a good example. He wears a big hoodie and a pair of baggy pants every day. He thinks he looks cool this way.

Q *How do teenagers entertain themselves?*

A: Oh, they do a wide range of things, like playing video games, doing various sports and um… a lot of other things. As for sports, many teenagers try extreme sports like skateboarding, riding a special kind of bicycle called BMX and parkour. They like these because they're young and they're drawn to things that are exhilarating and give them an adrenalin rush.

词汇 Key Words

baggy ['bægɪ] *adj.* 宽大的；宽松的

play a big part in sth. 在……中扮演重要角色

hoodie ['hʊdɪ] *n.* 帽衫

pants [pænts] *n.* 裤子

he looks cool this way 他这样看起来很酷

extreme sports 极限运动

skateboarding ['skeɪtbɔːdɪŋ] *n.* 滑板运动

BMX [ˌbiːem'eks] *n.* 小轮车

parkour [pɑːˈkʊə(r)] *n.* 跑酷

exhilarating [ɪgˈzɪləreɪtɪŋ] *adj.* 刺激的，令人激动的

🎤 Pets and animals

Q *What's your favourite animal?*

A: I think my favourite animal is the horse and this is only because I was born in the year of the horse according to the Chinese zodiac. I was born in 1990 and it was the year of the horse. So I always wanted to go and ride a horse, but I've never gotten an opportunity to do that.

Q *Have you ever had a pet before?*

A: Yeah, I have. When I was 10 or 11 years old…I was a fourth grader at that time…my parents bought me a puppy on my birthday and I really loved it. I would play with it every single day, and my experiences with her were so delightful. However, when I was 12, my parents gave her away because they wanted me to focus on my studies.

Q *What's the most popular animal in China?*

A: Our national treasure is the panda and everybody knows that. I'm just not sure if it's the most popular because pandas are only kept at zoos and we can't keep them at home. I suppose we love dogs the most; they are definitely the most well-liked pet in the world.

Q *Where would you prefer to keep your pet, indoors or outdoors?*

A: Can I say this question is a little silly because we definitely keep our pet indoors. A puppy, kitten or any other pet has to stay indoors most of the time. But when we want to play with our pet, we take it outdoors. So I think that's how it works.

真经点评：即使说考官的题目有点 silly 也没有关系，我们只是在自然地沟通。而且 Part 1 的题目并不是考官自己出的，而是考官从题库中抽取出来问考生的。考官自己都可能觉得有些题目 silly。

词汇 Key Words

I was born in the year of the horse 我是马年出生的

the Chinese zodiac 生肖

a fourth grader 四年级学生

puppy ['pʌpɪ] *n.* 小狗

delightful [dɪ'laɪtfl] *adj.* 令人高兴的，使人愉快的

give sth. away 把……送人

focus on my studies 关注我的学习

national treasure 国宝

be kept at zoos 被养在动物园里

silly ['sɪlɪ] *adj.* 傻的

kitten ['kɪtn] *n.* 小猫

that's how it works 是这么个情况 / 原理

🎤 Saving money

Q *Did you save money when you were young?*

A: No, I didn't. When I was growing up, whenever I wanted to buy something, I just went up to my parents and asked them for some money. They would always give me that, as long as I wasn't going to buy something very pricey.

Q *When was the last time you saved money to buy something?*

A: Well, I really wanted to buy the newest iPhone, the iPhone 13, but it is pretty expensive, so I just tightened my belt for a few months and I also borrowed some money from my parents, and then a coupe of weeks ago, I finally bought my iPhone 13 and I was on cloud nine when I got it.

Q *Have you ever given money to children?*

A: Yes, I have. In China, it's a tradition. On some special occasions, for example, during the spring festival, adults need to give money to children. We call this kind of money lucky money. Usually we put the money in a red envelope and then give it to kids.

Q *Do you think parents should teach children to save money?*

A: Yeah, I think so. It is a vital life skill for children to learn how to save up in order to buy something, because they will eventually grow up and they will have to deal with money and this kind of monetary skill is critical in everybody's life. I believe it's necessary that parents teach children this skill when they are at a young age.

词汇 Key Words

as long as 只要

pricey [ˈpraɪsɪ] *adj.* 昂贵的

tighten my belt 勒紧裤腰带（攒钱）

on cloud nine 超级开心的

lucky money 压岁钱

red envelope 红包

vital [ˈvaɪtl] *adj.* 非常重要的，至关重要的

deal with 处理；应对

monetary [ˈmʌnɪtrɪ] *adj.* 金钱的

🎤 Science

Q *Do you like science?*

A: Um, I don't know. Initially, I wanted to say "No, I don't like science", but...there's nothing about it that I don't like; it's my problem, it's not science's problem. I just find it super hard to learn those science subjects.

Q *When did you start to learn science?*

A: I think I was 8 or 9 years old. It's been ages, so my memory is a little vague, but it must have been when I was in primary school.

Q *What kinds of interesting things have you done with science?*

A: If you want me to pick out one thing to talk about specifically, I really can't. Like I said, it's been so long since I had a science lesson. I remember going to our laboratories in middle school and high school and using those pieces of scientific equipment to work out some chemical reactions and stuff like that, and perhaps that was fun.

Q *Which science subject do you find most interesting?*

A: Like I said over and over…I think you can already tell that I have no interest in science at all. So I don't find any science subject interesting.

词汇 Key Words

initially [ɪ'nɪʃəlɪ] *adv.* 最初，开始

find it hard to learn 觉得它很难学

it's been ages 已经很久了

my memory is a little vague 我的记忆已经有
　点模糊了

it must have been when I was in primary school
　那肯定是我在小学的时候

pick sth. out 挑出……

specifically [spə'sɪfɪklɪ] *adv.* 确切地，具体地

it's been so long since… 从……到现在已经很
　久了

laboratory [lə'bɒrətrɪ] *n.* 实验室

work sth. out 得到；解决

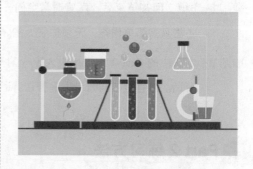

chemical reaction 化学反应

and stuff like that 等等

like I said over and over 就像我说了一遍又
　一遍的

tell [tel] *v.* 判断

have no interest in sth. 对……没兴趣

Part 2 回答九大准则

◆ **准则 1：** 考官并不关心考生是否按照顺序回答一道题目的四个小点，但是我们应该使用最简单的
　　　　方法 —— 从上到下逐点回答，每个小点单独扩展。

◆ **准则 2：** 把每一个小点看作一道 Part 1 题目，按照 Part 1 扩展方法来回答。

◆ **准则 3**：尽量按照顺序回答四个小点，但是如果漏掉了一个，或者因为两分钟时间到了而没说到最后一点，并不会扣分。

◆ **准则 4**：不好说的小点尽量少说，好说的小点可以充分扩展。通常，描述一件家具 / 一棵植物 / 一座建筑物等的外观较难回答，我们可以少说，花更多时间谈论与这一家具 / 植物 / 建筑物等有关的一次经历 / 故事。

◆ **准则 5**：不同的题目可以进行嫁接。如 "Describe a knowledgeable person" 可以与 "Describe a helpful person" 进行嫁接。如果内容合适，也可以与非人物类题目进行嫁接，如 "Describe a happy experience you had in your childhood"（小时候和爷爷聊天，爷爷教了我很多知识）。

◆ **准则 6**：答题之前的一分钟准备时间至关重要，考生应该在这一分钟内尽量写下足够多的关键词（尽量不要写词组或句子）。考生在备考期间要不断练习做笔记。

◆ **准则 7**：回答期间，没有必要一直和考官保持眼神沟通。考生可以不时低头看自己的笔记。

◆ **准则 8**：Part 2 回答结束后，考官通常会问一道与考生回答内容有关的题目。该题会非常简单，考生只需简单作答，无须扩展太多。

◆ **准则 9**：本书中的 Part 2 素材是供大家学习逻辑思路、积累词汇句型用的，大家尽量不要直接背诵。考官能够判断考生是否在背诵答案。

(((► Part 2 练习方法

◆ **方法 1**：熟练掌握 "流利度" 部分的逻辑扩展方法，把它运用到 Part 2 题目的小点扩展中。

◆ **方法 2**：学习本章 Part 2 例题的范例答案，积累词汇、句型、连接性表达。

◆ **方法 3**：听范例答案录音，改善发音；反复朗读范例答案，提高语感，并在此过程中掌握 Part 2 回答逻辑。

◆ **方法 4**：在 "学为贵雅思" App 上找到当季 Part 2 题库，按照题库准备自己的答案。

◆ **方法 5**：可以把自己的答案写下来，然后朗读几遍，再练习回答；也可以写下一些关键词，然后对照关键词练习回答。练习回答时要给自己计时（Part 2 回答时间是 1 ~ 2 分钟，考生应尽量说够 2 分钟）并录音。答完一遍之后，听自己的回答，把听到的词汇、语法、逻辑、发音等方面的问题记下来，并思考可以把哪些词汇和句型替换成更地道的语言。再录一遍、再听、再录、再听。每道题至少录音回答三次。

注意：我们不建议大家完全背诵范例答案。范例答案是为了帮助各位考生增加语言储备、学习逻辑思路的。大家应尽量说出自己的回答。

(((▶ **Part 2** 范例答案

> **Describe a time a child made you laugh.**
>
> **You should say:**
>
>   **when it was**
>
>   **who this child was**
>
>   **what he or she did**
>
> **and explain why it was funny.**

Well, a couple of years ago, in February, if my memory serves me correctly, I visited my uncle's family with my parents. We went over and had dinner with them.

My uncle had a five-year-old son and everyone calls him Xiaoqiang. To be honest, I hadn't seen Xiaoqiang in a long time because I was quite tied-up with work and I didn't often visit my uncle's family. It was then that I realised that he was such a hilarious boy and I believe he has the potential to be a comedian in the future.

When we met, Xiaoqiang had just learned some English at preschool, so he was so eager to show off his English in front of everyone. First, he said "Good morning" to us. But actually, what he said was something like "顾得猫腻". Then, he said "I love you", but it sounded like "爱老虎油". More interestingly, he told everyone his big ambition: he wanted to find an American girlfriend in the future simply because he thought he was really good at English. He really cracked everyone up.

Xiaoqiang made everybody burst out laughing mainly because he sounded so confident while saying those English words. But actually what he said didn't make any sense. Plus, he was thinking of getting a girlfriend. That was the funniest, I think.

词汇 Key Words

if my memory serves me correctly 如果我没记错的话

be tied-up with sth. 忙于……

hilarious [hɪ'leərɪəs] *adj.* 非常幽默的；非常搞笑的

potential [pə'tenʃl] *n.* 潜力

comedian [kə'mi:dɪən] *n.* 喜剧演员

be eager to do sth. 渴望……

show sth. off 炫耀……

ambition [æm'bɪʃn] *n.* 雄心；目标

crack sb. up 令某人发笑

burst out laughing 大笑出来

didn't make any sense 说不通；没人能懂

> **Describe a person who dresses well or a person who is fashionable.**
>
> **You should say:**
>
> **who this person is**
>
> **how you know this person**
>
> **what kind of clothes this person likes to wear**
>
> **and explain why you think this person dresses well.**

I'm going to talk about my friend, Andy. He's always well-turned out and to me, he's the trendiest guy I know.

Andy and I go way back. We used to be colleagues at a small company where I worked part-time, so it was 6 years ago already, if my memory serves me correctly. When I first met him, I was stunned by the way he dressed. He looked extremely smart and sharp.

Anyway, what kind of clothes he likes to wear... well, I'm not quite sure how to put it. I mean, he's always in a shirt, not a very baggy one. He usually wears a pair of jeans, really tight ones. And um, what else can I say...well, one thing I have to mention is that he wears glasses, but only the frame. I mean, he's not near-sighted at all. The glasses are just an accessory. Of course, he wears other kinds of clothes too, but no matter what he wears, he always looks good.

Andy dresses well mainly because he's fashion-conscious, I suppose. He reads fashion magazines and follows the latest trends. Plus, I guess he just has this exquisite taste in clothing. Maybe it's a gift, I'm not quite sure.

词汇 Key Words

well-turned out 衣着光鲜的 / 漂亮的

trendy ['trendɪ] *adj.* 时髦的

go way back 认识很多年

work part-time 兼职工作

be stunned by sth. 因……而吃惊

the way he dressed 他着装的方式

look smart and sharp 看起来很精神

I'm not sure how to put it 我不知道怎么说

baggy ['bægɪ] *adj.* （衣服）肥大的，松松垮垮的

a pair of jeans 一条牛仔裤

tight [taɪt] *adj.* 紧的

near-sighted ['nɪərs'aɪtɪd] *adj.* 近视的

accessory [ək'sesərɪ] *n.* 装饰品

fashion-conscious ['fæʃn'kɒnʃəs] *adj.* 注重时尚的

trend [trend] *n.* 趋势

have exquisite taste in clothing 在穿衣方面有品位

gift [gɪft] *n.* 天赋

> **Describe a person you know who can speak a foreign language.**
>
> **You should say:**
>
> > who this person is
> >
> > what foreign language he or she speaks
> >
> > how often he or she uses this language
>
> **and explain how this person mastered this language.**

Well, um, I'm going to talk about one of my closest friends, Joey. Joey and I go way back. Actually, we were high school classmates. At that time, I envied him so much because his English was already awesome.

So, as I said, Joey really excels at English. I mean, sometimes, when you talk with him in this language, you can't even tell whether he's Chinese or British. Oh, by the way, he has an amazing British accent which makes him sound pretty sexy when he talks. Last month, for example, we went to a café and hung out with a bunch of friends. There was a American girl there. She asked whether Joey had lived in the UK before and she was extremely shocked when he said no.

Um, how often he uses this language…well, to be honest, he doesn't use it that often. He only speaks English when he is with foreign friends. So I would say, two or three times a month.

Anyway, I asked Joey how he mastered English because I wanted to be fluent in this language too. As a matter of fact, my dream is to be multilingual in the future. What Joey told me was that he just watched English movies and he would always read English out loud. Plus, whenever he got a chance, he would practice speaking with a foreign friend. These things sound really simple, but just as the saying goes, "Practice makes perfect." I will try my best to master English too.

词汇 Key Words

envy sb. 羡慕某人

awesome ['ɔːsəm] *adj.* 极好的

excel at sth. 在某个领域非常杰出

tell [tel] *v.* 判断

sexy ['seksɪ] *adj.* 性感的

a bunch of… 一伙，一群（人）

shocked [ʃɒkt] *adj.* 非常惊讶的

master sth. 熟练掌握……

fluent ['fluːənt] *adj.* 流利的

read sth. out loud 读出声来

practice makes perfect 熟能生巧

try my best 尽我最大的努力

> **Describe a person who can do well at work.**
>
> **You should say:**
>
> > **who this person is**
> >
> > **how you know this person**
> >
> > **what kind of work this person does**
>
> **and explain why this person can do his or her work well.**

I'm going to talk about my friend, Yaohui. Her English name is Jenny.

We go way back. To be more accurate, it was about 7 years ago that we first met. I was still a high school student and I was preparing for an English-speaking contest. My cousin asked her to come and give me a hand with my English speech because she was really good at English. I was so stunned by how amazing her English was. I mean, I couldn't even tell whether she'd spend time in America before.

Anyway, what kind of work she does…well, she's an English teacher now. She's been doing it since she graduated from university. As far as I know, she's extremely popular with her students.

I think Jenny does her job really well primarily because she's a very driven person. I mean, she has been working incredibly hard to speak English well. She is very fluent in it now and she has this amazing American accent. In addition to this, she's a pretty positive person; I mean, she's a glass half full kind of girl, so whenever she runs into a problem at work, she just tries her best to think of ways to solve it. I think this quality is pretty rare among young people now. Sometimes, I think of Jenny as my role model.

词汇 Key Words

accurate ['ækjərət] *adj.* 准确的，确切的

English-speaking contest 英语演讲比赛

give sb. a hand 帮助某人

primarily because… 主要因为……

driven ['drɪvn] *adj.* 有上进心的

incredibly [ɪn'kredəblɪ] *adv.* 非常地；难以置信地

positive ['pɒzətɪv] *adj.* 积极的；有信心的

a glass half full kind of person 积极乐观的人

run into a problem 碰到一个问题

quality ['kwɒlətɪ] *n.* 品质

rare [reə(r)] *adj.* 罕见的

role model 榜样

> **Describe a person you know who always travels by plane.**
>
> **You should say:**
>
> > **who this person is**
> >
> > **what this person does**
> >
> > **why he or she always travels by plane**
>
> **and explain how this person feels about plane travel.**

I'm going to talk about my friend Andy. We're pretty tight together. I first met him on a trip to Japan because he was my tour guide. That trip was really an unforgettable experience.

As I said, Andy is a tour guide and he's been doing it for almost five years. Over the years, he's been to so many different places, cosmopolitan cities like Tokyo and New York, and places off the beaten track too. I think his job is pretty cool.

Why he always travels by plane…well, this is pretty obvious, right? What he mainly does is lead tourists from Beijing to other cities and even countries. There's no doubt that plane travel is his main form of transport.

I asked Andy once whether he enjoyed this job. He said that he couldn't love it more. For starters, being a guide allows him to travel to all kinds of places, which is the dream of so many people. For instance, he went to Yuanyang last year where you can see endless rice terraces. I've been longing to go there for a long time because the views are spectacular. Plus, he gets to get away from the hustle and bustle of city life and goes to many places that are both picturesque and peaceful. He loves his job a lot and I really envy him.

词汇 Key Words

tight [taɪt] *adj.* 亲近的

tour guide 导游

unforgettable [ˌʌnfə'getəbl] *adj.* 难忘的

over the years 这些年来

cosmopolitan city 国际化大都市

off the beaten track 人迹罕至的；游客不多的

obvious ['ɒbvɪəs] *adj.* 明显的

there's no doubt that… 毋庸置疑……

form of transport 交通方式

endless rice terraces 无尽的梯田

long to do sth. 渴望……

spectacular views 非常美丽的风景

get away from the hustle and bustle of city life 逃离城市的喧嚣

picturesque [ˌpɪktʃə'resk] *adj.* 风景如画的

peaceful ['piːsfl] *adj.* 宁静的，平静的

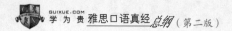
> **Describe a person whose job is important to the society.**
>
> **You should say:**
>
> > **who the person is**
> >
> > **what this person does**
> >
> > **what his or her job mainly involves**
>
> **and explain why you think this person's job is important.**

I'm going to talk about my friend Andy. We're pretty tight together. I first met him on a trip to Japan because he was my tour guide. That trip was really an unforgettable experience.

As I said, Andy is a tour guide and he's been doing it for almost five years. Over the years, he's been to so many different places, cosmopolitan cities like Tokyo and New York, and places off the beaten track too. I think his job is pretty cool, and really important. I'll talk about that in a while.

What his job mainly involves…well, what he mainly does is lead tourists from Beijing to other cities and even countries. When they're visiting a place of interest, like a historic site or a futuristic building, he's responsible for explaining everything about that particular place's history and everything. Also, he has to take care of other things too, like accommodation, food, transport and so on.

I think Andy's job is pretty important because in my country, people love travelling more and more and they need people like Andy to teach them and look after them. In my case, on my trip to Japan, the one I was talking about, I really learned a lot from Andy. It really helped to expand my horizons. Plus, travelling, in my opinion, is one of the best ways to unwind. What Andy does is make our trips more relaxing…

词汇 Key Words

in a while 过一会儿

historic site 历史遗迹

futuristic [fjuːtʃəˈrɪstɪk] adj. 未来风格 / 主义的

be responsible for sth. 负责……

particular [pəˈtɪkjələ(r)] adj. 特定的

take care of 照顾

accommodation [əˌkɒməˈdeɪʃn] n. 住宿

in my case 就我而言

expand my horizons 开拓我的视野

unwind [ˌʌnˈwaɪnd] v. 放松

> **Describe a family member you would like to work with.**
>
> **You should say:**
>
> > **who this person is**
> >
> > **what kind of person he or she is**
> >
> > **whether you've worked together before**
>
> **and explain why you would like to work with him or her.**

Well, I would like to work with my mom.

She is in her 50s but she is still pretty energetic every single day. I guess it's primarily because she has a positive outlook on life. For instance, when I was a child, she always told me that even though we would run into problems sometimes, they were great lessons for us to learn. Plus, she is a people person and gets along with everyone she knows. Oh, yeah, she also likes to tell jokes. Well, perhaps that's what makes her so popular with her friends.

I haven't worked with my mom before, but I guess it would be fantastic to work with her after I graduate because, for starters, what she does is what I'm interested in as well. She's an engineer and that's what I'm aiming to be in the future. Also, she's not the kind of person that always nags their children. Well, my dad is, so I doubt if I would ever want to be at the same company as he is. Hopefully, I'll be able to get a job at my mom's company in the future.

词汇 Key Words

in her 50s 五十多岁

energetic [ˌenə'dʒetɪk] *adj.* 精力充沛的

has a positive outlook on life 生活积极乐观

run into problems 遇到问题

a people person 擅长与人打交道的人

get along with sb. 与某人相处得好

tell jokes 讲笑话

fantastic [fæn'tæstɪk] *adj.* 极好的

be interested in sth. 对……感兴趣

engineer [ˌendʒɪ'nɪə(r)] *n.* 工程师

aim to do sth. 目标是做某事

nag sb. 念叨某人

hopefully ['həʊpfəlɪ] *adv.* 希望；但愿

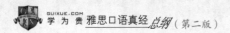

> **Describe a friend who you think is a good leader.**
>
> **You should say:**
>
> **who this friend is**
>
> **how you first met**
>
> **how other people behave towards him or her**
>
> **and explain why you think this person is a good leader.**

Well, I think my dad is a good leader. My dad and I are pretty close and we hang out a lot, so I guess I could say we're very good friends. My dad runs a small company. It specialises in selling children's clothing.

How other people behave towards him…well, actually, my dad is just like any other person at the company and other people don't treat him any differently. I think it's because he's the kind of person that likes to keep a low profile and doesn't want those working at the company to think of him as someone that they can't get along with. Once, I went with my dad to his office and on the way there, he met a couple of people who worked for him. To my surprise, they didn't say anything like "Manager Yang" or something like that. Instead, they all said "Lao Yang", which is something we say to very close friends.

In my opinion, there are a couple of reasons why he's a good leader. First of all, he's nice to everyone and treats people equally. Plus, he works extremely hard himself, so he sets a good example to others. Another reason could be that he throws a party at the company once in a while so that everyone can have fun and wind down after some busy days. So, yeah, I guess these are the reasons why my dad is a great leader.

词汇 Key Words

close [kləʊs] *adj.* 亲近的

run sth. 经营……

specialise in sth. 专门从事……

treat sb. 对待某人

keep a low profile 保持低调

to my surprise 令我惊讶的是

equally ['iːkwəlɪ] *adv.* 平等地

set a good example 树立好的榜样

throw a party 举办一个派对

once in a while 偶尔；有时

wind down 放松

> **Describe a famous foreign person who you would like to meet.**
>
> **You should say:**
>
> > **who this person is**
> >
> > **how you got to know this person**
> >
> > **why he or she is famous**
>
> **and explain why you would like to meet him or her.**

Well, I would really like to meet my all-time favourite actor, David Schwimmer. I'm not sure whether you're familiar with his name, but you've definitely heard of the most famous role he's played—Ross Geller in the sitcom, *Friends*.

I got to know David through the show *Friends*. One of my friends recommended the show to me because she said it was the funniest she had ever watched. I checked it out at once. I found Ross so adorable. You know, he plays a hopeless-romantic paleontologist and he just keeps getting married and then getting a divorce. Anyway, his dumbness makes him so lovable in the show.

As for why he is famous…well, I guess practically everyone knows him because of *Friends*. I know he has also starred in a bunch of other sitcoms and movies, but he gained worldwide recognition for playing Ross Geller.

Um, I would like to meet him simply because he's my favourite actor and I've been a big fan of his for a long time. I don't think anyone could ever replace him as my favourite. Also, you know, perhaps it would be great if I could learn a bit of acting from him if I were to meet David. You never know when that skill would come in handy.

词汇 Key Words

my all-time favourite actor 我一直以来最喜欢
　的演员

be familiar with... 对……很熟悉

play a role 扮演一个角色

sitcom ['sɪtkɒm] *n.* 情景喜剧

check it out at once 立刻看看

adorable [ə'dɔːrəbl] *adj.* 可爱的

a hopeless-romantic paleontologist 一个对爱情
　抱有美好畅想的古生物学家

get married 结婚

get a divorce 离婚

dumbness ['dʌmnɪs] *n.* 傻劲儿

practically ['præktɪklɪ] *adv.* 基本上；几乎

star in sth. 在……中担纲主演

gain worldwide recognition 获得全世界的认可

be a big fan of his... 非常喜欢某人（名人）
　（of 后通常会使用名词性物主代词）

replace... 代替……

acting ['æktɪŋ] *n.* 表演；演技

come in handy 有用

> **Describe a famous person in your country that you like.**
>
> **You should say:**
>
> **who this person is**
>
> **how you know this person**
>
> **what this person is famous for**
>
> **and explain why you like this person.**

I'm going to talk about Benny, who is a really well-known swimmer in China. Benny is his English name. By well-known, I mean, everybody knows him. If not everybody, then at least, every young girl knows this attractive champion swimmer.

I know him because two years ago, um, I remember one day, I was hanging out with a very good friend of mine in a mall and I saw his poster. When I saw his dashing looks, I got really attracted to him. I felt like I couldn't move my legs anymore. I asked my friend if she knew him, she said "Sure" and told me his name and what he does.

What he's famous for…well, I think Benny has gained great popularity nationwide over the past couple of years mainly because he's so good-looking. I mean, I'm not saying he isn't a good swimmer. Well, he is. He specialises in freestyle and he's one of the best in Asia. However, he has gained a large number of followers primarily because of his incredible physique and charming face. He has a six-pack, which absolutely makes most girls wanna scream when they see it. Plus, when he smiles…oh, my god, his smile is more beautiful than words can describe.

I really like him because…haha, I'm the same as most girls. I love how handsome he is. I hope my future boyfriend can be as good-looking as he is.

词汇 Key Words

well-known [ˌwel'nəʊn] *adj.* 有名的

by…, I mean… 我说……的意思是……

at least 至少

attractive [ə'træktɪv] *adj.* 有吸引力的

mall [mɔːl] *n.* 商场

poster ['pəʊstə(r)] *n.* 海报

dashing looks 迷人的面庞

gain great popularity nationwide 在全国范围内大受欢迎

good-looking [ˌɡʊd'lʊkɪŋ] *adj.* 好看的

specialise in freestyle 主攻自由泳

gain a large number of followers 获得大批追随者

incredible physique 令人难以置信的身形

charming ['tʃɑːmɪŋ] *adj.* 有魅力的，迷人的

a six-pack 六块腹肌

scream [skriːm] *v.* 尖叫

more…than words can describe 无法用言语形容

> **Describe a helpful person at work or school.**
>
> **You should say:**
>
> > **who the person is**
> >
> > **what kind of person she or he is**
> >
> > **how this person helps you**
>
> **and explain why you think this person is helpful.**

I'm going to talk about Feng who is the boss of a travel agency where I have been working for the past two years as a part-time tour guide.

He's well-read and well-spoken and he's extremely knowledgeable. Sometimes I just refer to him as a walking encyclopedia because he knows so much about Chinese culture, traditions and a lot about Chinese history. Plus, he's easy-going and approachable. He's always willing to go out of his way to help other people.

How he helps me…well, I'm only twenty years old, pretty young, right? As a tour guide, I really need to understand a lot about Chinese culture, but I don't. Sometimes, if there is something I can't make sense of, I just go to him for help. He has never failed to explain it to me in detail. I remember two years ago, he asked me to lead a tour to the Summer Palace. That was the second time that I went to the Summer Palace. I had only been there once myself, so I wasn't sure whether I was going to do a good job. Before going there, he just explained everything to me. He told me all that I was going to say and do in the Summer Palace, I mean, that was great help. Um, I can't say the tour was a complete success, but it went pretty smoothly.

I think Feng has helped me quite a lot over the past two years, because I have improved considerably as a person, as a tour guide, and also as a communicator. I'm really grateful to him.

词汇 Key Words

travel agency 旅行社

part-time tour guide 兼职导游

well-read ['wel'red] *adj.* 知识渊博的

well-spoken ['wel'spəʊkən] *adj.* 能言善辩的

refer to sb. as… 把某人称为……

a walking encyclopedia 行走的百科全书

easy-going ['iːzɪ 'gəʊɪŋ] *adj.* 随和的，平易近人的

go out of one's way to help others 竭尽全力帮
　助别人

make sense of sth. 理解，弄明白

never fail to do sth. 总能够……

in detail 详细地

go smoothly 进行得比较顺畅

improve considerably 大幅提升

communicator [kə'mjuːnɪkeɪtə(r)] *n.* 沟通者

grateful ['greɪtfl] *adj.* 感激的

> **Describe someone who is older than you that you admire.**
>
> **You should say:**
>
> **who this person is**
>
> **how you know this person**
>
> **what kinds of things you like to do together**
>
> **and explain why you admire this person.**

The person that I'm going to talk about is one of my neighbours whose name is Mr. Peng. He is in his mid-40s, 45 or 46 years old. But he's already retired. According to some other neighbours, Mr. Peng is financially independent now. He used to run a company selling kites. He made so much money that he was able to retire several years ago. I really envy his life. Although we have a big age difference, we are actually pretty good friends.

I know him because I moved to this neighbourhood about 4 years ago, and I think it was a fine spring day. That day I walked out of my apartment building and saw a notice. It was a notice recruiting people for a cycling club in our neighbourhood. I have always enjoyed cycling, so I signed up and then I learned that Mr. Peng was the organiser of this club.

What kinds of things we like to do together? We just cycle everywhere, like in some large parks, also along rivers in the north of the city. There's also a really beautiful, absolutely gorgeous hiking trail in the west of our city where we like to ride our bikes. We go there several times a year. We have a great time cycling and chatting and doing some other stuff.

I think I really admire Mr. Peng mainly because not only does he ride a bike for fun, he actually does it for the environment. He says that this form of transportation is really green. It's zero-emission. When we ride our bikes, we are actually leaving zero carbon footprint, which is the best for the environment. Because of that, I just really admire him.

词汇 Key Words

in one's mid-40s 四十五六岁

financially independent 财务自由的

envy ['envɪ] v. 羡慕

age difference 年龄差距

a fine spring day 一个晴朗的春日

recruit sb. 招募某人

a cycling club 骑行俱乐部

sign up 报名参加

I learned that... 我了解到……

organiser ['ɔːgənaɪzə(r)] n. 组织者

absolutely gorgeous 非常美丽的

hiking trail 徒步路线

for fun 为了开心

form of transportation 交通方式

green [griːn] adj. 环保的

zero-emission ['zɪərəʊ ɪ'mɪʃn] n. 零排放

leave zero carbon footprint 留下零碳足迹

（不污染环境）

> **Describe a creative inventor or musician.**
>
> **You should say:**
>
> **who this person is**
>
> **what this person does**
>
> **how you know this person**
>
> **and explain why you think this person is creative.**

I'm going to talk about a very famous singer in China, whose name is Shaun. He's so well-known that everyone knows him, including my mom. My mom is already 56 years old, but she claims to be Shaun's biggest fan.

Like I said, he's a singer, so he sings, releases albums, goes on tour and so on. In fact, just before this test, in order to calm myself down, you know, this is such a nerve-wracking experience…In order to get rid of the nerves, I just listened to one of his songs time and time again—*Love is Blind*, which is a really beautiful song.

Anyway, I know Shaun because…I remember very clearly, ten years ago, I was hanging out with a good friend of mine one day in a shopping mall, and then a song grabbed my attention. My friend told me the singer was Shaun, so after I got home, I found all his albums on the internet and bought all of them.

I think he is such a creative musician because…well, he composes and sings many different songs, of various styles—R&B, rap, rock and roll, jazz and so on. Plus, he gets inspiration from literally everything…

词汇 Key Words

well-known [ˌwel'nəʊn] *adj.* 有名的

claim [kleɪm] *v.* 声称

release albums 发行专辑

go on tour 巡回演出

calm myself down 令我镇静 / 平静

nerve-wracking ['nɜːvˌrækɪŋ] *adj.* 令人非常紧张的

get rid of the nerves 缓解紧张情绪

time and time again 一遍又一遍

grab my attention 吸引我的注意力

album ['ælbəm] *n.* 专辑

compose [kəm'pəʊz] *v.* 作曲

inspiration [ˌɪnspə'reɪʃn] *n.* 灵感

literally ['lɪtərəlɪ] *adv.* 简直

> **Describe a person who moved in with you.**
>
> **You should say:**
>
> > **who this person is**
> >
> > **when he or she moved in**
> >
> > **why he or she moved in with you**
>
> **and explain how it affected your life.**

I'm going to talk about my roommate, Nancy. We've developed a really close bond since she moved in with me.

We've been living together for 2 years. If I remember correctly, it was in July that she began living with me.

Anyway, she moved into my apartment because she had just graduated from college and had been looking for a place to live. She was actually a friend of a friend, so she was told that there was a room available in my apartment. Plus, I couldn't afford the rent on my own. You know, I needed to pay 5,500 Yuan for this apartment and I really needed to tighten my belt, so I was on the lookout for a roommate at that time too. Luckily, I found her and she found me.

How it affected my life…well, I've got a new friend, of course. We hang out every day now and she has brought a lot of joy into my life. Plus, she is an amazing cook. She makes the best spaghetti I've ever tasted. Well, I used to cook on my own, but the food she cooks is far better than mine. So yeah, it's great that she moved in with me.

词汇 Key Words

develop a really close bond 关系变得非常好

look for 寻找

a friend of a friend 一个朋友的朋友

afford the rent 付得起租金

on my own 独自；靠自己的力量

tighten my belt 勒紧裤腰带；省钱

on the lookout 寻找

joy [dʒɔɪ] *n.* 快乐

spaghetti [spə'getɪ] *n.* 意大利面

> **Describe a foreign country that you would like to visit but haven't been to.**
>
> **You should say:**
>
> **where this place is**
>
> **what it is like**
>
> **what you could do in this country**
>
> **and explain why you would like to visit the country.**

Well, I would like to visit Japan in the near future. Japan is pretty close to China and it only takes about 4 or 5 hours to get there by plane, so visiting this country is actually really easy and convenient.

What it is like…well, honestly, I'm not sure where to start. Um, I guess I could say Japan is both modern and historical. I mean, if you go to Tokyo, there are many skyscrapers there, as well as upscale restaurants and chic clothing stores. However, if you go to Kyoto, you will see that it's full of history. I mean, it's filled with historic architecture.

If possible, my boyfriend and I would go to several cities in Japan. First of all, we would definitely go to Tokyo to do some shopping. Plus, I heard that Okinawa is a fantastic tourist destination because the views there are breathtaking and we could go snorkelling, which is something that I've been longing to do for ages.

I would like to visit Japan because…well, there are tons of reasons actually. For starters, it's close to China and it's much easier to go there than other countries. Another reason is that the cosmetics there are extremely cheap and more importantly, of great quality. I would do a lot of shopping there if I really went.

词汇 Key Words

modern ['mɒdn] *adj.* 现代的

historical [hɪ'stɒrɪkl] *adj.* 历史的

skyscraper ['skaɪskreɪpə(r)] *n.* 摩天大楼

upscale [ˌʌp'skeɪl] *adj.* 高端的

chic [ʃiːk] *adj.* 时髦的

Kyoto ['kjəʊtəʊ] *n.* 京都

historic [hɪ'stɒrɪk] *adj.* 有历史意义的

architecture ['ɑːkɪtektʃə(r)] *n.* 建筑式样；建筑
风格

Tokyo ['təʊkjəʊ] *n.* 东京

Okinawa [ˌəʊkɪ'nɑːwə] *n.* 冲绳

tourist destination 旅游目的地

breathtaking views 非常美的风景

go snorkelling 去浮潜

long to do sth. 渴望……

for ages 很久

tons of… 很多……

> **Describe a place where you can read or write (not your home).**
>
> **You should say:**
>
> where it is
>
> when you go there
>
> who you go there with
>
> and explain why you like to go there.

I'm going to talk about a bookshop that is quite close to my apartment. It's just about 300 metres away, so I find it really convenient to go and hang out there, either alone or with my friends. Apart from being a bookshop, there's also a small café inside, so I think it's a great place where I can do some reading and stuff.

I go there **on a regular basis**, I mean, about two or three times a week.

I usually **pass the time** there with my girlfriend. Um, the two of us **have a lot in common** and we particularly enjoy reading. We're really fond of **biographies**. For instance, we went to this bookshop three days ago and we sat in the café for three hours. We were reading Steve Jobs' biography together. Besides that, we also had a discussion about Steve. We really had an enjoyable time there.

Why I like to go there…well, I think it's primarily because I'm a big **bookworm**. I mean, I'm quite into reading and it's **an essential part of my life**. I find this bookshop a really nice place to read and think. Plus, I like it because of its café. The **atmosphere** there is great and um, the **latte** they make is so good.

词汇 Key Words

apart from… 除了……

on a regular basis 定期；经常

pass the time 打发时间

have a lot in common 有很多共同点

biography [baɪˈɒɡrəfɪ] n. 传记

bookworm [ˈbʊkwɜːm] n. 书虫；喜欢读书的人

an essential part of my life 我生活中非常重要的一部分

atmosphere [ˈætməsfɪə(r)] n. 气氛；氛围

latte [ˈlɑːteɪ] n. 拿铁咖啡

Describe a street that you like to visit.

You should say:

    where it is

    how often you go there

    what you like to do there

and explain why you like it.

Well, I'm going to talk about a very famous and popular street in Beijing, called 王府井. It draws loads of shoppers and tourists—I mean, tourists both from other cities and countries. It's located right in the heart of the city, not very far from Tian'anmen Square.

I only go there from time to time, something like 2 or 3 times in a couple of months. I wish I could go there more often, but my home is not near there at all and also, I'm always tied-up with my studies.

I can do tons of things there, like sightseeing, shopping and so on. I can do some sightseeing because there are a few historic sites. The most popular

one is a Catholic cathedral which dates back to 100 years ago. Plus, there are many chic clothing stores, boutiques as well as name-brand factory stores there, so it's a fantastic place to shop. For instance, the last time I went, I bought a pair of Nike shoes at the Nike factory store.

I think I really like this street simply because, as I mentioned earlier, there's a variety of things you can do and all of them are so much fun. I suppose this is what makes it so popular.

词汇 Key Words

draw [drɔː] v. 吸引

right in the heart of the city 在城市的正中心

be tied-up with my studies 忙于我的学业

sightseeing ['saɪtsiːɪŋ] n. 观光

historic site 历史遗迹

Catholic cathedral 天主教堂

date back to… 追溯至……

chic [ʃiːk] adj. 时髦的

boutique [buːˈtiːk] n. 精品店

name-brand factory store 名牌工厂店

a variety of… 多种多样的……

> **Describe a street market or an outdoor market you've been to.**
>
> **You should say:**
>
> > **what it is like**
> >
> > **when you went there**
> >
> > **why you went there**
> >
> > **and explain how you felt about it.**

I'm going to describe a street market that was really famous in my hometown when I was a kid and it was named Dog's market, 狗市 in Chinese, but actually the official name was 花鸟鱼虫市场, a market of flowers, birds, fish and dogs. You can probably tell that there were a variety of things that were sold there, but I guess that market was most famous for all the cute dogs that people wanted to buy. A lot of dog lovers would go there. They would see different breeds, like Chihuahuas, labradors, corgis, and so on.

I remember when I was 9 years old, because I really wanted a corgi, I thought it was the most adorable dog in the world… My parents actually took me there one weekend, and they bought me a corgi for my birthday. I was on cloud nine when I got that adorable pup.

When I went to this market? I went there a lot in primary school, almost every month. Sometimes even more often than that. However, I stopped going there after graduating from primary school, because my family moved away from that area. I just haven't been back there ever since, and honestly, I don't even know whether this market still exists.

I went to this market just to have fun with my parents or with my little friends, because it was such a bustling market. You could hear a lot of sellers shouting to get people's attention to look at their products, flowers, birds, dogs, and so on. And also, you could see people haggling down prices. It was just so fun. Every time I went there, I would have a blast.

词汇 Key Words

be named 被叫作……

official [əˈfɪʃl] *adj.* 官方的；正式的

breed [briːd] *n.* 品种

pup = puppy 小狗，可爱的狗狗

Chihuahua [tʃɪˈwɑːwə] *n.* 吉娃娃

labrador [ˈlæbrədɔː(r)] *n.* 拉布拉多

corgi [ˈkɔːgɪ] *n.* 柯基

adorable [əˈdɔːrəbl] *adj.* 可爱的

on cloud nine 非常开心

more often than that 比那还要经常

I haven't been back there ever since 自从那
　　时我就没有回过那里

have fun 开心

bustling [ˈbʌslɪŋ] *adj.* 热闹的，熙熙攘攘的

get people's attention 吸引人们的注意力

haggle down prices 砍价

so fun 很有意思

have a blast 玩得很开心

> **Describe a café or restaurant that impresses you.**
>
> **You should say:**
>
> **where it is**
>
> **how often you go there**
>
> **what kind of food they serve there**
>
> **and explain why you like this place.**

I'm going to talk about a café called 明轩. In Chinese, I guess it translates as "bright place". It's within walking distance of my home, so I go there pretty often and pass the time by reading a book or doing my homework.

Since this café is really close to my apartment, I go there on a quite regular basis, I mean, about 2 or 3 times a week.

Anyway, as I said, it's a café, so it's not really famous for its food. What they make the best is the coffee. I particularly like their latte. But there's food too and it's mainly western, like spaghetti, pizza and risotto.

I really like this place primarily because of its atmosphere. They play some soft music, which is very soothing and relaxing. So whenever I have time, I just go there alone and do some reading. It really helps me take my mind off things. Another reason why I'm really fond of it is that, as I mentioned earlier, their coffee is awesome. Actually, I brought a couple of friends there and they also thought the coffee was among the best they had ever tasted. Anyway, this place is my favourite place to hang out and I always tell people about it if I get a chance.

词汇 Key Words

within walking distance of... 到……的距离在步行范围内

pass the time 打发时间

on a regular basis 定期；经常

spaghetti [spə'getɪ] *n.* 意大利式细面条

risotto [rɪ'zɒtəʊ] *n.* 意大利烩饭

soothing ['suːðɪŋ] *adj.* 令人安静的

relaxing [rɪ'læksɪŋ] *adj.* 令人放松的

take my mind off things 让我不想烦心事

be fond of sth. 喜欢……

awesome ['ɔːsəm] *adj.* 极好的

> **Describe a historical building in your country.**
>
> **You should say:**
>
> > **where it is**
> >
> > **how you got to know this building**
> >
> > **what it is like**
>
> **and explain why it is important to your country.**

I'm going to talk about the Temple of Heaven, which is situated in the southeastern part of central Beijing. It was the place where emperors of the Ming Dynasty and Qing Dynasty held the Heaven Worship Ceremony. Now it's open to the public as a park and residents nearby can go for a walk inside. Plus, it's not uncommon for elderly people to do tai chi, play chess and other traditional Chinese activities there.

I got to know the Temple of Heaven when I was just a small kid. I was just 7 or 8 years old then, if I remember correctly. My mom told me about it and brought me there later.

What it is like…well, it's pretty hard to describe. Well, this temple is even larger than the Forbidden City. It's enclosed by a long wall. The northern part within the wall is semicircular, symbolising the heavens and the southern part is square, symbolising the earth. The main altar lies in the heart of the whole temple and it was where emperors held worship ceremonies.

I think this temple is extremely important to my country mainly because it's a link between the past and the present. I mean, when you stand inside the temple, it just feels like all the history is around you and it reminds Chinese people of our rich past. In addition to this, everything inside this temple is so beautifully designed and decorated, so it's just like a gorgeous work of art.

词汇 Key Words

the Temple of Heaven 天坛

be situated in… 位于……

emperor ['empərə(r)] n. 皇帝

dynasty ['dɪnəstɪ] n. 朝代

Heaven Worship Ceremony 祭天仪式

residents nearby 附近的居民

not uncommon 很普遍

elderly people 老年人

the Forbidden City 故宫

be enclosed by a long wall 被一道很长的墙围起来

semicircular [ˌsemɪ'sɜːkjələ(r)] adj. 半圆的

symbolise sth. 象征……

square [skweə(r)] adj. 方的

altar ['ɔːltə(r)] n. 祭坛；神坛

in the heart of sth. 在……的中心

a link between the past and the present 一条连接过去和现在的纽带

rich past 璀璨的历史

beautifully designed and decorated 设计和装饰得很精美

gorgeous ['gɔːdʒəs] adj. 非常美丽的

work of art 艺术品

> **Describe a tall building in your hometown you like or dislike.**
>
> **You should say:**
>
> > **where it is**
> >
> > **what it is used for**
> >
> > **what it looks like**
>
> **and explain why you like or dislike it.**

I'm going to talk about my dormitory building, which is on my university campus. It's in the south of the university, not very far from the south gate. My university is in the northwestern suburb of my hometown, not in the city centre, so if I'm not mistaken, this 23-storey building is the tallest in the area.

Like I said before, it's a dormitory building. It accommodates about 1,000 students, freshmen and sophomores. All junior and senior students live in another building, close to the north gate of the university.

What it looks like…well, it's just a regular-looking building, greyish in colour. Grey is the most common colour when it comes to buildings in China. But what's special about this building is that the windows are pretty big. They're extraordinarily big so they can let in more sunshine and air. All rooms in this building are well-ventilated, which is pretty good.

I like this building a lot because…well, first of all, I've been living there for 2 years, so I'm quite attached to it. Apart from that, I live on the 7th floor, which I think is perfect. Most of the time, I take the elevator, but from time to time, I take the stairs and walk up. It's great cardiovascular exercise, I suppose. Walking up and down helps me keep fit and stay in shape.

词汇 Key Words

dormitory building 宿舍楼

on campus 在校园里（注意介词 on）

suburb ['sʌbɜːb] *n.* 郊区

if I'm not mistaken 如果我没说错的话

23-storey ['twentɪriː'stɔːrɪ] *adj.* 23 层的

accommodate [ə'kɒmədeɪt] *v.* 容纳

freshman ['freʃmən] *n.* 大一学生

sophomore ['sɒfəmɔː(r)] *n.* 大二学生

junior ['dʒuːnɪə(r)] *n.* 大三学生

senior ['siːnɪə(r)] *n.* 大四学生

regular-looking ['regjələ(r) 'lʊkɪŋ] *adj.* 外表普通的

greyish ['greɪɪʃ] *adj.* 有点灰色的

when it comes to… 当提到……的时候；关于……

extraordinarily [ɪk'strɔːdnrəlɪ] *adv.* 不同寻常地

let in sunshine and air 使阳光和空气进来

well-ventilated ['wel'ventɪleɪtɪd] *adj.* 通风很好的

be attached to sth. 非常喜欢……，热爱……

from time to time 偶尔；有时

cardiovascular exercise 有氧运动

keep fit and stay in shape 保持健康、保持身材

> **Describe a park or garden you visited that you like.**
>
> **You should say:**
>
> > **where it is or was**
> >
> > **what it looks or looked like**
> >
> > **what people do or did there**
>
> **and explain why you like this park/garden.**

I'm going to talk about a park that is quite close to my apartment. It's actually within walking distance, so if I'm not busy, I go there every day.

This park is gorgeous. There are so many trees inside, like gingkos, willows, and a lot of pines. Oh, my granddad once told me that some of the gingkos there are even hundreds of years old. Plus, there's a big lake in the centre of the park and you can row a boat on it. Of course, you have to rent one from the boat shed.

What people do there…well, we can do many things. For instance, some people like to go for a stroll there after dinner and others, especially elderly people, enjoy doing tai chi, playing mahjong and also chess with their friends. In my case, I often go jogging there. Yesterday, for example, I ran for 30 minutes and I found it pretty relaxing.

I really like this park mainly because it's a wonderful place to unwind. You know, I'm always tied-up with my studies and it really stresses me out, so having a park near my home and doing some leisure activities definitely does me good. I feel that walking or jogging a little in this park helps me take my mind off things. Besides, I really like the peace and quiet there.

词汇 Key Words

gingko ['gɪŋkəʊ] *n.* 银杏树

willow ['wɪləʊ] *n.* 柳树

pine [paɪn] *n.* 松树

row a boat 划船

boat shed 船棚

go for a stroll 去散步

mahjong [mɑːˈdʒɒŋ] *n.* 麻将

go jogging 去慢跑

unwind [ˌʌnˈwaɪnd] *v.* 放松

tied-up ['taɪd ʌp] *adj.* 很忙的

stress me out 令我倍感压力

leisure activity 休闲活动

do me good 对我有好处

peace and quiet 安静，宁静

> **Describe an important place (like stadium, swimming pool) in your city.**
>
> **You should say:**
>
> > **where it is**
> >
> > **how often you go there**
> >
> > **what people do there**
>
> **and explain why you think it is important.**

I'm going to talk about the public swimming pool in the southwest of my hometown. It's right next to our public library, which is a landmark in the city, so it's really easy to find.

I like to go to this place in the summer because I go to university in another city; I can't go there when I'm at uni. But when the term ends, especially during the summer holiday, I go there pretty regularly, something like 2 or 3 times a week.

Obviously, people just go swimming there. You can see people of all ages at the pool—old people, young people, kids. Many children go there too. In fact, this is exactly what I did when I was a child. When I was 4 or 5 years old, my dad took me there to teach me how to swim. He said that swimming was a walk in the park, but I found it super difficult. It took me weeks to master it.

Anyway, I think this swimming pool is a really important place in the city because it provides the local residents with a place to work out, to live a healthy life. In my opinion, swimming is the best sport because it's relaxing, it doesn't make you too tired and it trains all parts of your body.

词汇 Key Words

right next to... 正挨着……

landmark ['lændmɑːk] *n.* 地标

uni ['juːnɪ] *n.* 大学（= university）

when the term ends 在学期结束之后

regularly ['regjələlɪ] *adv.* 定期；经常

a walk in the park 很简单的事

master sth. 熟练掌握……

local residents 当地居民

work out 健身，锻炼

train all parts of your body 锻炼你全身所有
　部位

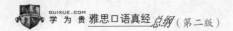
> **Describe a change that would improve the area where you live.**
>
> **You should say:**
>
>   **what change it would be**
>
>   **why you think there should be this change**
>
>   **what people would have to do**
>
> **and explain whether you think you would see this change.**

There's a big problem in my hometown and it's the awful traffic. I really hope that it can be improved in the not-too-distant future. So I suppose if we could all take the public transport more, our roads wouldn't be too congested. So this is the change I'm going to talk about.

There should be this change primarily because, as I said, there are simply too many vehicles on the road, which means when you go to work or go to school, it always takes you a long time. Last Wednesday, for instance, I went to the Summer Palace. Although my home isn't far at all from the Summer Palace, it took me over one and a half hours to get there by bus. I found the busy traffic extremely annoying.

What people have to do...well, as I mentioned earlier, it would be fantastic if we could all take the public transport because, in that case, there would be fewer cars on the road. Also, perhaps we could try carpooling. I mean, for example, if my neighbour and I went to the same part of the city for work, we could share the same car.

I believe our traffic will be better in the near future because almost everyone is fed up with all the congestion in Beijing. In order to reduce all the traffic, people will definitely take action.

词汇 Key Words

awful ['ɔːfl] *adj.* 非常糟糕的

in the not-too-distant future = in the near future
  在不远的未来

congested [kən'dʒestɪd] *adj.* 拥堵的

primarily because 主要因为

vehicle ['viːɪkl] *n.* 车辆

annoying [ə'nɔɪɪŋ] *adj.* 令人厌烦的

carpool ['kɑːpuːl] *v.* 拼车

be fed up with... 厌烦……

take action 采取行动

> **Describe a long journey you went on by car.**
>
> **You should say:**
>
> **where you went**
>
> **who you went there with**
>
> **what you did during the journey**
>
> **and explain why you went on the journey by car.**

I'm going to talk about the time when I drove to Inner Mongolia. I'm from Beijing and the place we went to was about 600 kilometres away, so I drove almost 10 hours. It was exhausting yet really rewarding.

I went with my girlfriend. It was her who decided that we should drive there. Actually, up until then, I'd already been to Inner Mongolia a couple of times, but she hadn't, so she was eager to go.

What we did on the journey…well, it was driving most of the time, of course. But we pulled over from time to time because I had to rest every once in a while. I wasn't a very experienced driver after all. Plus, it was really gorgeous along the way, so we always stopped to take photos. Oh, there's something else I shouldn't forget to tell you. My girlfriend is an amazing singer, so she kept singing all the way in order to make the drive not so boring. I think the journey was a blast.

Anyway, as for why we drove there…um, well, it was mainly because we both had four days off, so we had plenty of time to spend on the way there. Also, we were convinced that the journey would be very enjoyable, what with all the views and stuff. It turned out that we were right. We really had a ball.

词汇 Key Words

exhausting [ɪgˈzɔːstɪŋ] *adj.* 令人筋疲力尽的

rewarding [rɪˈwɔːdɪŋ] *adj.* 令人满意的；令人有收获的

be eager to do sth. 渴望做某事

pull over 靠边停车

from time to time = once in a while 偶尔；有时

experienced [ɪkˈspɪəriənst] *adj.* 经验丰富的

after all 毕竟

gorgeous [ˈgɔːdʒəs] *adj.* 非常美丽的

a blast 令人开心的事

have…off 休息……（一段时间）

convinced [kənˈvɪnst] *adj.* 确信的

what with 由于……

it turned out that… 事实证明

have a ball 玩得很开心

> **Describe a long walk you ever had.**
>
> **You should say:**
>
> > **when this happened**
> >
> > **where you walked**
> >
> > **who you walked with**
>
> **and explain how you felt about the walk.**

I'm going to talk about the time when I had a long walk on the Great Wall. It was the only time I'd been to the Great Wall and it was a blast. It was 2 years ago that I went there. At that time, I was really tied-up with my studies because I was busy preparing for the final exams. I decided to take a day off and go hiking somewhere to put everything behind me.

The section of the Great Wall I went to is located in the northeastern part of Beijing, quite close to Hebei Province. This section doesn't draw many tourists, so it felt great walking there, with very few other hikers.

Who I walked with…well, to be honest, I was just on my own. I went for this walk simply because I wanted to get away from it all and have some time completely to myself.

I felt very good about it because it really helped me take my mind off things. I wasn't thinking about my studies or my relationships. I was just really focusing on finishing the 4-hour hike. It was really exhausting, but it felt awesome. Plus, the views there were stunning. At one point, I had to trek in the mountains and it was great…

词汇 Key Words

a blast 令人开心的事

be tied up with my studies 忙于我的学习

put everything behind me 把一切抛在脑后

(be) close to… 离……很近

draw many tourists 吸引很多游客

get away from it all 摆脱所有烦恼

have some time completely to myself 有一些完全独处的时间

take my mind off things 让我不想烦心的事

exhausting [ɪɡ'zɔːstɪŋ] *adj.* 令人筋疲力尽的

awesome ['ɔːsəm] *adj.* 非常棒的

stunning ['stʌnɪŋ] *adj.* 令人震惊的

at one point 在某一时刻

trek in the mountains 在山里行走

> **Describe a paid job you did or someone you know did.**
>
> **You should say:**
>
> > **what it was**
> >
> > **how you or this person found this job**
> >
> > **how long you or this person did this job**
>
> **and explain how you felt about this job.**

I was a part-time tour guide a couple of years ago. I was an English tour guide and the people taking part in my tours were mainly westerners.

I was a sophomore at university when I began this job. One of my teachers referred me to a small company called China Culture Centre. This company specialises in introducing foreigners to Chinese culture and apart from tours, they also give courses and talks on different aspects of Chinese culture, like traditional Chinese food, Peking Opera, Fengshui and so forth.

This job lasted two years. I'm extremely thankful for these two years because I went to tons of places in China, such as Tibet, Inner Mongolia and Xinjiang. Being a tour guide really helped to expand my horizons. While telling foreigners about our country, I learned a lot as well. Plus, this experience allowed me to hone my communication skills. To be honest, I had always been pretty shy around people, but since I had no choice but to talk with my guests all the time, I gradually got more extroverted.

How I felt about this job…well, it was a very valuable experience for me. I mean, as I mentioned earlier, I learned so much during that period. I'm really grateful to my teacher and to China Culture Centre for having given me this opportunity.

词汇 Key Words

part-time [ˌpɑːt'taɪm] *adj.* 兼职的

take part in sth. 参加……

sophomore ['sɒfəmɔː(r)] *n.* 大二学生

refer sb. to 把某人推荐给……

specialise in 专门从事……

aspect ['æspekt] *n.* 方面

last [lɑːst] *v.* 持续

be thankful for 对……表示感激

expand my horizons 开拓我的视野

hone my communication skills 锤炼我的沟
　　通技巧

extroverted ['ekstrəvɜːtɪd] *adj.* 外向的

valuable ['væljuəbl] *adj.* 有价值的；有益的

be grateful to sb. 对某人表示感激

> **Describe a skill that was difficult for you to learn.**
>
> **You should say:**
>
> > **when you learned it**
> >
> > **why you learned it**
> >
> > **how you learned it**
> >
> **and explain how you felt when you learned it.**

The skill that I'm going to talk about is speaking French. And I learned it about 5 years ago, during the summer vacation after my second year of high school.

I had performed really well in school during that year, so my parents decided to give me a reward of taking me to French on vacation. And we went there in mid-August. I just learned French because of that. I wanted to be better able to communicate with the locals, to better understand the culture.

How I learned French…I was using several Apps, including Duolingo, Rosetta Stone, and a couple of other Apps. The one that proved the most effective was Rosetta Stone, because while I was using that App, there was a lot of listening and speaking, and those were the skills that I really wanted to improve and perfect.

How I felt when I learned it…Honestly, your topic is to describe a skill that was difficult for me to learn. It was indeed really hard, super tough. I think the main reason is that when you're learning French, when you're memorising words, it's like, it's not a walk in the park, mainly because there are feminine words, there are masculine words, and there's no rule to tell which one is feminine, and which one is masculine. For example, une table, a table is feminine. And un lit, a bed is masculine. You never know, right? That's really confusing. That's why when I was learning this language, I had a hard time memorising the genders of those individual words and it took me a long time to learn only 100 words.

词汇 Key Words

reward [rɪ'wɔːd] *n.* 奖赏

mid-August [mɪd 'ɔːgəst] *n.* 八月中旬

be better able to… 能够更好地……

the locals 当地人

prove + *adj.* 证明是……的

effective [ɪ'fektɪv] *adj.* 有效的

perfect sth. 使……完美

tough [tʌf] *adj.* 困难的

memorise sth. 记忆……，背……

a walk in the park 简单的事

feminine ['femənɪn] *adj.* 阴性的

masculine ['mæskjəlɪn] *adj.* 阳性的

tell [tel] *v.* 判断

confusing [kən'fjuːzɪŋ] *adj.* 令人困惑的；

　费解的

have a hard time doing sth. 做某事很困难

> **Describe a success in your life.**
>
> **You should say:**
>
>   **when and where this happened**
>
>   **who you were with**
>
>   **what you did**
>
> **and how you felt about the success.**

I'm going to talk about the time when I succeeded in losing weight. Three years ago, I was a really chubby girl. I was not obese, but I already felt that I had to do something. So I began to lose weight.

I did everything alone. There was nobody else that was trying to shed pounds with me. But I had the support of my family and friends. They always encouraged me and um, I suppose I owe some of my success to them.

Anyway, what I did…well, I did a combination of things. For starters, I had to cut down on my calorie intake, so basically I stopped eating junk food, such as hamburgers, French fries and ice cream. Instead, I ate a lot of fruit every day, like apples, lychees, strawberries and so on. Plus, I think what was fundamental in my success was that I went jogging on a daily basis. I would jog in the park for 30 minutes both in the morning and in the evening. After about half a year, I successfully lost 30 pounds. Actually, now, I still can't believe I did it.

How I felt about the success…well, I'm pretty proud of myself. You know, I really put a lot of effort into it and as I said, it's unbelievable that I didn't give up. I feel much more confident now than before.

词汇 Key Words

chubby ['tʃʌbɪ] *adj.* 比较胖的

obese [əʊ'biːs] *adj.* 非常胖的

shed pounds 减肥

owe sth. to sb. 把……归功于……

do a combination of things 做一些事（组合）

cut down on my calorie intake 减少卡路里摄入量

junk food 垃圾食品

fundamental [ˌfʌndə'mentl] *adj.* 主要的；基本的

effort ['efət] *n.* 努力

unbelievable [ˌʌnbɪ'liːvəb(ə)l] *adj.* 难以置信的

give up 放弃

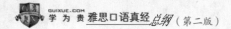
> **Describe a team you have been part of.**
>
> **You should say:**
>
>   **when this team was formed**
>
>   **who were on the team**
>
>   **what you did together**
>
> **and explain whether you liked to be on that team.**

Well, I'm going to talk about the time when I gave a presentation with several classmates. It was back in college and I was a sophomore. Our English teacher divided us into groups of five and each group would give a presentation about an aspect of Chinese culture.

I just teamed up with four of my best friends in the class. You know, we were really tight, so basically we did everything together.

Honestly, preparing for that presentation was not a walk in the park. We decided to talk about Fengshui, or more specifically, why there was always a river or lake built to the north of an important building. We read many books about it and then we wrote down everything that we were going to say. Luckily, the presentation went really well and we were on cloud nine when our teacher made some very positive comments.

Whether I liked to be on that team…well, yeah, sure. I mean, as I said, I worked with my closest friends and we felt really comfortable working together. Although our opinions might differ sometimes, we never had a falling out. So yeah, it was really enjoyable working with them.

词汇 Key Words

give a presentation 做报告 / 展示 / 演讲

team up with sb. 和某人组队

tight [taɪt] *adj.* 亲近的

a walk in the park 简单的事

on cloud nine 非常开心的

positive comments 积极评价

differ ['dɪfə(r)] *v.* 不同

have a falling out 争吵，不和，闹翻

> **Describe a time when you felt surprised to meet someone.**
>
> **You should say:**
>
> > **when it was**
> >
> > **who you met**
> >
> > **what you did together that day**
>
> **and explain why you thought it was a surprise to meet this person.**

I'm going to talk about the time when I met my primary school classmate, Jack. It was two years ago, in July, if my memory serves me correctly. I went on a trip to Dalian, a coastal city in the north of China.

Who I met…well, as I said, I met Jack. You know, we used to be really close friends when we were young. We would hang out together every day, playing soccer, basketball and many other games. We always had a ball together. But then, we went to different secondary schools and we gradually lost touch. I met Jack in a big shopping mall on my second day in Dalian. When I saw him, I just thought this guy looked pretty familiar and we looked at each other for a while until I recognised him. I was so surprised and more importantly, happy as a clam.

Anyway, we went to a Starbucks later and did a lot of catching up. We talked about how our lives had been and where we were living and working. Oh, by the way, he told me that he was going to get married in October and invited me to his wedding. I was on cloud nine that day.

I think it was a big surprise primarily because Jack was my primary school classmate and we hadn't seen each other in years. Also, it was not in Beijing, I mean, we both went to Dalian at the same time. It was such a small world.

词汇 Key Words

if my memory serves me correctly 如果我没记错的话

coastal city 海滨城市

have a ball 玩得很开心

gradually lose touch 逐渐失去联系

familiar [fə'mɪlɪə(r)] *adj.* 熟悉的

recognise sb. 认出某人

happy as a clam 非常开心的

do a lot of catching up 了解近况；叙旧

get married 结婚

> **Describe a person who impressed you most when you were in primary school.**
>
> **You should say:**
>
> > who he or she was
> >
> > how you got to know him or her
> >
> > why he or she impressed you most
>
> **and explain how you felt about him or her.**

The person that I'm going to talk about was a middle school student. This topic says describe a person who impressed me most when I was in primary school. At that time, we were not classmates or schoolmates. I was in primary school. He was in middle school. He was already in his third year of middle school, which means his high school entrance examinations were coming, but he didn't seem to be very concerned about those exams. Actually, they were supposed to be really important, but he just had this nonchalant demeanor. And to me, that was really cool.

I got to know him when I was 10 or 11 years old, when I was a 5th or 6th grader. At that time, we were neighbours and his parents and my parents would always hang out with each other. I still remember the first time I visited his apartment. He had locked himself up in his own room playing the guitar. I didn't see him, but he was playing the guitar and that was just really charming to me.

I think the main reason he impressed me most is just because he was able to play a musical instrument and that was the guitar. Anybody that could play anything like the piano or keyboard or the drums was cool to me. As a teenager, I wanted to learn something like that as well, because I wanted to impress other people, especially girls. And then he was able to play the guitar. So yeah, he was really cool. Like I said over and over and over, he impressed me a lot with those musical skills.

词汇 Key Words

in his third year of middle school 初三

high school entrance examinations 中考

seem to... 看起来……

be concerned about sth. 对……很担心

be supposed to... 应该……

nonchalant demeanor 漠不关心的举止

a 5th or 6th grader 五年级或六年级学生

hang out 待着；玩；休闲地做一些事

lock himself up 把他自己锁起来

charming ['tʃɑːmɪn] *adj.* 有魅力的

musical instrument 乐器

keyboard ['kiːbɔːd] *n.* 键盘乐器

play the drums 打架子鼓

as a teenager 作为一个青少年（13～19 岁）

as well 也

over and over and over 一遍一遍又一遍

> **Describe a time that you and your friend had a disagreement.**
>
> **You should say:**
>
> > **when this happened**
> >
> > **who you disagreed with**
> >
> > **what you and your friend argued about**
>
> **and explain whether you two solved the disagreement in the end.**

I'm going to talk about the time when I had a disagreement with my friend, Yaohui. His English name is Peter. It was a couple of weeks ago, on a Saturday, if I remember correctly. I was free that day and I didn't know what to do to pass the time.

I asked Peter what he had in mind. Peter and I are really tight friends; we're as thick as thieves and we like to do everything together. We'd never had a falling out or anything, so I didn't expect that we'd have an argument that day.

What he wanted to do was to go to a bakery to learn how to make a cake. I was quite shocked when he said it because he had never expressed any interest in baking. However, he was pretty adamant. I told him that what I thought would be a great idea was to go on a picnic in Beihai Park, which is pretty close to the Forbidden City. The problem was, neither of us would budge.

Well, at last, we reached an agreement. Since it was Saturday, we could go to the park that day and go to the bakery on Sunday. After all, we're best friends; we wouldn't be angry with each other forever.

词汇 Key Words

pass the time 打发时间

as thick as thieves 关系特别好

bakery ['beɪkərɪ] *n.* 面包房

shocked [ʃɒkt] *adj.* 非常惊讶的

adamant ['ædəmənt] *adj.* 坚定的

go on a picnic 去野餐

budge [bʌdʒ] *v.* 让步

reach an agreement 达成一致

after all 毕竟

Describe a time when you were friendly to someone you didn't like.

You should say:

> **when and where it happened**
>
> **who he or she was**
>
> **why you didn't like this person**

and explain why you were friendly to him or her on that occasion.

I'm going to talk about a time when I was at a wedding ceremony. It was 2 years ago, in June. To be accurate, it was June the 6th. That day was also a Saturday, a lot of sixes right? Saturday is the 6th day in a week according to the Chinese calendar. A lot of sixes...which was perfect for a Chinese wedding, because the number six is one of the luckiest numbers in our culture. And the place where that wedding ceremony was held is actually where I was born, 23 years ago. This place is about 40 kilometres from where I currently live. My parents had to drive about an hour to get in there.

This person that I didn't quite like is actually one of my cousins who I have only seen 2 or 3 times in my entire life.

The reason I didn't like him is just because we were at the wedding, we were eating and drinking and chatting, and then he just kept bragging about his successes. For example, he talked about how many girls he had dated. Like one time there was a girl that he was seeing, and then he dumped her and began to see another girl. That was not very nice to hear. Another thing is that he just kept swearing. He used a lot of curse words, like the Chinese equivalent of dropping the f-bomb.

But I still had to be friendly to him, mainly because we're relatives. And we were at a wedding...it was supposed to be a happy event, so I couldn't be angry or rude to him.

词汇 Key Words

at a wedding ceremony 在一场婚礼上

to be accurate 确切地说

calendar ['kælɪndə(r)] *n.* 日历

be held 被举行

kilometre ['kɪləˌmiːtə] *n.* 千米，公里

where I currently live 我现在住的地方

drive about an hour 开差不多一个小时的车

keep doing sth. 一直做……

brag about sth. 吹嘘……

be seeing a girl 正在和一个女孩约会

dump her 甩了她

swear [sweə(r)] *v.* 说脏话

curse words 骂人的话，脏话

the Chinese equivalent of... 相当于中文中的……

drop the f-bomb 说脏话

relative ['relətɪv] *n.* 亲戚

a happy event 一场开心的活动

rude [ruːd] *adj.* 粗鲁的

> **Describe an artistic activity you did at school.**
>
> **You should say:**
>
> > **when this happened**
> >
> > **who you did it with**
> >
> > **what you did in the activity**
>
> **and explain how you felt about this activity.**

I'm going to talk about the time when I performed at the New Year Party at high school. It was already 7 years ago now, but I still remember it vividly because it was the first time that I had performed in front of a big crowd of people. I was extremely nervous.

My performance was a hip-hop dance, and I did it with four other students. In my first year of high school, one of my classmates formed a dance crew and asked me to join. I could do a little popping and I thought "Why not". The thing is, I never imagined we would give such a nerve-wracking performance one day.

Anyway, um, the dance lasted about 5 minutes, but it felt like hours to me. There were about 300 people in the audience and they gave us a big round of applause after our performance. To be honest, my heart was still beating really fast then.

How I felt about it…well, it's hard to say, because right after the performance, I thought I would never dance in front of so many people again. But, a few minutes later, I was actually pretty happy that I had done it. I mean, I was really proud that I was the centre of attention then. It felt really good.

词汇 Key Words

remember sth. vividly 清晰地记得……

dance crew 舞团

popping ['pɒpɪŋ] *n.* 机械舞

nerve-wracking ['nɜːvˌrækɪŋ] *adj.* 令人无比紧张的

300 people in the audience 300 名观众

a big round of applause 热烈的掌声

beat fast (心脏)跳动得很快

centre of attention 关注的焦点

Describe a natural talent (sport, music, etc.) that you want to improve.

You should say:

what this talent is

when you discovered this talent

how you want to improve it

and explain why you want to improve it.

I'm going to describe singing. Music has been a big part of my life ever since I was a little kid. And now I listen to it on a daily basis. When it comes to the kinds of music I like to listen to, I've been particularly into rock music recently and there's a really famous and popular singer in China, whose name is Xu Wei. He's a rock musician. And when you listen to his songs, you can kind of feel that he is sad and he has definitely experienced a lot of ups and downs in his life. So yeah, I listen to his music every day now.

When I discovered this talent of singing…Honestly, I don't suppose I should say that I discovered this talent because I'm really not good at singing, but I've been singing my entire life, perhaps ever since I was a toddler. My mom told me that I used to hum a lot of songs every day, especially those famous and popular nursery rhymes, like *Twinkle Twinkle Little Star*, like *London Bridge is Falling Down*. I'm probably out of tune now. But anyway, I used to sing those rhymes a lot. And now I don't sing them, but I still sing some other songs.

The next two questions are how I want to improve this talent and why I want to improve it. I have to be totally honest with you. I don't want to improve this talent. The reason I'm talking about this is just because when I saw this topic, this is the first thing that came to mind. I feel perfectly fine being at the level of singing that I am right now. I don't really see the need to improve.

词汇 Key Words

music has been a big part of my life 音乐一直
    是我生活中重要的一部分
on a daily basis 每天
when it comes to… 关于；在……方面
I've been into…recently 我最近比较喜欢……
musician [mjuˈzɪʃn] *n.* 音乐家；音乐人
ups and downs 跌宕起伏
toddler [ˈtɒdlə(r)] *n.* 学步的孩童

hum songs 哼歌
nursery rhymes 儿歌
out of tune 跑调
the first thing that came to mind 我立刻想到
    的东西
feel perfectly fine 感觉很好，不觉得有问题
see the need to… 觉得有必要……

> **Describe an educational trip you went on.**
>
> **You should say:**
>
> > **where you went**
> >
> > **who you went there with**
> >
> > **what you did during the trip**
>
> **and explain why you thought this trip was educational.**

I'm going to talk about the time I went to the History Museum with my classmates. The trip was organised by our high school teacher, Mr. Li. He taught us history. He brought us there so that we could gain a better understanding of our country's past. Well, this museum is situated in the very heart of Beijing, I mean, right next to the Forbidden City. But unfortunately, we didn't go there. We just spent the entire afternoon in the museum.

What we did there…well, we took a walk inside the museum with a guide who was an expert on Chinese history. We started from the section where weapons and pottery from 2,000 years ago were on display. Our guide talked about the first dynasty in our country, the Qin Dynasty. Oh, by the way, the Great Wall was built then. After that, the guide showed us around sections that were dedicated to the following dynasties like the Tang Dynasty, Song Dynasty and so forth. Although we were really busy taking notes and memorising stuff, we still had a ball there.

I think this trip was really educational primarily because we, at least, I, gained a great deal of knowledge about our history. Also, to be honest, history wasn't really my cup of tea then, but this trip sparked my interest in this subject and I decided to learn it better.

词汇 Key Words

gain a better understanding of sth. 更深入了解……

be situated in... 位于……

the very heart of... ……的正中心地带

right next to sth. 紧挨着……

section ['sekʃn] *n.* 部分

weapon ['wepən] *n.* 武器

pottery ['pɒtərɪ] *n.* 陶器；陶瓷器皿（不可数）

on display 展出

dynasty ['dɪnəstɪ] *n.* 朝代

be dedicated to... 专门用于……

take notes 记笔记

memorise sth. 记忆……，背诵……

have a ball 玩得很开心

gain a great deal of knowledge 学到很多知识

not my cup of tea 我不喜欢……

spark my interest in sth. 激起我对……的兴趣

> **Describe an article on health you read in a magazine or on the internet.**
>
> **You should say:**
>
> > **what the article was about**
> >
> > **where you read it**
> >
> > **why you read it**
>
> **and explain how you felt about it.**

I'm going to talk about an article about sleep. This article talks about the reasons why a lot of people nowadays are suffering from insomnia, why they are tossing and turning every night, and why they have a lot of unwanted wake-ups. At the end of the article, it also touches on some possible solutions to the problems I mentioned just now. For example, if you are tossing and turning, if you are waking up so many times during the night, you shouldn't fight it. If you want to go to the bathroom, just go, don't argue with your bladder. If you want to go and read a book in the living room, just go and do it. But one thing to note is that perhaps you shouldn't read a very interesting book. You have to make sure that the book is slightly boring so that you will not be very fascinated by the content of the book. You will want to come to bed.

I read this article online. I don't actually remember from which website. Last Sunday, I didn't have any class. I decided to take a nap, but before doing that, I was browsing on the internet and then I came across this article.

There's no particular reason why I read it. Like I said just now, it was by accident that I read it. Normally, I'm a good sleeper. I don't really experience a lot of insomnia. I'm just not an insomniac, but I'm still really happy that I read this article because who knows what's gonna happen in the future, right? Maybe I will have difficulty falling asleep. Maybe I will have those unwanted wake-ups that are talked about in the article. When that happens, it'll come in handy.

词汇 Key Words

suffer from insomnia 失眠

toss and turn 辗转反侧

unwanted wake-ups 不希望出现的醒来

touch on sth. 涉及……

fight sth. 与……抗争

don't argue with your bladder 别和你的膀胱争
论（想去厕所就去）

one thing to note is… 要注意的一件事是……

slightly boring 有一点点无聊

be fascinated by the content of the book 被
书的内容所吸引

take a nap 午睡；小憩

browse [braʊz] v. 浏览

come across… 偶然碰到……

by accident 偶然地；意外地

an insomniac 失眠者

it'll come in handy 那会很有用

> **Describe something you do to stay healthy.**
>
> **You should say:**
>
>   **what you do**
>
>   **when you started doing this**
>
>   **how often you do this/how much time you spend doing it**
>
> **and explain how it helps you stay healthy.**

Well, honestly, I'm not really an outdoorsy type. I don't like sports at all, so I don't think there's anything physical that I can talk about. But I really enjoy eating fruit. I mean, different kinds of fruit, so this is what I'm going to talk about.

When I started doing this...God, how am I supposed to answer this? I started eating a great amount of fruit 3 or 4 years ago. I used to eat a lot of junk food every day and I put on so much weight. Then, I made up my mind to lose weight and I began eating a variety of fruit, like cherries, lychees, Hami melon and so on. You can see that I'm in shape, right? I suppose I owe it to my fruit-eating habit.

Ever since I started this habit, I've been eating different kinds of fruit every day. You know, sometimes, I even put some apples or grapes in my backpack so that I can eat them even on the bus.

Anyway, eating fruit helps me stay healthy because...well, I guess it's primarily because fruit doesn't contain much fat and it's low in calories, so as I said, it helps me lose weight. Plus, no matter what kind of fruit it is, it contains many types of vitamins, which is definitely very beneficial to my health...

词汇 Key Words

an outdoorsy type 喜欢户外运动的人	in shape 身材好
a great amount of sth. 大量……	owe sth. to sth. 把……归功于……
junk food 垃圾食品	contain fat 含有脂肪
put on weight 增重；增肥	low in calories 低卡路里
make up my mind 下定决心	vitamin ['vɪtəmɪn] *n.* 维生素
a variety of sth. 多种多样的……	

> **Describe an activity that you feel excited about.**
>
> **You should say:**
>
> > **what it is**
> >
> > **where you can do it**
> >
> > **how you do it**
>
> **and explain why you feel excited about it.**

I'm going to talk about hiking, which is my favourite leisure and outdoor activity. Hiking is becoming more and more popular in China and a lot of people around me have taken it up in recent years, so we just often go hiking together.

There are many places in and around my hometown where I can hike, but my favourite spot is the 金山岭 section of the Great Wall, which is situated in the northeast of Beijing. It borders Hebei Province and is really picturesque. I really love this place because hiking there is extremely challenging. I mean, I have to walk for at least four hours to another section named 古北口, both on and off the wall. Each time after the hike, I feel worn-out, but proud as well.

How I do it…um, I'm not sure how to answer this…well, before a hike, I have to fill my backpack with several bottles of water in case I get dehydrated. Plus, sunscreen is a necessity as well. After all the preparation, I just begin walking…and um, that's it.

I feel pretty excited about walking because it allows me to be in the great outdoors, which gives me the best feeling, I think. You know, seeing all the stunning views and meeting all kinds of difficulties while hiking is pretty exhilarating.

词汇 Key Words

take sth. up 开始做某事

spot [spɒt] *n.* 地点

section ['sekʃn] *n.* 部分

be situated in... 位于……

border sth. 和……相邻

picturesque [ˌpɪktʃə'resk] *adj.* 风景如画的

challenging ['tʃælɪndʒɪŋ] *adj.* 有挑战性的

worn-out ['wɔːn'aʊt] *adj..* 非常疲劳的

in case 以免；以防

dehydrated [ˌdiːhaɪ'dreɪtɪd] *adj.* 脱水的

sunscreen ['sʌnskriːn] *n.* 防晒霜

necessity [nə'sesətɪ] *n.* 必要的东西

the great outdoors 大自然；户外

stunning views 非常美的风景

exhilarating [ɪg'zɪləreɪtɪŋ] *adj.* 刺激的；令人激动的

> **Describe a (jigsaw) puzzle you like.**
>
> **You should say:**
>
> > **what it is**
> >
> > **how easy or difficult it is**
> >
> > **how long it takes you to solve**
>
> **and explain why you like it.**

I'm going to describe the crossword puzzle, which is pretty popular in English-speaking countries like America, Canada, the UK, Australia, and so on. I know that there's always a crossword puzzle or even more than one in newspapers and magazines. For example, there's a pretty famous magazine in America called *Reader's Digest*. There's always a crossword puzzle on one of the pages towards the end of the magazine.

I think it's actually pretty tough, especially for non-native speakers like me, because I don't have a big English vocabulary. And even the words I do know, I don't know them like the back of my hand.

When I have to do this kind of puzzle, those words don't pop into my head very easily. And because of that, it always takes me pretty long to solve the puzzle. For example, if it's 10 words, 5 across, 5 down, perhaps it might take me over an hour.

And why I like this puzzle…I don't like it, to be honest. The reason I'm talking about crossword puzzles is because when I saw this topic, this is the only thing that came to mind. Honestly, I don't like learning English, either. English has been pretty challenging for me. But I've been trying to better my English recently because of this test. I have to do well in this test. I will also have to use English when I go and study abroad. It has been pretty frustrating for me, because the last time I took the IELTS test, I only got 6 in IELTS writing, but I need a 6.5 to meet the requirements for my dream university, the University of Manchester.

词汇 Key Words

crossword puzzle 纵横填字游戏

English-speaking country 英语国家

Reader's Digest《读者文摘》

towards the end of... 接近……的末尾处

non-native speaker 非母语者

a big vocabulary 很大的词汇量

know sth. like the back of my hand 了如指掌

pop into my head 被我想到，进入我的大脑

5 across, 5 down 5 个横着的，5 个竖着的

come to mind 被我想到

better sth. 提升……

study abroad 出国留学

frustrating [frʌ'streɪtɪŋ] *adj.* 令人沮丧的

meet the requirements 达到要求

> **Describe something you would like to do if you were given a day off.**
>
> **You should say:**
>
>   **what you would like to do**
>
>   **who would you like to be with**
>
>   **where you would like to do it**
>
> **and explain how you would feel at the end of the day.**

If I had a day off, I would most likely stay at home and learn English. I'm not lying, this is definitely what I would do if my teacher told me that I didn't have to go to school tomorrow, because I've gotten quite fond of learning English recently. You know, I've been preparing for this IELTS test for the past couple of months and I've realised learning English is a lot of fun. Normally, every day after I get up, I will read several BBC articles and then note down some useful words and phrases. Then, I will watch one or two episodes of *Friends*, you know, the American sitcom. I've found that my English has improved dramatically over the past several months.

Who I would like to be with…well, I guess I would just be alone, because most of my friends don't like learning English. They find it boring and difficult.

I guess I would go to the café within walking distance of my home. It's where I often go and pass the time. Plus, their coffee is pretty good, and more importantly, really cheap.

How I would feel at the end of the day…well, to be honest with you, I wouldn't feel anything special because this is something that I've been doing for months. If I had to give an answer, I'd say I would feel that my day was not wasted.

词汇 Key Words

a lot of fun 很有意思

note sth. down 把……记下来

episode ['epɪsəud] *n.* （电视节目）一集

sitcom ['sɪtkɒm] *n.* 情景喜剧

improve dramatically 大幅提升

pass the time 打发时间

> **Describe a situation where you waited for something.**
>
> **You should say:**
>
>   **when and where it happened**
>
>   **who you were with**
>
>   **how long you waited for it**
>
> **and explain how you felt about the waiting.**

I'm going to talk about a time when I waited for the sunrise. It was two years ago, during the winter vacation, actually. My parents and I went to Yuanyang, which is a small county in Yunnan Province. Yuanyang is famous for its spectacular rice terraces. My dad is a huge fan of photography, so he really wanted to capture the sunrise there.

Anyway, who I was with…well, apart from my parents, there were also hundreds of people waiting for the sun. The platform where we were standing was overcrowded and at one point, I couldn't even see whether the sun was up or not, because after all, I'm pretty short.

We waited two hours because it was pretty foggy that day and although it was already 7 o'clock, the sun was still not in sight. Then, it suddenly cleared up and finally, everybody got what they wanted. We were all super happy.

How I felt about the waiting…well, to be honest, I felt extremely cold at that time. Haha, just kidding. Well, I think it was well worth it, because after all, my dad got some amazing photos. We showed them to some neighbours after we got back and they were really stunned by the breathtaking views.

词汇 Key Words

sunrise ['sʌnraɪz] *n.* 日出	after all 毕竟
·county ['kaʊntɪ] *n.* 县	foggy ['fɒgɪ] *adj.* 有雾的
spectacular/breathtaking views 非常美的风景	in sight 在视线以内
rice terraces 梯田	clear up 变得晴朗
capture the sunrise 捕捉日出的景象（拍照）	well worth it 很值得
overcrowded [ˌəʊvə'kraʊdɪd] *adj.* 过度拥挤的	be stunned by sth. 因……而吃惊

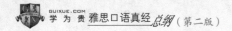

> **Describe something you've wanted to do for a long time but haven't done yet.**
>
> **You should say:**
>
> **what it is**
>
> **where you want to do it**
>
> **how easy or difficult it is**
>
> **and explain why you want to do it.**

I'm going to talk about yoga, which, as everybody knows, is one of the most popular forms of relaxation as well as physical activity. In recent years, it's been growing fast in popularity in China and many of my friends are doing it on a regular basis. I've wanted to take up yoga for quite a long time.

As far as I know, there's a gym not far from my home which offers yoga classes. I haven't checked it out yet, but if I finally decide to practice yoga, I might go and see if their classes suit me. Plus, I bet I will also buy a yoga mat and practice at home since I might want to do it every day and going to a class on a daily basis would be a little pricey for me.

In terms of the level of difficulty...um, I'm convinced that doing yoga is extremely difficult, at least for me, I think, because there's a lot of stretching involved and I'm not very flexible. But no matter how dreadful it may sound, I'll try my best if one day I make up my mind to begin doing it.

I've wanted to practice yoga for ages mainly because of its calming and relaxing effect. Over the past few years, I've constantly felt a great amount of anxiety and my stress levels can be quite high sometimes. I've been told that yoga has an amazing effect on calming people's nerves, so I think it's worth a try.

词汇 Key Words

form of relaxation 放松方式

grow in popularity 越来越流行

on a regular basis 定期；经常

take sth. up 开始做某事

check sth. out 去看看……

suit sb. 适合某人

yoga mat 瑜伽垫

on a daily basis 每天

pricey ['praɪsɪ] adj. 昂贵的

stretch [stretʃ] v. 拉伸；伸展

flexible ['fleksəbl] adj. 柔韧的；灵活的

dreadful ['dredfl] adj. 可怕的

for ages 很久

anxiety [æŋ'zaɪətɪ] n. 焦虑

calm sb.'s nerves 放松某人紧张的神经，
　　使某人不焦虑

worth a try 值得尝试

> **Describe a time when you were very busy.**
>
> **You should say:**
>
> **when it happened**
>
> **where you were**
>
> **what you did**
>
> **and explain how you felt about it.**

I'm going to talk about the time when I was busy gearing up for my final exams. I think it was 6 years ago, when I was in my second year of university. To be honest with you, I hadn't studied hard enough that semester. You know, I had skipped a lot of classes and so was really worried about the finals.

In order to prepare for the exams, I went to our school library every single day for two weeks. I would run there at 7 o'clock in the morning and stay there for the whole day and just, you know, cram!

Anyway, what I did…um, well, I just read and read and made a lot of notes and memorised them. I also took photos of the things I had to learn so that when I was waiting in line to buy food or while I was eating, I could study too. So yeah, I just seized every opportunity to learn.

How I felt about it…well, I obviously felt worn-out every day, with all the hard work that I put into the exam preparation. Plus, I felt that I was indeed an idiot because I had wasted so much time not studying. If I had studied more before, I wouldn't have been that exhausted every day.

词汇 Key Words

gear up for sth. 为……做准备	wait in line 排队
skip classes 逃课	seize every opportunity 抓住每个机会
final ['faɪnəl] *n.* 期末考试	worn-out ['wɔːn'aʊt] *adj.* 筋疲力尽的
cram [kræm] *v.* （为应考）临时死记硬背；填鸭式学习	indeed [ɪn'diːd] *adv.* 确实
鸭式学习	idiot ['ɪdɪət] *n.* 傻瓜

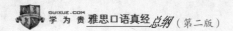

> **Describe a time when you got up early.**
>
> **You should say:**
>
> > **when it was**
> >
> > **who you were with**
> >
> > **what you did**
>
> **and explain why you got up early that day.**

I'm going to talk about a time when I got up at 5:00 am. It was 2 months ago, on a Monday, if I remember correctly. I had seen a video about an interview where a successful person said that he gets up in 4:30 every single day to have a head start when everybody else is still asleep. He works out in the morning, reads a book and then gets some work done. I found that video really inspiring and decided to do the same.

I was with nobody that morning. I had asked all of my dormmates to do the same with me, but none of them said "yes".

What I did that morning is…at 5:00 am, my alarm went off. I dragged myself out of bed and went to our schoolyard. I ran there for about half an hour. And then I found a place to do some reading. In fact, that book I was reading that day happened to be a motivational book.

The reason I got up early that day is because I didn't want to slack off anymore; I just wanted to make good use of every single day, every single hour, because I am someone that has really big aspirations. However, that day, the entire day, I felt really groggy, and then the next day I got up at 6:00 am.

词汇 Key Words

if I remember correctly 如果我没记错的话

a head start 起步前的优势；领先

work out 健身

get some work done 完成一些工作

I found that video inspiring 我觉得那个视频很

 激励人

dormmate ['dɔ:meɪt] *n.* 舍友

none of them said "yes" 没有一个人同意

my alarm (clock) went off 我的闹钟响了

drag myself out of bed 挣扎着起床

schoolyard ['sku:ljɑ:d] *n.* 学校操场

happen to… 碰巧……

slack off 松懈，懈怠，不努力

make good use of… 很好地利用……

aspiration [ˌæspə'reɪʃn] *n.* 抱负，志向

groggy ['grɒgɪ] *adj.* 昏昏沉沉的

> **Describe a positive change in your life.**
>
> **You should say:**
>
> > **what the change was**
> >
> > **when it happened**
> >
> > **how it happened**
>
> **and explain why you think it was a positive change.**

I'm going to talk about the time when I fell in love with travel. Travel is an integral part of my life now and I do it whenever I have several days off. For instance, I'm planning on going to Thailand for a few days next month.

I fell in love with it three years ago. As a matter of fact, I'd never been that into travel before that. I always thought it was a waste of money and I would just rather stay home and watch some movies if I wanted to do something to unwind. But this totally changed in that summer three years back.

How it happened…well, my girlfriend and I went to Saipan on vacation. I'm not sure if you know this place, but it's absolutely one of the most picturesque islands in the world. The views there are so stunning that when I got off the plane after arriving there, the beauty literally took my breath away. My girlfriend and I swam in the sea, went snorkelling and did tons of other fun things. It was definitely a once in-a-lifetime experience. It was then that I realised that travel was actually one of the most relaxing and enjoyable things.

I think this was a positive change mainly because travel has made my life more fun and more exciting than before. I'm not the boring, dull person that I was three years ago now. Plus, I've also realised that I understand the world better.

词汇 Key Words

fall in love with… 爱上……

travel ['trævl] *n.* 旅行（travel 也可以作名词）

an integral part of my life 我生活中不可分割
   的一部分

be into… 喜欢……

unwind [ˌʌn'waɪnd] *v.* 放松

picturesque [ˌpɪktʃə'resk] *adj.* 风景如画的

stunning views 非常美的风景

literally ['lɪtərəlɪ] *adv.* 简直

take my breath away（美丽、奇特、壮观得）
   令我窒息

go snorkelling 去浮潜

a once-in-a-lifetime experience 一生中仅有
   一次的经历；难忘的经历

dull [dʌl] *adj.* 无聊的

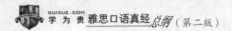

> **Describe a time when someone or something made a lot of noise.**
>
> **You should say:**
>
> > **when it was**
> >
> > **who/what was making the noise**
> >
> > **what kind of noise it was**
>
> **and explain how you felt about it.**

I'm going to talk about the time when a student made a lot of noise in my school library. It was three months ago, on a Friday, if I remember correctly. I think it was around 2 o'clock in the afternoon and I was in the library preparing for my final exams.

Then, I heard a student talking very loudly. Can you believe that? We were in the library and he was talking so loudly that I couldn't concentrate on studying any more. So yeah, that noise was really annoying at first. Since I couldn't concentrate any more, I just began to listen to what he was saying. Well, it seemed like that he was on the phone with his girlfriend.

In terms of what they were talking about, well, I think his girlfriend just wanted to break up with him, because he said something like, "Are you kidding me? We've been going out for 3 years and now you wanna end this? I can't believe what I just heard."

How I felt about this noise…well, as I was saying, at first, I was pretty annoyed by it, but a few minutes later, I got more and more curious. I really wanted to know why the girl wanted to split with the guy and whether they're still together now.

词汇 Key Words

annoying [ə'nɔɪɪŋ] *adj.* 令人很烦的

break up with sb. 和某人分手

Are you kidding me? 你在和我开玩笑吗?

be going out (with sb.) (和某人)交往、谈
恋爱

annoyed [ə'nɔɪd] *adj.* 感到很烦的

curious ['kjʊərɪəs] *adj.* 好奇的

> **Describe a time when you lost your way.**
>
> **You should say:**
>
> > **where you were**
> >
> > **what happened**
> >
> > **how you found your way**
>
> **and explain how you felt about it.**

I'm going to talk about the time when I lost my way in the Summer Palace, which was the place where the royal family of the Qing Dynasty would go to spend their summer months. This place is massive and tens of thousands of people visit it every day, and I believe a lot of those people lose their way too inside the Summer Palace. And of course, this is exactly what happened to me. It happened 2 years ago when I was still a freshman at university. I had just begun my university life and several weeks into that, my roommates and I decided to go to the Summer Palace together. We were all new in Beijing. We had never been to the Summer Palace, so we just wanted to go there to see what it was like.

What happened there was that my roommates went there first because I had some other stuff to do. And then I entered the Summer Palace through the east gate. I should have made a right turn, but I made a left turn. And then I was just totally lost. I couldn't find my roommates.

How I found my way…It was actually pretty easy. I called my roommates. They told me that they were at the Marble Boat. And then I just began asking those people around me. I asked them where the Marble Boat was. Some of them knew the way, and they just told me how to get there. They told me to go straight and then turn right and turn left and stuff like that. About 15 or 20 minutes later, I found my roommates.

I didn't feel anything special about it because, I don't know, I didn't feel bad about it. I was still pretty happy. And then after finding them, we just began having a good time inside the Summer Palace.

词汇 Key Words

royal ['rɔɪəl] *adj.* 皇家的

dynasty ['dɪnəstɪ] *n.* 朝代

massive ['mæsɪv] *adj.* 非常大的

tens of thousands of… 几万……

this is exactly… 正是……

freshman ['freʃmən] *n.* 大一学生

several weeks into… ……开始几周之后

be totally lost 完全找不到路

Marble Boat 颐和园中的石舫

and stuff like that 等等

> **Describe a time you got a little angry.**
>
> **You should say:**
>
> > **when it happened**
> >
> > **where it happened**
> >
> > **who you were with**
>
> **and explain why you were angry.**

I'm going to talk about the time when I got overcharged by a taxi driver.

It happened two months ago, on a Saturday, and I went to a dinner organised by one of my high school classmates. In fact, most of my high school classmates and I hadn't seen each other in years, so I was really happy that day that we could get together and catch up.

The place where we had dinner was a really fancy restaurant in the north of the city, which is pretty far from my home. I live in the south, so after we finished our dinner, I took a taxi home.

The taxi driver seemed to be a rather nice guy because when I first got into the taxi, I felt it was pretty chilly and he just turned the heat up. Then, at some point during the ride, he began to smoke. I seriously hate the smell of cigarettes, so I said I'd rather he not smoke and he just stopped it immediately. I thought that was really nice of him. After about 55 minutes, I arrived home. The total taxi fare was 160 yuan. I gave him the money, asked for a receipt and got out.

The problem was, when I told my mum that it cost me 160 yuan to come back from the north of the city, she said that I had been ripped off. It should have only cost 100 yuan. I had no idea why I had been overcharged that extra 60 yuan, and I was really angry.

词汇 Key Words

be/get overcharged by sb. 被某人多收钱

get together 聚会

catch up (with sb.) 了解某人近况；与某人叙旧

fancy restaurant 高级饭店

chilly ['tʃɪlɪ] *adj.* 寒冷的

fare [feə(r)] *n.* 路费；车费

receipt [rɪ'si:t] *n.* 收据；发票

be ripped off 被敲竹杠

Describe a time when you received good service.

You should say:

    what the service was

    when you received it

    who you were with

and explain why you think it was good service.

I'm going to talk about the time when I went hiking on the Great Wall, the Jinshanling section of the Great Wall, which is located in the northeast of Beijing. And the person that provided some really good service for us, my friends and I actually, was a guide, a farmer who lived at the foot of the mountains where the Great Wall is located. He was leading the way the entire time—telling us where to go, which direction to walk in, where to turn and stuff like that. At one point, we had to go off the Great Wall and into the mountains, so he just told us everything about that.

I received this service 3 years ago when I was a sophomore at university. It was already towards the end of my summer vacation. Several days before the new semester began, I thought I just wanted to do something fun and exciting before the new semester began. I talked with some of my friends and we decided that we would go hiking and camping on the Great Wall. And then we found this guide on the internet.

I was with some of my friends, like I said just now. They were my university friends and high school friends. Actually, everybody spoke really highly of this guide.

And I think that was very good service, mainly because that hike lasted about 5 hours, so it was so strenuous, super physically demanding, but he was with us the entire time. And also, sometimes he would slow down for us because we were walking really slowly. Another thing is that he was very patient. So yeah, he was indeed a really good guide. If I ever went back to that part of the Great Wall, I would contact him again.

词汇 Key Words

go hiking/camping 去徒步旅行 / 野营

section ['sekʃn] *n.* 部分

guide [gaɪd] *n.* 向导

at the foot of the mountains 在山脚下

lead the way 带路

the entire time 全程；一直

go off the Great Wall 走下长城

go into the mountains 走进山里

sophomore ['sɒfəmɔː(r)] *n.* 大二学生

semester [sɪ'mestə(r)] *n.* 学期

like I said just now 就像我刚才说过的

speak highly of sb. 称赞某人

strenuous, physical demanding 非常费力的

slow down 慢下来

patient ['peɪʃnt] *adj.* 耐心的

indeed [ɪn'diːd] *adv.* 确实

contact sb. 联系某人

> **Describe a situation where someone gave you a piece of useful advice.**
>
> **You should say:**
>
> > **what the situation was**
> >
> > **who gave it to you**
> >
> > **what the advice was**
>
> **and explain why you think the advice was useful.**

I'm going to talk about a piece of advice I received at university.

Ever since I was a kid, I had always been a shy and reserved boy that didn't quite like socialising. Plus, I was very reluctant in terms of making changes in life. Being like this didn't do me any good.

During my sophomore year at university, my best friend Andy gave me a piece of advice that fundamentally changed my life. What he told me was that I should be more open to people and the world. His exact words were: Open yourself to the rest of the world, and the world will open itself to you.

I found his advice really useful and at that point, I made up my mind to hang out with people more and explore the world more. Actually at present, it's more of exploring the country. I've been to a bunch of places in China and my horizons have been greatly expanded. In addition, whenever I see a friend, I will greet him or her with a broad smile on my face, which, in return, has won me great popularity among friends. What I feel is that I'm much happier than before and more confident while chatting with people. I'm really thankful to Andy.

词汇 Key Words

reserved [rɪˈzɜːvd] *adj.* 内敛的

socialise [ˈsəʊʃəlaɪz] *v.* 社交，与人交往

reluctant [rɪˈlʌktənt] *adj.* 不情愿的

do me good 对我有好处

sophomore [ˈsɒfəmɔː(r)] *adj.* 二年级的

fundamentally [ˌfʌndəˈmentəlɪ] *adv.* 根本性地

make up my mind 下定决心

explore sth. 探索……

at present 目前

a bunch of... 一堆，一群……

expand my horizons 开阔视野

in return 作为回报

popularity [ˌpɒpjuˈlærətɪ] *n.* 声望；受欢迎度

chat with sb. 跟某人聊天

be thankful to sb. 感激某人

> **Describe a habit your friend has that you want to develop.**
>
> **You should say:**
>
> > **who your friend is**
> >
> > **what habit he or she has**
> >
> > **when you noticed this habit**
>
> **and explain why you want to develop this habit.**

Well, the habit that I'm going to talk about is reading and the person that has this habit is one of my friends from middle school, whose English name is Sean. We have known each other for 10 years.

The habit is, like I said, reading, which is a really simple and common habit. The first thing Sean does in the morning is read for about 30 minutes. He does this even before brushing his teeth, washing his face and having breakfast. So yeah, he reads for about 30 minutes in the morning, and it means that he can read about 50 books in a year. It's a really staggering number to me considering he only reads for just half an hour every single day.

I noticed this habit about 3 years ago, and I think it was around that time that he began having this habit. One day, I think it was in the summer, we were chatting with each other about our daily routines. And he shared that he had this habit. I thought it was really cool and admirable.

I really want to develop this habit, mainly because I know all the benefits of reading. The problem with me is that I'm not a consistent reader. I read sometimes, but other times I just feel that I don't have enough time. Of course, this is an excuse—it's a cop-out. In the future, I think I'm just going to get up a little bit earlier in the morning so that I can have 20, 30 or 40 minutes every day to do some reading too.

词汇 Key Words

brush one's teeth 刷牙

staggering ['stægərɪŋ] *adj.* 令人大吃一惊的，
　令人震惊的

considering... 考虑到……

around that time 大约在那个时候

daily routine 日常生活，日常生活习惯 / 流程

I thought it was admirable 我认为这非常令
　人钦佩

a consistent reader 可以坚持读书的人

cop-out ['kɒp aʊt] *n.* 借口

> **Describe a gift for others that took you a long time to choose.**
>
> **You should say:**
>
> > **what it was**
> >
> > **who you gave it to**
> >
> > **why it took you a long time to choose**
>
> **and explain why you chose this gift in the end.**

I'm going to talk about a book that I gave to my one-year-old niece on her birthday. It's called 《熟睡的小兔子》. I guess it could be translated as *The Rabbit That's Sound Asleep*. It's written by a psychologist and linguist. Sorry, I don't remember the author's name.

This gift took me a long time to choose because I had several options then. For example, I wanted to give her a Barbie doll because I thought most baby girls would be fond of it. The thing is, most of the gifts I thought of were not creative at all, so I really racked my brains to try to think of a good one.

At last, I decided to buy this book for her coz a lot of moms were raving about it. It shot to the top of Amazon's best-seller list right after it came out. I heard that if you read this book to your baby, they will soon be sleepy and oh, here's something very important: while reading the book, you should also yawn from time to time. It will get your kid to fall asleep really fast. After I read some reviews on Amazon, I decided that this book would be the best gift because my niece was having difficulty falling asleep at night. Last time I checked, it's not as hard as before to put her to sleep now. I feel really happy about it.

词汇 Key Words

psychologist [saɪˈkɒlədʒɪst] *n.* 心理学家

linguist [ˈlɪŋgwɪst] *n.* 语言学家

author [ˈɔːθə(r)] *n.* 作者

option [ˈɒpʃn] *n.* 选项

creative [kriˈeɪtɪv] *adj.* 有创意的

rack my brains 绞尽脑汁

rave about sth. 对……大加赞赏

shoot to the top of... 迅速达到……的顶端

best-seller list 畅销书排行榜

come out 出版；发行；上映

yawn [jɔːn] *v.* 打哈欠

from time to time 偶尔；有时

fall asleep 入睡

review [rɪˈvjuː] *n.* 评论；评价

put sb. to sleep 哄某人睡觉

> **Describe an electronic device you want to buy.**
>
> **You should say:**
>
> > **what it is**
> >
> > **when you got to know this device**
> >
> > **what specific features it has**
>
> **and explain why you want to buy this electronic device.**

I would really like to buy a Kindle, you know, the most popular e-book reader at the moment. Actually, no matter where you go now, you can see many people using it to read.

I got to know this device about five years ago, so it's been quite a long time. I remember one day, I was reading a book on the subway. I noticed that the passenger next to me was also reading, but he was reading on an electronic device. Out of curiosity, I asked him what it was and this is how I got to know it.

Anyway, as for its features…well, as a matter of fact, I don't think I know much about it, as all I know is that I can use it to do some reading. I suppose it would be possible for me to make notes and bookmark pages too.

I would like to buy a Kindle primarily because I'm a big bookworm; I'm crazy about reading. I find that reading has a soothing effect on my nerves. I think my phone screen is too small, so I only read printed books now, but sometimes, my backpack gets really heavy if I have several books with me at the same time. If I had a Kindle, I could download many books into it and it would allow me to read any book at any time.

词汇 Key Words

e-book reader 电子书阅读器

passenger ['pæsɪndʒə(r)] *n.* 乘客

out of curiosity 出于好奇

bookmark pages 收藏页面；设定书签

bookworm ['bʊkwɜːm] *n.* 喜欢读书的人

have a soothing effect on my nerves 有令我
    放松的作用

printed book 纸质书籍

Describe a photo of yourself that you like.

You should say:

> **where this photo was taken**
>
> **when it was taken**
>
> **how it was taken**

and explain how you felt about the photo.

I'm going to talk about a photo of myself that hangs on my bedroom wall. It's one of my favourite photos, so I just put it on the wall right opposite my bed so that every morning when I wake up, I can see it.

This photo was taken in the swimming pool just around the corner from where I live. I always go there to swim for an hour or so, especially on the weekend.

It was taken last year, in September, if I remember correctly. One day, I went there with my girlfriend and while we were walking by the pool, she kicked me down into the water and when I was struggling, she took this photo with her cellphone. When I finally stood up in the water and looked at her, she was laughing really hard…

I didn't feel so good when I fell into the pool, of course, but now, I just find the photo pretty amusing. I don't know why but I just have a strange liking for weird photos, so this one is one of my favourites, like I mentioned earlier…

词汇 Key Words

hang [hæŋ] *v.* 悬挂

opposite sth. 在……对面

an hour or so 一小时左右

amusing [əˈmjuːzɪŋ] *adj.* 逗人笑的；好笑的

have a strange liking for sth. 对……有奇怪的
喜好

weird [wɪəd] *adj.* 奇怪的

> **Describe a piece of equipment in your home.**
>
> **You should say:**
>
> **what it is**
>
> **how often you use it**
>
> **who you use it with**
>
> **and explain why you like using this piece of equipment.**

I'm going to talk about my coffeemaker, which is probably my favourite item in my apartment. It was actually a gift from my boyfriend. I had revealed to him that it would be fantastic if I could have a coffeemaker of my own, so he bought me one as a birthday gift last year.

I use it every single day now, in the morning, of course. I usually drag myself out of bed around 6:30, and then I'll put some coffee beans in the maker and let it work. Then, I'll sip some coffee that I made myself while watching the morning news. This whole process feels extremely enjoyable.

Who I use it with… um, well…I live alone, so most of the time, it's only me that uses this coffeemaker. But from time to time, I invite some of my close friends over to my apartment and I make some coffee for them if they feel like it.

I love this coffeemaker a lot simply because I'm a coffee aficionado. I won't say that I'm addicted to it but it's definitely a big part of my life. Drinking a cup or two in the morning is a great pick-me-up and with this coffeemaker that my boyfriend gave me, I can do it at home.

词汇 Key Words

coffeemaker ['kɒfɪˌmeɪkə] *n.* 咖啡机

reveal [rɪ'viːl] *v.* 透露

sth. of my own 我自己的……

drag myself out of bed 挣扎着起床

coffee beans 咖啡豆

sip sth. 小口地喝……

feel like sth. 想要……

aficionado [əˌfɪʃəˈnɑːdəʊ] *n.* 狂热爱好者

be addicted to sth. 对……上瘾

pick-me-up ['pɪk miː ʌp] *n.* 提神的东西

> **Describe an item on which you spent more than expected.**
>
> **You should say:**
>
>   **what it is**
>
>   **how much you spent on it**
>
>   **why you bought it**
>
> **and explain why you think you spent more than expected.**

The item that I'm going to talk about is a standing desk. This concept of having a standing desk is getting more and more popular in China, and also around the world. It's something that I can place on my own desk and then because it's higher, I can just stand up while working or studying. This is actually very good because it helps prevent people from developing and living a sedentary lifestyle.

I spent 300 yuan on the standing desk. I bought it last week. I remember it was last Friday. I had read an article about all the benefits of having a standing desk. For example, if you just sit at your desk most of the time, it's an inactive lifestyle. And there are many health problems associated with that, like an increased risk of developing cardiovascular disease, heart problems, back pain, and so on. I didn't want any of those and that's why I just decided to buy the standing desk. I got it delivered to my apartment last Sunday.

I bought this desk mainly because of everything I said just now. I want to live an active lifestyle, but this desk was more expensive than I had expected because before buying it, I had thought that it was only going to cost about one or two hundred yuan. However, it cost me 300 yuan, which is okay actually, because considering that it's really beneficial to me, I still bought it, and I've been using it for a week. I really like it.

词汇 Key Words

standing desk 站立式书桌

concept ['kɒnsept] *n.* 概念

around the world 在全世界

place sth. on... 把……放置在……上

live a sedentary/an active lifestyle 过一种经常
    坐着的／经常运动的生活

most of the time 大部分时间

an inactive lifestyle 一种不怎么运动的生活方式

(be) associated with sth. 与……相联系

an increased risk of...……更高的风险

develop cardiovascular disease 患心血管疾病

back pain 背部疼痛

I got it delivered to my apartment 我收到了
    （快递）

just now 刚刚，刚才

considering... 考虑到……

beneficial [ˌbenɪ'fɪʃl] *adj.* 有益的

> **Describe a piece of local news that people were interested in.**
>
> **You should say:**
>
> > **what it was about**
> >
> > **where you saw or heard it**
> >
> > **who was involved**
>
> **and explain why people were interested in it.**

I'm going to talk about a piece of news I read last month. It was a Saturday or a Sunday, because I remember that day, I didn't have anything important to do. I was actually going out of my apartment for a leisurely walk. But then I saw a notice about a garden that was about to be set up in our neighbourhood. It was going to be a community garden, which means anybody can contribute to it. We can go there to plant some fruits, veggies, herbs or any other type of plant.

I saw this notice on the notice board right outside of our apartment building. Most of the time, I don't pay any attention to it, but that day, I don't know why, I just looked at it, and then I saw this news.

Who was involved in it…um, I think anybody could be part of this community garden. I think it could be like a team sport, which anybody could take part in. Anybody that is gregarious, anybody that wants to make friends could go to this garden and work with other people.

After coming back home, I told my dad about it and he was particularly interested in it. My dad loves taking care of plants. We have a lot of house plants, but now he just works in solitude. With this community garden, he could go and work with other people and potentially make a lot of friends. I think other people are interested in this piece of news for a similar reason. It could be a social activity and that would be great.

词汇 Key Words

a leisurely walk 一次悠闲的散步

notice ['nəʊtɪs] *n.* 通知；告示

be set up 被建立

contribute to sth. 为……出力；为……做贡献

veggies ['vedʒɪz] *n.* 蔬菜（＝vegetables）

herbs [hɜːbs] *n.* 草药；香草

notice board 布告栏

right outside of our apartment building 就在我

　　们公寓楼外面

pay attention to sth. 注意……

team sport 团体运动

take part in sth. 参加……

gregarious [grɪ'geərɪəs] *adj.* 爱交际的；合

　　群的

take care of… 照顾……

house plants 家居植物；室内植物

in solitude 独自

potentially [pə'tenʃəlɪ] *adv.* 潜在地；可能地

for a similar reason 因为一个类似的原因

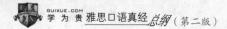

> **Describe an educational TV programme you've watched.**
>
> **You should say:**
>
> > **what programme it is**
> >
> > **how often you watch it**
> >
> > **what type of people enjoy this programme**
>
> **and explain why this programme is educational.**

I'm going to talk about a TV programme called *Modern English*. It's an English-teaching show and you can learn a lot of natural and useful words and phrases as well as sentence structures from it. I've been a huge fan of this show for about 2 years.

I watch this programme on a daily basis. It lasts 30 minutes every day, from 6:30 to 7:00, so no matter what I'm doing then, I will stop to watch the show.

What kind of people like watching it…well, people who want to master English are usually pretty fond of this programme. For instance, like me, my friend Jason is really into this show too. His dream is to be multilingual, but his English is not very good now, so in order to be fluent in it, he watches this show every single day.

I think this programme is very educational mainly because I can learn a lot of things from it. For example, I can learn many idioms, which are pretty interesting. Oh, last week, I learned the phrase "under the weather" which means "not feeling well". I find this idiom very useful and I even used it when I was talking with Jason the other day. Another reason is that I get to know a little about western culture as well by watching this show.

词汇 Key Words

master sth. 熟练掌握……

be fond of sth. = be into sth. 喜欢……

multilingual [ˌmʌltɪˈlɪŋgwəl] *adj.* 会多种语言的

be fluent in... 流利使用（某种语言）

idiom [ˈɪdɪəm] *n.* 习语；成语

under the weather 身体不舒服

> **Describe a movie that you like.**
>
> **You should say:**
>
> **what the movie is**
>
> **when and where you watched it**
>
> **what it is about**
>
> **and explain why you like it.**

The movie that I'm going to talk about is *Fast and Furious* 7. *Fast and Furious* is definitely my favourite movie franchise and the 7th instalment is absolutely the one that I love the most. Everybody knows that there are several characters in this movie series. And Brian and Mia are the two characters that I like the most. They are so in love with each other and I really like that.

I think the first time I watched this movie was 5 years ago. Honestly, I don't really remember when exactly it was or where exactly I was when I first watched it, but I have watched this movie many times ever since. For example, two months ago, it was actually on a Saturday, I was flying to Shanghai with my wife. It was a 2-hour flight. I took advantage of that time to watch this movie one more time and I really enjoyed it.

What this movie is about…um, everybody knows that there's a lot of racing and fighting.

However, what I love the most about this movie series is their focus and emphasis on family. Many of the characters are not directly related, but they consider themselves family members. For example, in the last scenes of *Fast and Furious* 7, Brian, Mia and their son are playing on the beach and all of the other characters are watching them. Everybody is happy, everybody is blissfully happy, and I just really like that.

词汇 Key Words

Fast and Furious 《速度与激情》

franchise ['fræntʃaɪz] *n.* (电影) 系列

instalment [ɪn'stɔ:lmənt] *n.* (系列电影中的)

　一集

character ['kærəktə(r)] *n.* 人物；角色

be in love with each other 彼此相爱

a 2-hour flight 两小时飞行时间

take advantage of… 利用……

race [reɪs] *v.* 赛车

focus and emphasis on… 对于……的关注和

　强调

directly related 直接相关的，在这里表示

　"真正的家人、亲人"

consider sb. sb. 将……看作……

scene [si:n] *n.* 场景

blissfully happy 幸福快乐的

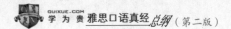

> **Describe something you would like to learn more.**
>
> **You should say:**
>
> > **what it is**
> >
> > **how you would learn it**
> >
> > **where you would learn it**
>
> **and explain why you would like to keep learning it.**

Well, I'm going to talk about learning French. I started learning this language three years ago, but I'm far from being fluent in it, so I will definitely keep learning.

I suppose what I would mainly do is try to watch as many French movies and TV shows as possible, because that would be a great way to pick up some natural words and phrases. Plus, if possible, I would try to make some French friends. If I could always talk with them, it would be much easier for me to learn this language.

Where I would learn it…well, to be honest, I guess I could learn this language anywhere. As I said, watching movies and TV shows would be my main method, so I don't think there would be a place where I couldn't do it, since as long as I have an internet connection, I can watch a movie no matter where I am.

I would like to keep learning French primarily because I've been to France on holiday a couple of times and I've found that the people there don't really like to converse with others in English. If I could speak French, it would be a lot easier to integrate with the locals and understand their culture.

词汇 Key Words

pick sth. up 学习……

converse with sb. 与某人交谈

integrate with the locals 融入当地人的生活

> **Describe a small and successful company you know.**
>
> **You should say:**
>
> > **what the company is called**
> >
> > **how you got to know it**
> >
> > **what kind of business it does**
>
> **and explain why you think this company is successful.**

The company I'm going to talk about is called BC Camping. This company offers camping holidays on the outskirts of Beijing.

I got to know it two years ago. At that time, my nephew wanted to go on a camping holiday with me and so I searched for some information on the internet. This is how I found the company.

What kind of business it does…well, basically, you go with them to a mountainous region where they have a campsite. Then, you can stay there for a couple of days. During your stay, there are many fun activities to do. For instance, if I'm not mistaken, each day kicks off with a sports match, like football or volleyball. Then, there are some interesting things for children, like poster competition, model making and so forth.

I suppose this company is pretty successful mainly because their staff are well-qualified and really enthusiastic. When you have a request or a complaint, they always deal with it immediately. I think another reason is that their activities really meet people's demands. I mean, nowadays, a lot of people are really busy with work and so they want to spend their weekends doing something fun with their children. BC Camping offers tons of activities that people can do with kids…

词汇 Key Words

on the outskirts of… 在……的郊区

camping ['kæmpɪŋ] *n.* 野营

search for information 搜索信息

mountainous region 山区

campsite ['kæmpsaɪt] *n.* 野营地

kick off with sth. 以……作为开始

poster ['pəʊstə(r)] *n.* 海报

model making 模型制作

well-qualified [wel'kwɒlɪfaɪd] *adj.* 有资格的；
完全能胜任的

enthusiastic [ɪnˌθjuːzɪ'æstɪk] *adj.* 热情的

request [rɪ'kwest] *n.* 要求；请求

complaint [kəm'pleɪnt] *n.* 抱怨；投诉

deal with sth. 处理……

meet people's demands 满足人们的需求

tons of… 很多……

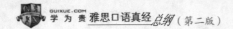

> **Describe a song that means something special to you.**
>
> **You should say:**
>
> **what this song is about**
>
> **when you listened to this song for the first time**
>
> **how often do you listen to this song**
>
> **and explain why you think it is special to you.**

The song I'm going to talk about is called *Around the Corner*. In this song, a young man and a young woman are on the verge of a breakup, but the man doesn't want it to happen. He tells his girlfriend that he is still madly in love with her and she means the world to him.

I first listened to this song when I was still in secondary school. At first, I just thought it was pretty catchy and so I learned to sing it. At that time, I had some feelings for my deskmate. One day, I sang this song to her and she told me that she really loved it. I was on cloud nine when she told me so. Then, she became my girlfriend and we were together for about half a year until my mom found out about it. I was forced to break up with her.

Anyway, how often I listen to this song…well, I still listen to it now, but not as often as before because it's been so many years since I first listened to it and there have been many other songs that I've loved.

I think this particular song is really special to me mainly because I sang it to my deskmate then. She was my first girlfriend, and our puppy love was pretty precious.

词汇 Key Words

on the verge of a breakup 在分手的边缘

be madly in love with sb. 疯狂地爱着某人

mean the world to sb. 对某人来说意味着一切

catchy ['kætʃɪ] *adj.* 朗朗上口的

have feelings for sb. 对某人有感觉；喜欢某人

on cloud nine 非常开心的

puppy love 早恋；少男少女短暂的爱情

precious ['preʃəs] *adj.* 宝贵的

> **Describe a kind of weather you like.**
>
> **You should say:**
>
> **what it is**
>
> **where you usually experience it**
>
> **what you will do in this kind of weather**
>
> **and explain why you like this kind of weather.**

I'm going to talk about rainy weather, which is my favourite.

I know many other IELTS candidates talk about sunny days because on a sunny day, you can go out and about and do a lot of outdoor activities. However, the thing is, I'm not a fan of the sunshine. I've always been crazy about the rain.

You know, on a rainy day, I can do quite a few things that are pleasurable. For example, the first thing that comes to mind is that if it's only a sprinkle of rain out there, I like to go to the basketball court on my university campus and play basketball alone, I mean, completely on my own, for about an hour or so. I believe many other people will consider this to be really weird and goofy. When I play basketball in the rain, I will be drenched from head to toe. However, I don't care, because when I do it, I get a kick out of it. Another thing I like to do on a rainy day, especially when it's raining heavily out there is that I often sit on the balcony and do some reading. I find it pretty enjoyable when I watch the rain trickling down the window and listen to the pitter-patter of raindrops. It's just really therapeutic.

I think I'm crazy about rainy weather mainly because…um, here is a word that I used about ten seconds ago, therapeutic. When I sometimes feel stressed out, the sound of raindrops just puts me in a better mood and puts my mind at ease.

词汇 Key Words

IELTS candidate 雅思考生

go out and about 出去走走、转转

pleasurable ['pleʒərəbl] *adj.* 令人愉快的

a sprinkle of rain 小雨

basketball court 篮球场

goofy ['guːfɪ] *adj.* 愚蠢的；可笑的

be drenched from head to toe 从头到脚湿透

get a kick out of sth. 从……中获得乐趣

rain heavily 雨下得很大

trickle down the window 顺着窗户流下来

the pitter-patter of raindrops 雨滴的噼啪声

therapeutic [ˌθerə'pjuːtɪk] *adj.* 治愈的；使人放松的

feel stressed out 感到压力很大

put me in a better mood 令我心情变好

put my mind at ease 令我放松；让我感到安心

> **Describe an important invention which has changed our lives.**
>
> **You should say:**
>
> > **what it is**
> >
> > **what it does**
> >
> > **why it's popular in all age groups**
> >
> **and explain how people feel about it.**

I'm going to talk about shared bicycles, which are a relatively new invention, but they've already taken the country by storm. No matter which city you go to, you can see many shared bicycles scattered around the city.

In terms of what they do…Well, they just offer an alternative mode of transport. Shared bicycles are fairly easy to operate—you just find one, scan the QR code, hop on it and go. When you arrive at your destination, you can park the bike anywhere. It's super convenient.

I think this invention is extremely popular mainly because of its convenience. Like I said, they're everywhere, so you don't have to make an effort to find a bike. Plus, cycling is a good workout—it's really good exercise riding a bike from one place to another. At least, it's better than sitting in a cab for 10 minutes, right?

I think generally speaking, people have positive opinions about shared bicycles, but they do create a problem. Sometimes they look like a mess when there are so many of them in one small place. Perhaps there should be some regulations put in place by the government to deal with this problem.

词汇 Key Words

relatively ['relətɪvlɪ] *adv.* 相对地

take…by storm 风靡……

(be) scattered around the city 分散在城市各处

an alternative mode of transport 一种替代性的

交通方式

operate sth. 操作……

scan the QR code 扫描二维码

hop on (the bike) 跳上（自行车）

park [pɑːk] *v.* 停车

convenient [kən'viːnɪənt] *adj.* 方便的

convenience [kən'viːnjəns] *n.* 方便性

a good workout 一种好的健身方式

a mess 一片混乱的景象

put in place some regulations = put some

　　regulations in place 推行一些规章制度

> **Describe a sport you like that is a little expensive.**
>
> **You should say:**
>
> > **what it is**
> >
> > **how much it usually costs**
> >
> > **who you usually do it with**
>
> **and explain why you like to do this sport.**

I'm going to talk about skydiving, which I think is one of the most thrilling sports.

I'm not sure how much it costs in other countries, but…I did it in Fiji. My wife and I went there on holiday and we skydived. It cost about 1,000 US dollars, so 7,000 RMB, I think. But if we had gone higher… um, we jumped from a point of 10,000 feet, and if we had jumped from 12,000 feet or 14,000 feet, it would have cost us more.

Who I usually do it with…well, honestly, like I said before, I've only done it once. I think skydiving is just a once-in-a-lifetime experience. You just have to do it once and brag about it your entire life. I did it with my wife. She is a thrill-seeker, an adventurous person. I remember one of our instructors asked us whose crazy idea it was to skydive, I said it was hers. It was indeed.

I really loved this sport mainly because it gave me an adrenaline rush; it was so exciting and I felt proud of myself. Plus, as I was saying, I can brag about it for the rest of my life now and I feel really good when I tell people I've done it before and they're very envious of me.

词汇 Key Words

skydiving ['skaɪdaɪvɪŋ] *n.* 高空跳伞

thrilling ['θrɪlɪŋ] *adj.* 刺激的，扣人心弦的

a once-in-a-lifetime experience 一生仅有一次
的经历；难忘的经历

brag about sth. 吹嘘、夸耀……

thrill-seeker [θrɪl 'si:kə(r)] *n.* 寻求刺激的人

adventurous [əd'ventʃərəs] *adj.* 喜欢冒险的

instructor [ɪn'strʌktə(r)] *n.* 教练；指导员

give me an adrenaline rush 让我肾上腺素飙升

for the rest of my life 在我的余生里

be envious of sb. 羡慕某人

> **Describe a historical event in your country.**
>
> **You should say:**
>
> > **when and where it happened**
> >
> > **how you know it**
> >
> > **what happened**
> >
> > **and explain how you feel about this event.**

I'm going to talk about the only time when our men's national football team competed in the World Cup.

It happened in 2002, in June, to be exact. That year, the World Cup was held jointly by Japan and Korea. Sorry, since it was so long ago, my memory's already a little vague, so I don't remember exactly in which country China played all its three matches.

I know this event because…um, well, I think this is pretty obvious because everyone in China knows about it. It was a significant event. China had tried for decades to get into the World Cup, only to fail each and every time. But that year, we finally succeeded, so it was absolutely a big thing.

What happened…well, sadly, we lost all three matches and got knocked out. That's what happened, but even so, I was really proud of my country. In fact, it was that event that made me fall in love with football and it's been an integral part of my life since then. Now, I often play on the pitch in my university. Football is such a fun and exhilarating sport and I always get a buzz out of it. I believe I'll keep playing football for the rest of my life.

词汇 Key Words

national football team 国家足球队

jointly ['dʒɔɪntlɪ] *adv.* 共同地

vague [veɪg] *adj.* 模糊的

significant [sɪg'nɪfɪkənt] *adj.* 重大的；有意义的

only to fail each and every time 但是每次都失败

succeed [sək'siːd] *v.* 成功

get/be knocked out 出局；被淘汰

fall in love with… 爱上……

an integral part of my life 我生活中不可分割的一部分

pitch [pɪtʃ] *n.* 足球场

exhilarating [ɪg'zɪləreɪtɪŋ] *adj.* 刺激的；令人激动的

get a buzz out of sth. 从……中得到乐趣

for the rest of my life 在我的余生里

(((▶ Part 3 回答七大准则

◆ **准则 1**：观点不重要，不要因为过多思考观点而迟迟不作答，要在考官问题问完之后，立刻张嘴说话。即使没有观点也要开始说英文，说出当时自己脑中出现的想法。

◆ **准则 2**：可以先告诉考官"题目很难""没有想过这个问题"等，然后对自己所表达的"题目很难""没有想过"进行扩展——为什么觉得题目难？为什么没有想过？事实上，当考生谈论这些内容的时候，同样是在讨论题目。

◆ **准则 3**：如果没有听清、听懂考官的问题，考生应立刻提问，请考官重复或解释题目。考生可以说 "I'm sorry, I'm not quite sure what...means." "I'm sorry, what do you mean by...?" "Excuse me. Could you please repeat that?" "Excuse me. Would you please explain that a little bit?" 等。

◆ **准则 4**：考生在给出一个观点之后，应尽量对这个观点进行扩展，而非立刻罗列其他观点或者给出第二个，甚至第三个观点。若想扩展一个观点，可以解释自己提出这个观点的原因或用一个例子证明自己的观点等。

◆ **准则 5**：在 Part 3 中给出的例子最好是社会化、大众化的例子。个人的例子也是可以的，但是不要在答案开始就立刻给出，也不要把个人的例子说得过长。不过，如果刚开始回答时没有观点、想法，可以稍微聊一下自己的生活、经历来拖延时间，同时思考观点。同样，这样的内容也不要太长。

◆ **准则 6**：不要担心考官不同意你的观点。Part 3 是"讨论"，考官可以提出自己的想法、质疑，甚至"反驳"，但这不意味着考官会给你扣分。你的分数不是由观点决定的，而是由你说出的英文决定的。

◆ **准则 7**：Part 3 的很多题目与雅思写作 Task 2 的题目有很大的相似性，考生也可以通过写作范文积累 Part 3 题目的观点、句型和词汇。建议在备考雅思口语 Part 3 时，搭配《雅思写作真经总纲(精选版)》中的写作范文一起学习。

(((▶ Part 3 练习方法

◆ **方法 1**：学习本章 Part 3 例题的范例答案，积累词汇、句型、连接性表达。

◆ **方法 2**：反复朗读《雅思写作真经总纲(精选版)》中的写作范文，积累词汇、句型、连接性表达。

◆ **方法 3**：用《雅思写作真经总纲(精选版)》中的写作范文进行复述练习，提升口语水平。复述不是背诵，复述内容无须和原文完全相同。

◆ **方法 4**：听范例答案录音，改善发音；反复朗读范例答案，提高语感，并在此过程中掌握 Part 3 回答逻辑。

◆ **方法 5**：练习回答本章 Part 3 例题，练习时均以录音的方式进行：给自己的回答录音，答完一遍之后，听自己的回答，把听到的词汇、语法、逻辑、发音等方面的问题记下来，并思考把哪些词汇和句型替换成更地道的语言。再录一遍、再听、再录、再听。每道题至少把这个过程重复三次。

◆ **方法 6**：找一个同样在准备雅思考试或英语口语较好的同学协助自己练习。让这位同学充当雅思考官的角色，提出问题，模拟雅思考试现场。

◆ **方法 7**：Part 3 中出现的很多题目很可能是考官在现场根据考生的回答临时想出的，考生无法完全预测考试题目。建议大家平时多阅读关于社会性话题的英语文章，积累更多的想法、观点和英文。

注意：我们不建议大家完全背诵范例答案。提供范例答案是为了帮助各位考生增加语言储备、学习逻辑思路。大家应尽量说出自己的回答。

下面，我们来学习一些 Part 3 高分答案。在这些答案中，有一些是"正常逻辑"，即先给出观点、然后通过原因和例子扩展观点；也有一些是"不正常逻辑"——在最开始无法给出观点，而是通过说出自己当时想法的方式与考官进行沟通、聊天，在后面给出了一些观点。

(((▶ **Part 3 范例答案**

🎙 **Work, careers, companies**

Q *Do you think it's important for people to take some time off work occasionally?*

A: Yeah, definitely. I think it's vitally important for people to take some time off from time to time in order to relax. People these days, especially those living and working in large cities, tend to work nonstop, which puts a great deal of pressure on them. Taking a day or two off once in a while is extremely important. They can use the time to hang out with friends, bond with family members, go and catch a film or just stay home alone, chilling out. All of these can help them relax.

词汇 Key Words

vitally important 非常重要

take some time off 休息一小段时间

work nonstop 不停地工作

put a great deal of pressure on sb. 给某人很大压力

bond with sb. 和某人增进感情

catch a film 去看场电影

chill out 放松

Q *Should people make career choices based on money or what they're interested in?*

A: Well, I think the most significant consideration should be whether what they will do is something they take pleasure from because only when they like what they do can they do well in their jobs. Personally, I'm fanatical about fashion design and I majored in that at university. Now, I find everything I do at work quite exciting and I derive a lot of fun from that every day. However, if, for instance, I were working at a bank, which I wouldn't like at all, no matter how much money I made, I wouldn't feel happy. Of course, it's definitely best if what we do is both interesting and high-paying, but interest should come first.

词汇 Key Words

the most significant consideration 最重要的考虑
　因素

take pleasure from sth. 从……中得到乐趣

be fanatical about sth. 非常热爱……

sth. should come first ……应该是第一位的

Q *Why do some people like their jobs while others don't?*

A: There could be tons of reasons for this. First of all, perhaps they don't really get along with their colleagues. In that case, they won't feel comfortable at all at work. For instance, if you walk into the office and everyone gives you a cold shoulder, I don't think you will like this job. Another reason might be…perhaps some people think they're underemployed and deserve a higher salary. So I guess it's likely that these people don't find what they do rewarding, which will make them less enthusiastic about their jobs.

词汇 Key Words

get along with 与……相处得好

give sb. a cold shoulder 对某人冷淡

be underemployed 大材小用的；工作不符合
　自己能力的

deserve [dɪ'zɜːv] v. 应得

rewarding [rɪ'wɔːdɪŋ] *adj.* 令人满意的；令
　人有所收获的

be less enthusiastic about one's jobs 对工作
　没有那么热情

Q *Is it difficult for university graduates to find a job in your country these years?*

A: Well, I think it is. It's getting more and more difficult for them to land a job, especially a high-paying one. I guess it's due to the size of our population. I mean, millions of students graduate and enter the job market, but there are not enough openings for them at companies. In addition to this, most of those who've studied at college think they're well-educated and so should only work at big companies or even multinationals; they don't want to work in small towns or rural areas. Very few university graduates would want to work as farmers, although it might pay even more than having a nine-to-five job in an office.

词汇 Key Words

land a job 找工作

enter the job market 进入工作市场

opening ['əʊpənɪŋ] *n.* 空缺的职位

well-educated ['wel'edjuːkeɪtɪd] *adj.* 受过良好
    教育的

multinational [ˌmʌltɪ'næʃnəl] *n.* 跨国公司

a nine-to-five job 一份朝九晚五的工作

Q *In your culture, what kind of people can be leaders?*

A: In my culture? Well, to be honest, I believe it's the same in any culture. First, this person needs to be passionate about their job. They have to be enthusiastic about what they do every day. Only in this case will those who work for him or her be willing to devote themselves to whatever they do. I believe this is the most important quality a leader should have. Also, communication is crucial, so a leader has to be able to communicate ideas well. If they can't, the whole team might not be on the same page and this will definitely result in problems.

词汇 Key Words

be willing to do sth. 愿意做……

devote oneself to sth. 奉献 / 致力于……

on the same page 意见一致

result in sth. 导致……

Q *Many women are earning more money now, does it mean they can be leaders?*

A: Well, women can definitely be leaders. In fact, they can be great leaders. In our world today, many successful women occupy high positions in a company or even in a government and it's not uncommon at all. For instance, the former Prime Minister of the UK, Teresa May, is a woman. My mom is also an example. She runs a small clothing company and there are over 100 people working for her. So yeah, I don't think it's because women are earning more that they can be leaders. Men and women are the same and as long as you're capable, you can be a leader, regardless of your gender.

词汇 Key Words

occupy a high position 占据高位	regardless of 不论
not uncommon 很普遍	gender ['dʒendə(r)] *n.* 性别
capable ['keɪpəbl] *adj.* 有能力的	

Q *Why do some people keep changing their jobs?*

A: Well, I suppose there could be many reasons. First of all, perhaps it's because they're always unsatisfied with their salaries. When they change jobs, they want to find better-paid ones. Another reason could be that they find it hard to get along with their colleagues. Maybe it's because they have flawed personalities. In my case, I get on really well with the people I work with, so I'm not seeking to find another job even if my current one doesn't pay that well.

词汇 Key Words

be unsatisfied with 对……不满意	get on well with 和……相处融洽
better-paid ['betə(r) peɪd] *adj.* 薪酬更高的	seek to do sth. 寻求做……
flawed personality 有缺陷的性格	

Q *What kinds of jobs are easy to get in foreign countries?*

A: Um, this is a really weird question. To be honest with you, I thought about what questions I would possibly get on this speaking test and one of them was "What kinds of jobs are popular in China?". I never expected I'd get one like this. But um, let me think about it. In foreign countries? Well, since I'm Chinese and Chinese is my first language, I'd say that if I ever wanted to find a job in a foreign country, it would be pretty easy for me to become a Chinese teacher. I would definitely have a competitive edge over the locals in that country who learned Chinese as a second language. And I'm convinced that it would be a high-paying job because with China becoming more and more influential on the world stage, an increasing number of people are learning this language. I'm sure that I would have many students and therefore earn a decent salary.

词汇 Key Words

on the test 在考试中（美式）	on the world stage 在世界舞台上
in the test 在考试中（英式）	more and more = an increasing number of 越
a competitive edge 竞争优势	来越多的
second language 第二语言	earn a decent salary 挣一份不错的薪水
influential [ˌɪnflu'enʃl] *adj.* 有影响力的	

Q *What factors can affect a company's development?*

A: Well, off the top of my head, I'd say it's extremely important that the leader of a company is able to make sensible decisions. For instance, they should make a wise decision as to whether the company should target a particular market or aim to make their products popular with people from all economic and social backgrounds. Another factor is cooperation. There has to be good cooperation and coordination between departments. Otherwise, the company won't develop well.

词汇 Key Words

make sensible decisions 做明智的决定

target a particular market 瞄准一个特定市场群体

aim to 目的在于

people from all economic and social backgrounds
具有不同经济和社会背景的人

coordination [kəʊˌɔːdɪˈneɪʃn] *n.* 协调

Q *What are the benefits of giving prizes?*

A: Well, in my opinion, giving prizes to people who have worked extremely hard to win something makes them more motivated, so they will keep working hard. For example, the students who do well in an exam or competition can get a prize or something and I believe they will make every effort to get it the next time too. In order to do that, what they have to do is keep studying as hard as they can. In addition, I think giving prizes to some people makes them good role models for others. In this case, they set a good example for other people.

词汇 Key Words

motivated ['məʊtɪveɪtɪd] *adj.* 有动力的

do well in an exam or competition 在一次考试或
    比赛中表现出色

make every effort to do sth. 竭尽全力做……

role model 榜样

set a good example 树立好的榜样

Q *How do companies reward employees for special achievements?*

A: Well, I suppose there could be a couple of ways. First of all, managers might consider giving these employees a pay raise. This is the most obvious, of course, but I believe it works the best. Although some members of staff say they don't work for money, and they try to get job satisfaction and a sense of achievement, money still gives them more motivation, I think. Plus, these employees could be given a promotion. This is exactly what happened to my dad. He got promoted to department manager after working out a way to increase sales by over 20 percent.

词汇 Key Words

give sb. a pay raise 给某人涨工资

members of staff 员工

get job satisfaction 得到工作满足感

a sense of achievement 成就感

motivation [ˌməʊtɪˈveɪʃn] *n.* 动力

a promotion 升职

work out a way to increase sales 想出一种
提高销售额的方法

Q *What factors can affect a company's development?*

A: Well, I believe loads of factors can contribute to a company's success, but I might have to think a little. Um, first of all, I guess it's crucial that the leader of a company is always able to make smart decisions because in today's world where competition is extremely fierce, a small mistake might result in the loss of a lot of money. Besides, I've always believed that it's of great importance that all members of staff get along with each other. Imagine you walk into your office and see everyone smiling at you, this kind of environment really fosters a good team spirit and this is necessary to the development of any company.

词汇 Key Words

contribute to sth. 促成……；有助于……

fierce competition 激烈的竞争

all members of staff 所有员工

foster a good team spirit 培养一种良好的团
队精神

Q *Would you work for a small but successful company in the future?*

A: Yeah, I guess I would, because, firstly, there's better work efficiency. I mean, if you wanna work on a project, you can go to your boss directly and tell him or her what you're trying to do and how the company can help you with that. However, if you work for a big organisation, this is probably impossible. Also, it feels great to work in a place where you're familiar with everyone. Honestly, if I worked in a huge multinational company where I hardly knew anyone, I wouldn't feel comfortable at all.

词汇 Key Words

work efficiency 工作效率

be familiar with 对……熟悉

multinational company 跨国公司

🎙 Family, friends, neighbours, roommates, socialising, teamwork

Q *What are the qualities of a good friend?*

A: Well, first of all, I believe a good friend has to be reliable, because, for example, if you were supposed to meet your friend for coffee, but you got stood up, you would feel really bad. Also, if you text your friend and they never reply, I don't really think this is a good friendship. Plus, your friends and you have to see eye to eye on most things. Take Americans for example, I guess it's pretty hard for a democrat and a republican to be long-time friends.

词汇 Key Words

reliable [rɪˈlaɪəbl] *adj.* 可靠的

be supposed to do sth. 本应该做……

get stood up 被放鸽子

see eye to eye on sth. 在……上意见一致

democrat [ˈdeməkræt] *n.*（美国）民主党人

republican [rɪˈpʌblɪkən] *n.*（美国）共和党人

Q *Are friends more important than family?*

A: No, I don't think so. Friends come and go, but your family will be there all the time, whether you like it or not. Maybe, for some reason, friends will betray you or something at some point in your life, but your family members will never do anything like that. Instead, they will always love you, care for you and be supportive of you. So, friends are never as important as family.

词汇 Key Words

betray [bɪˈtreɪ] *v.* 背叛

at some point in one's life 在人生的某个时刻

be supportive of 支持

Q *What do you think is the ideal time for people to get married?*

A: Um, by "ideal time", do you mean at what age should people get married? Well, to be honest, I'm not quite sure about this. I know that in China, the age limit for people to tie the knot is…um…it's 22 or older for men and 20 or older for women. In some European countries, as far as I know, it's a lot younger—16 or even less. What I think is that if people get hitched way too early, they're actually not mature enough to handle some problems in life, like financial difficulties and raising children, and this might give rise to more serious problems in their marriage. So yeah, thinking about it, I think the Chinese age limit is pretty good.

词汇 Key Words

by…, do you mean…? 说到……，你的意思是……吗?

get married 结婚

as far as I know 据我所知

way too… 太……，过于……

mature [mə'tʃʊə(r)] *adj.* 成熟的

handle ['hændl] *v.* 处理；应对

financial difficulties 财务问题

raise children 抚养孩子

give rise to 导致；引起

marriage ['mærɪdʒ] *n.* 婚姻

Q *Do you think expensive gifts are a sign of true friendship?*

A: No, I don't think so. We always say "it's the thought that counts", and it's right, because not everyone can afford gifts that are pricey. Plus, some presents are of great sentimental value even if they are inexpensive. For example, I'm a big bookworm and I would love it if my friends gave me a good book on my birthday or some other special occasions.

词汇 Key Words

it's the thought that counts 心意最重要

pricey ['praɪsɪ] *adj.* 昂贵的

be of great sentimental value 有很大的情感价值

a big bookworm 一个很爱读书的人

on some special occasions 在一些特殊场合

Q *In general, what do you think is the significance of giving gifts?*

A: Well, truth be told, I haven't given it a lot of thought. I think most people just follow the trend. You know, we give gifts coz everybody does it. But I suppose, by giving presents to others, we make them happy and we can derive pleasure from it too. I guess it's also a way of enhancing our relationship with whomever we give gifts to. You know, if I give my friend something he or she really likes, it's likely that we will be closer. It's the same with relatives and family members, I think.

词汇 Key Words

truth be told 说实话

I haven't given it a lot of thought 我没想过这个

follow the trend 跟风

derive pleasure from sth. 从……中得到快乐

enhance our relationship 增进我们的关系

closer ['kləʊsə] *adj.* 更亲近的

Q *Do you think it's important that people have a good relationship with neighbours?*

A: Well, absolutely. It's of great significance that people get along with their neighbours, due to the fact that only when we have a good relationship with them can we feel a sense of community, and this is really beneficial to everyone. Sometimes, if we're in need of help, those living next door can give us a hand. For instance, they can help us fix the toilet, babysit our children while we're away, take care of our pets and so forth. If we don't get on well with them, we might feel pretty helpless when something urgent happens.

词汇 Key Words

a sense of community 社区归属感；社区意识

give sb. a hand 给予某人帮助

babysit children 替人临时照看孩子

Q *Why are virtual communities becoming more and more popular nowadays?*

A: Well, the reasons are manifold, I think. Firstly, since technology has come such a long way, it has become much easier for us to make friends online. We don't have to go to the trouble of going to a bar, a café or a party to meet someone new. Instead, it can be done on the internet. Secondly, some people are really into virtual communities because they can pretend to be someone that they are not and experience something they can't have in the real world. For instance, if a man is physically unattractive and poor, he can still claim that he is a charming guy by posting some pictures of other people. So, these are the reasons I can think of.

词汇 Key Words

manifold ['mænɪfəʊld] *adj.* 多方面的

technology has come such a long way 科技取得
了很大发展

go to the trouble of doing sth. 不怕麻烦费心做……

physically unattractive 相貌平平

charming ['tʃɑːmɪŋ] *adj.* 有魅力的

post a picture (on the internet) （在网上）发
布一张照片

Q *Do you think there are any advantages to sharing an apartment with people who are not your family members?*

A: Well, I've never really thought about it before. It's really hard to think of an advantage, I think, because I suppose most people would like their roommates or flatmates to be family or friends. Maybe it's beneficial for people to stop being too reliant on their parents and start taking responsibility for themselves. Another advantage might be that they get to develop communication skills and it makes them more sociable because when living under the same roof, people definitely have to interact with their flatmates and try to get along with them. If they don't, they will have a hard time living together.

词汇 Key Words

be reliant on sb. 依赖某人

take responsibility for sth./sb. 对……负责

communication skills 沟通技巧

sociable ['səʊʃəbl] *adj.* 善于社交的

live under the same roof 同住一个屋檐下

interact with sb. 和某人互动

have a hard time doing sth. 做……很困难

Q *What are the differences between doing something in a group and doing things alone?*

A: Well, off the top of my head, I'd say people might be more motivated in a group. No matter what they do, be it a sport or a project assigned by their teachers or employers, they know if they don't try their best, the whole team will not function to the full. In that case, the results might not be optimal and they might let others down. However, by contrast, when you're doing something on your own, you might feel the urge to slack off because no one is working side by side with you and you're likely to feel that it won't hurt if you don't give it your best shot.

词汇 Key Words

be more motivated 更有动力的

no matter what..., be it...or... 不管怎样，无论
  是……还是……

try one's best 尽最大努力

function to the full 充分发挥作用

optimal ['ɒptɪməl] *adj.* 最理想的

on one's own 独自地

feel the urge to slack off 有松懈的冲动

work side by side 共同工作

it won't hurt 无妨

give it one's best shot 尽最大努力

🎤 Transport, commuting

Q *Do people in your country prefer to use public transport or private transport?*

A: As far as I'm concerned, most people like to take public transport. I think there are a couple of reasons for this. First of all, public transport is extremely cheap in most cities. Take Beijing for example, it only costs several yuan to ride the subway. Another reason might be that the traffic in large cities in China is awful, so it drives people crazy sometimes if they use their own car. For this reason, if it's available, the subway sounds like a much better choice.

词汇 Key Words

ride/take the subway 坐地铁

drive people crazy 令人发疯，把人逼疯

Q *Why do some people have to travel a long distance to work?*

A: Well, um, it only takes me half an hour to get to my company, so I haven't given it a lot of thought. Well, I suppose, there could be many reasons. For starters, many people go to work in the city but live in the suburbs because housing prices are sky-high in the city. Besides, some parents live far away from work because they live in close proximity to their children's schools. This way, it's convenient for their children, but they have to travel a long distance every day. Honestly, I would feel terrible if I had to drive a long time to get to work. It would drive me up the wall if I had to do it on a daily basis.

词汇 Key Words

in the suburbs 在郊区（注意复数形式）

in close proximity to… 离……很近

sky-high ['skaɪ'haɪ] *adj.* 超高的

Q *Do you think the government should control the number of cars on the road?*

A: Well, I think it should, if it's extremely congested on the road. If the government doesn't do anything, the traffic conditions will just keep worsening and an entire city will simply be a big parking lot. Take Beijing for example, every weekday, a certain percentage of cars are not allowed to be used, so there's less traffic and it's slightly better than if there weren't this policy at all.

词汇 Key Words

congested [kən'dʒestɪd] *adj.* 堵塞的

a certain percentage of cars 一定比例的车辆

worsen ['wɜːsn] *v.* 恶化；变坏

less traffic 车辆较少

parking lot 停车场

🎤 Countryside and cities, accommodation, buildings

Q *What are the advantages of living in the countryside?*

A: Well, there are obviously a ton of advantages of living in the country and the first one that comes to mind is that due to the absence of cars and factories…um…I think I may have exaggerated it a little bit…well, there are certainly some cars and factories in the countryside, but since there are not

that many, people living in the country don't inhale a lot of toxic fumes. This is clearly one of the main advantages of country life over city dwelling. In Beijing, where I'm from, there are millions of vehicles running on the streets every day, which gives rise to air pollution from time to time, and that's why some people are considering moving away. Another benefit of country life is the slow pace of life. Time runs more slowly in the country, which doesn't make people feel under too much pressure. In the city, however, everyone tends to rush from one place to another and it's extremely stressful.

词汇 Key Words

a ton of 很多

the absence of... 没有……；缺少……

exaggerate [ɪɡ'zædʒəreɪt] v. 夸张

inhale toxic fumes 吸入有毒气体

city dwelling 城市居住

give rise to 导致

pace of life 生活节奏

rush from one place to another 从一个地方

　急忙赶到另外一个地方

Q *What kind of people like city life?*

A: Well, I believe most young people do, because cities are more vibrant and dynamic and there are many bars, clubs, and tons of other places where young people can entertain themselves. By contrast, these places are few and far between in the countryside. Plus, career-minded people might be more into city life, coz cities provide more job opportunities and usually in those jobs, there's more room for promotion. For instance, if you want to pursue a career in advertising, I can't imagine living in a rural area being good for you.

词汇 Key Words

vibrant and dynamic 活跃、有激情

entertain sb. 娱乐某人

few and far between 稀少的

career-minded people 有事业心的人

more room for promotion 更大的晋升空间

pursue a career 干一番事业

Q *What are some of the problems of living in the city?*

A: Well, I think there are loads of problems. For starters, people are always under a huge amount of pressure, because the competition in the job market is extremely fierce, and also, the cost of living is sky-high in cities. Another problem is that there's a lot of pollution like air pollution and noise pollution. Millions of cars lead to these problems and they also give rise to traffic congestion. Personally, I'm not a big fan of living in the city, although there's not much I can do about it.

词汇 Key Words

under a huge amount of pressure 有很大压力	cost of living 生活成本
fierce competition 激烈的竞争	lead to = give rise to 导致
job market 工作市场	traffic congestion 交通堵塞

Q *Why do so many people like to go to places with water?*

A: Well, off the top of my head, it's because of the appeal of those fun activities that can be done on or near water. For instance, a lot of people enjoy swimming in the sea, snorkelling, kayaking, lying on the beach and so on. All of these things bring people a great amount of joy. Personally, I'm a huge fan of snorkelling and I wouldn't miss any opportunity to go to a seaside city if I could snorkel there. Another reason could be the views. No matter where it is, as long as it's close to a lot of water, it's gorgeous.

词汇 Key Words

appeal [ə'piːl] *n.* 吸引力	miss sth. 错过……
snorkel ['snɒkl] *v.* 浮潜	view [vjuː] *n.* 风景
kayak ['kaɪæk] *v.* 划独木舟 / 皮艇	as long as 只要
bring sb. a great amount of joy 给某人带来很多的快乐	gorgeous ['gɔːdʒəs] *adj.* 非常美丽的

Q *Are expensive buildings a waste of money?*

A: Oh, that's something I've never thought about before. Um, expensive buildings…No, I don't think they're a waste of money because one building that comes to mind is the Trump Tower in New York, built by the former president of the United States, Donald Trump. I bet it cost him millions of dollars to build it, but it absolutely generates enormous revenues now. There are loads of famous stores in it, many hotel rooms and even a large number of tourists visit it every day, so it's definitely a profitable building. So yeah, thinking about this…I don't agree that expensive buildings are a waste of money.

词汇 Key Words

a waste of money 浪费钱的行为	generate enormous revenues 产生巨大的收益
come to mind 被想到	profitable ['prɒfɪtəbl] *adj.* 盈利的
I bet 我敢肯定；我确信	

🎤 Hobbies, relaxation, lifestyles, sports, travel

Q *Why do some people like taking photos and some don't?*

A: Um, well, off the top of my head, I don't suppose there's anybody that doesn't like taking photos, coz photography is amazing, right? It allows us to have a record of where we have been and what we have done. I believe everybody loves snapping photos of interesting, unusual, weird things and beautiful scenery. I guess those who say they don't love photography must be people who don't like taking selfies. Perhaps they don't think they're photogenic and so don't want to be seen by others in a picture. In my opinion, it's important for those people to be more confident about their look.

词汇 Key Words

take photos = snap photos 照相

have a record of... 有一个对于……的记录

where we have been 我们去过的地方

what we have done 我们做过的事情

unusual [ʌnˈjuːʒʊəl] *adj.* 不寻常的

take selfies 自拍

photogenic [ˌfəʊtəʊˈdʒenɪk] *adj.* 上相的

Q *Why do people take selfies?*

A: Well, that's an interesting question and…actually, I just took a selfie and posted it on Weibo, the Chinese equivalent of Twitter, this morning. After posting, I even stuck around for a few minutes to see if I could get some likes and comments. So, what I think is that people take selfies because they wanna feel loved; they want to get people's attention. You know, not many people take selfies only for the sake of taking them; they're more likely to post them on social media, and if they get a lot of likes and comments, it definitely boosts their ego. Yeah, ego, that's the reason behind many things.

词汇 Key Words

the Chinese equivalent of Twitter 中国的 Twitter

stick around 逗留；停留

get people's attention 获得人们的关注

for the sake of... 为了……

social media 社交媒体

boost one's ego 提升某人的自信心 / 自尊

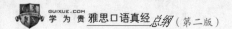

Q *Why do people like to take many photos when they're travelling?*

A: Well, haha, this is a really interesting question. We really do take way more photos on a trip than we're at home or work. Um, I believe this is because what we do and see while travelling is totally different from what we do and see most of the time, and in order to have a record of these special things, we take a lot of photos. For instance, if you go on holiday to a seaside city, you can go swimming and snorkelling in the sea, watch the sunrise over the sea, lie on the beach and so on, which are not things you can do on a regular basis. Snapping photos of these things will help you record these memories.

词汇 Key Words

way more… 更多的……	sunrise over the sea 海上日出
go on holiday 去度假	lie on the beach 躺在海滩上

Q *Where do people go to relax in your country?*

A: Well, it varies from person to person. Some people like to go to cafés to do some reading or just chat with their friends. You can see that there are more and more cafés both in cities and in the suburbs and it's not uncommon for people to go and grab a cup of coffee and hang out there with friends. Others might like to go and sing karaoke, hang out at bars and clubs and go to the gym. I think it's a pretty positive trend that we have more ways to wind down after a busy day at work.

词汇 Key Words

grab a cup of coffee 买杯咖啡	a positive trend 一个很好的趋势
sing karaoke 唱卡拉 OK	a busy day at work 忙碌工作的一天

Q *What can people learn from travelling overseas?*

A: Overseas travel can help people learn a bunch of things. For starters, travellers can get a glimpse of what the local life of a country is like and therefore, it helps to understand why the locals do some particular things and we can learn what they do well in. If you travel to Japan, for example, you will see how people recycle things and how they are really polite to one another. Of course, we can learn these things from them. We can also pick up a bit of their language if we stay in another country for a relatively long period of time, say 2 or 3 months.

词汇 Key Words

a bunch of 一些

get a glimpse of 瞥见；稍微了解

recycle [ˌriː'saɪkl] v. 回收

pick up a bit of their language 学习一点他们的语言

for a relatively long period of time 在一段相对长的时间内

Q *What do you think are the advantages and disadvantages of travelling in a tour group?*

A: Well, off the top of my head, being looked after is definitely a benefit. When you go somewhere with a tour guide, not only will they introduce you to the place you're visiting, but they can also help you solve problems on the trip. For instance, if there's something wrong with the accommodation, food, etc., you can rely on them to sort things out. However, if you're travelling alone, you have no choice but to do these on your own, which could be a hassle. When it comes to disadvantages, I'd say, you don't get to do all you want in a group. You always have to follow the guide and it lacks a bit of flexibility.

词汇 Key Words

be looked after 被照顾

introduce you to a place 向你介绍一个地方

rely on sb. 依靠某人

sort things out 解决问题

a hassle 一件麻烦事

lack a bit of flexibility 缺少一点灵活性

🎤 Entertainment, celebrities, role models

Q *Do you think entertainment will be mainly home-based in the future?*

A: Yeah, I do think so. This is mainly because of the rapid development of the internet, which is responsible for a lot of what we do for fun nowadays. For instance, there are many websites now where we stream all kinds of videos. This is what a large number of people do for pleasure these days. Additionally, virtual reality technologies are progressing pretty fast too. I went to a VR centre a couple of weeks ago  and had a ton of fun there playing games. We can even buy our own VR devices and play those fun games at home.

词汇 Key Words

rapid development 快速发展	virtual reality = VR 虚拟现实
be responsible for sth. 是……的原因; 促成……	progress [prəʊ'gres] *v.* 进步
stream videos 在线看视频	have a ton of fun 玩得很开心
for pleasure 为了消遣	device [dɪ'vaɪs] *n.* 设备

Q *How do people become famous in your country?*

A: Well, people become famous in various ways, and um, I don't really know where to start. Um, for starters, a lot of people who wanna become famous overnight take part in talent shows, like *The Voice of China, China's Got Talent* and so on. If they're indeed super talented and are great singers or actors or comedians, they may rise to stardom in an instant. Another thing I can think of now is that athletes in different fields train really hard for years in order to win a medal at the Olympics. Those who really win can grab a lot of attention nationwide and even worldwide. Benny is a good example here. He's a fantastic swimmer that specialises in freestyle and um, I'm not sure about the details, but I think he won a couple of medals at the last Olympics and everybody in China knows him now.

词汇 Key Words

in various ways 通过不同的方式	medal ['medl] *n.* 奖牌
for starters 首先	the Olympics 奥运会
become famous overnight 一夜成名	grab a lot of attention 吸引很多注意力
talent show 选秀	nationwide [ˌneɪʃn'waɪd] *adv.* 在全国范围内
rise to stardom 成名	worldwide ['wɜːldwaɪd] *adv.* 在全球范围内
in an instant 迅速	specialise in... 专攻……
another thing I can think of 我能想到的另外一件事	freestyle ['friːstaɪl] *n.* 自由泳
for years 多年	a couple of 两三个

Q *What are the disadvantages of being famous?*

A: Oh, it has loads of disadvantages and the first one that comes to mind is that you can't get a break, ever. What I mean is that, of course, you go to work and act in a movie or record a song, but that's not it. Even when you're off work and going shopping or grabbing a coffee, you may be recognised by your fans and they run after you and want to get your autograph or take pictures with you. So yeah, being a celebrity is extremely tiring and stressful. In addition to this, you don't know who your real friends are. Perhaps the person that you're very close to today will reach out to a gossip magazine and spill some beans about you tomorrow.

词汇 Key Words

loads of 很多

get a break 休息；停歇

be off work 下班

grab a coffee 喝杯咖啡

be recognised 被认出来

autograph ['ɔ:təɡrɑ:f] *n.* 亲笔签名

tiring ['taɪərɪŋ] *adj.* 令人感到疲倦的

stressful ['stresfl] *adj.* 给人以很大压力的

be close to sb. 和某人很亲近

gossip magazine 八卦杂志

spill the beans 泄密

Q *What kinds of people can become role models?*

A: Off the top of my head, I think those people who are extremely hard-working must be very good role models. In my opinion, diligence is the most important quality in a person and no matter what someone wants to achieve, he or she has to work hard. The person I really look up to is Jackie Chan, who I'm sure you know. He just received an honorary Oscar award for his contributions to the film industry. I believe the main reason he's become so well-known and respected today is that he worked incredibly hard. Honestly, compared to him, a lot of actors and actresses now really lack the kind of work ethic that he has, so they just can't be good role models.

词汇 Key Words

hard-working ['hɑ:d'wɜ:kɪŋ] *adj.* 刻苦努力的

diligence ['dɪlɪdʒəns] *n.* 勤奋

quality ['kwɒlətɪ] *n.* 品质

achieve [ə'tʃi:v] *v.* 达成

look up to 敬仰

contribution [ˌkɒntrɪ'bju:ʃn] *n.* 贡献

respected [rɪ'spektɪd] *adj.* 受人尊敬的

incredibly [ɪn'kredəblɪ] *adv.* 难以置信地

lack [læk] *v.* 缺乏

work ethic 职业道德（努力工作的精神）

🎤 Internet, technology

Q *How can people find reliable friends online?*

A: Um, honestly, I believe the answer is "they can't". The online world is very different from the real world that we live in. You know, in the real world, if we want to make friends,

we can go to a bar or party or any other place where we can meet various kinds of people. We can see others in person and make some sort of judgment as to whether these people are reliable or not. Although this kind of judgment may not be 100% accurate, it's still much better than making friends online. I mean, on the internet, we might assume that we're chatting with a 20-year-old girl, but it might turn out that it's actually a 50-year-old pervert. So yeah, I just don't think it's possible to find reliable friends online.

词汇 Key Words

be different from... 和……不同	accurate ['ækjərət] *adj.* 准确的
meet various people 遇到不同的人	assume [ə'sjuːm] *v.* 认为
in person 当面	turn out 结果是
as to 至于，关于	pervert ['pɜːvɜt] *n.* 变态
reliable [rɪ'laɪəbl] *adj.* 可靠的	

Q *Which do you think provides useful learning materials, the internet or books?*

A: The internet or books...well I believe they're both very valuable tools that can help people learn a wide range of things. As for books, they are without a doubt the most important source of information. Our wisdom has been passed down from generation to generation through books. But at the same time, we shouldn't neglect the importance of the internet. An example comes to mind now. In China, a very popular website is Wangyi Open Class which provides people with tons of valuable and precious learning resources. We even have access to classes from prestigious universities in the United States, the UK and Australia. So yeah, I believe that books and the internet are both essential in helping people learn in this day and age.

词汇 Key Words

valuable ['væljuəbl] *adj.* 有价值的	be passed down from generation to generation
a wide range of things 很多东西	一代一代传下来
without a doubt 毋庸置疑	have access to sth. 能够获得……
source of information 信息来源	prestigious [pre'stɪdʒəs] *adj.* 有名望的
wisdom ['wɪzdəm] *n.* 智慧	in this day and age 在当今时代

Q *How has technology changed our lives?*

A: Technology has been improving rapidly over the past couple of decades and because of that, we spend…or um…I suppose a better way to put it would be we waste a lot more money on high-tech stuff, either out of our own will, or because we're kinda forced by the trend. A good example would be the iPhone. Apple releases a new iPhone every year, or even two, and in order to always look trendy, whenever a new model hits the market, many people go and buy it. In fact, a new iPhone just came out several days ago and um, it's almost identical to the ones that were unveiled last September, except this new one is a little bigger. I bet a lot of people will go to the Apple store and buy it in spite of the fact that they already have several iPhones in their possession.

词汇 Key Words

rapidly ['ræpɪdlɪ] *adv.* 很快地

over the past couple of decades 在过去的二三十年中

a better way to put it 一种更好的表达方式

high-tech stuff 高科技的东西

out of one's own will 出于自愿

trend [trend] *n.* 趋势，潮流

release [rɪ'liːs] *v.* 发布

trendy ['trendɪ] *adj.* 时髦的，时尚的

model ['mɒdl] *n.* 型号

hit the market 上市

be identical to… 跟……一样

unveil [ʌn'veɪl] *v.* 公布；使……公之于众

in spite of the fact that… 即使……

in one's possession 拥有

Q *What are some problems that people face on the internet?*

A: Well, the first problem that comes to mind is something that we see every day and everywhere——internet trolling. I have no idea why this is so prevalent now, but you definitely see it in all kinds of places online. In my country, the most popular social networking site is Weibo, the Chinese equivalent of Twitter, and under each and every one of those popular posts, you see tons of vicious comments. For instance, I saw one comment calling a new-born baby extremely ugly yesterday and um…of course, this guy got what he deserved. Many people condemned him and said he looked like a pig as well. But then again, that's trolling too.

词汇 Key Words

prevalent ['prevələnt] *adj.* 普遍存在的；盛行的

social networking site 社交网站

equivalent [ɪ'kwɪvələnt] *n.* 相等的东西；对应物

vicious ['vɪʃəs] *adj.* 恶毒的

comment ['kɒment] *n.* 评论

a new-born baby 一个新生婴儿

deserve [dɪ'zɜːv] *v.* 应得

condemn [kən'dem] *v.* 谴责

but then again 然而，不过

Q *What electronic devices and household appliances do people use now?*

A: Oh, we use tons. As for electronic devices, we use the computer and the smartphone and they're like an essential part of our life now. Also, it's not uncommon for us to use some tablets to play games and read and stuff. Household appliances…well, there are loads of them, like the washing machine, the dishwasher, the refrigerator and…I could simply go on and on and on. I think these machines and devices have improved our lives dramatically and everything is super convenient now.

词汇 Key Words

electronic device 电子产品

tablet ['tæblət] *n.* 平板电脑

household appliance 家用电器

dishwasher ['dɪʃwɒʃə(r)] *n.* 洗碗机

improve sth. dramatically 使……大幅提高

Q *Do you think teachers will be replaced by technology in the future?*

A: No, I can't agree with those who hold this view, because I believe there's no substitute for the guidance of a good teacher. Traditionally, teachers and students interact with each other face to face and teachers can see whatever is going on in the classroom. If they realise that a student is having difficulty making sense of what they teach, they can either stop to explain everything or tutor this student in person later. I don't think technology can do what I described just now.

词汇 Key Words

there's no substitute for sth. 没什么能替代……

interact with sb. 和某人互动

have difficulty doing sth. 做……有困难

make sense of sth. 弄懂……的意思

🎤 Children, young people, old people

Q *Do you think it's beneficial for children to take part in group activities?*

A: Yeah, absolutely. I'm convinced that it's good for them and there are loads of benefits. For starters, the most evident one would be that children are more likely to make friends in a group. Another benefit I can think of is that they can develop social skills from an early age. We need to deal with people from all walks of life on a daily basis and I think it's good if children can hone their skills as early as possible. For example, when kids play football,

not only should they be able to play well as an individual, but they're also required to communicate effectively with teammates. This, I believe, is pretty beneficial to them.

词汇 Key Words

develop social skills 培养社交技能

from an early age 从小

deal with people from all walks of life 和各行各
业的人打交道

hone their skills as early as possible 尽早磨
炼他们的技能

Q *What are the benefits of team sports for children?*

A: Well, there are tons of benefits of course, and one of them is that team sports train children to cooperate with others. This is extremely important in today's world. Everyone, including children, tends to be egocentric in some way, but their "my way or the highway" attitude will have to stay in check when they're doing a team sport like soccer, basketball or hockey.

词汇 Key Words

train [treɪn] *v.* 训练

cooperate [kəʊˈɒpəreɪt] *v.* 合作

egocentric [ˌegəʊˈsentrɪk] *adj.* 以自我为中心的

in some way 在某个 / 某些方面

my way or the highway 顺我者昌，逆我
者亡；非照我的意思去办不可

stay in check 加以控制

Q *Are there any differences between old people and young people when it comes to travelling?*

A: Sure, there are definitely tons of differences between them. For starters, when young people choose to go travelling somewhere, it's more likely that they will go on their own instead of signing up for a tour group, because most young people would like the trip to be challenging and full of excitement. If they go with a tour group and a tour guide, they might not feel the freedom they'll have when travelling alone. Old people tend to travel with others. They don't have to think too much about accommodation and flights and so on. These things might prove to be a hassle for them if they don't often use the internet. Apart from that, young people might want to go to places off the beaten track, whereas older people generally want to go to key tourist attractions, I think.

词汇 Key Words

go on one's own 自己去

sign up for a tour group 报名参加旅行团

a hassle 一件麻烦事

places off the beaten track 人迹罕至的地方

whereas [weərˈæz] *conj.* 然而 (用在句中)

key tourist attractions 重点旅游景点

Q *Why don't young people like educational programmes?*

A: Well, firstly, I'd like to **point out** that some young people do enjoy educational shows, coz I, **for one**, am crazy about a couple of programmes that teach spoken English, and also, quite a few of my friends are into watching documentaries. But **it's fair to say** that **the majority of** young people are not fans of these kinds of programmes. I suppose this is because what they do on a daily basis is **be educated**, or they've just left school or university, and therefore they still **remember vividly** those hard days sitting in a classroom, **busy learning** or preparing for exams. In fact, I remember thinking to myself "I don't ever wanna study anymore" the very day I graduated from university. The whole year after that, I **was** so **addicted to reality shows** and game shows. It was two years later that I realised that I had to keep learning in order to **stand out** at work.

词汇 Key Words

point out 指出	remember vividly 清楚地记得
for one 作为其中一个；举例来说	(be) busy doing sth. 忙于做……
it's fair to say… 这么说并不过分；说句公道话	be addicted to… 对……上瘾
the majority of… 大多数……	reality show 真人秀
be educated 受教育	stand out 杰出；突出

注意：上述答案中的 "what they do is be educated…" 中，be 动词前面是 do，be 动词后面可以使用动词原形，也可以使用 to do，但 native speakers（以英语为母语的人）使用动词原形的情况更多。例如 "All you do is eat." "All I wanna do is take a nap." "What I'm going to do is note down a few details." 等。

Q *How do you think the problem of youth crime could be tackled?*

A: Well, that's a **tough** question. Um, in my opinion, the **fundamental** solution to any social problem is education. Of course, people would claim that **one** effective **approach to tackling** youth crime is a much **stricter** system of penalties and punishments…well, that might **work**, but we really have to seriously think about how to prevent young people from committing crimes rather than only about punishing them after **offences**. As for education, we should do two things. One is to **inform** young people about the dangers of committing crimes and the other is to **equip them with sufficient** knowledge and skills to find **decent jobs** and earn enough money to live good lives. I believe if these things are done well, youth crime could be **dramatically** reduced.

词汇 Key Words

tough [tʌf] *adj.* 困难的

fundamental [ˌfʌndə'mentl] *adj.* 根本的

one approach to doing sth. ……的一个方法

tackle ['tækl] *v.* 解决

strict [strɪkt] *adj.* 严格的

work [wɜːk] *v.* 起作用

offence [ə'fens] *n.* 违法行为

inform sb. 告知某人

equip sb. with sth. 使某人具备……

sufficient [sə'fɪʃnt] *adj.* 足够的

decent jobs 体面的工作

dramatically [drə'mætɪklɪ] *adv.* 显著地

Q *Why do young people tend to waste money?*

A: Well, in my view, it's not that young people often waste money on purpose. They do spend a lot and splurge on some things occasionally because they want to live in the present by trying out fun things and having a great time. When you're in your 20s, you certainly want to enjoy yourself by partying, singing karaoke, travelling and so on, and these things are usually very costly. So, as I was saying, young people don't want to waste money; they just end up spending a lot on things that they believe can bring them a great amount of joy.

词汇 Key Words

on purpose 故意

splurge on sth. 在……上花很多钱

live in the present 活在当下

try out… 尝试……

in one's 20s 在某人二十多岁的时候

party ['pɑːtɪ] *v.* 参加派对

costly ['kɒstlɪ] *adj.* 昂贵的

as I was saying 就像我刚才说过的

end up doing sth. 最终……；以……告终

joy [dʒɔɪ] *n.* 快乐

Q *How can we teach elderly people new technology?*

A: Um, well, off the top of my head, I really want to say that it's extremely difficult to teach old people new things, let alone technology, which is generally harder to learn than many other things. This is because senior citizens have lived their entire lives doing the things that they're used to, that they're familiar with. So most elderly people are reluctant to learn new things. Thinking about it, if we want to teach old people new technology, it's crucial that we get them to understand it's necessary to learn it. For example, my mom only agreed to learn to use WeChat, the Chinese equivalent of WhatsApp, because I told her that I would be on it all the time, and she could send me text messages and voice messages anytime she wanted. If it hadn't been for that, I suppose she still wouldn't be able to use WeChat today.

GUIXUE.COM

词汇 Key Words

let alone 更不用说

senior citizens 老人

be used to sth. 习惯……

be familiar with sth. 熟悉……

be reluctant to do sth. 不情愿做……

crucial ['kru:ʃl] *adj.* 至关重要的

text message 文字信息 / 短信

voice message 语音信息

🎤 Food

Q *Are there many vegetarians in your country?*

A: Yeah, I think so. Although there are not many vegetarians around me, I mean, only two of my friends are, the fact is, I know more and more people decide to eat a vegetarian diet nowadays. I guess this can be seen from the increasing number of vegetarian restaurants in China, especially in large cities, where people are generally better off and more open-minded about this kind of diet. Around my neighbourhood, for instance, three vegetarian restaurants have opened in the past year and they're all pretty popular.

词汇 Key Words

more and more = an increasing number of 越来越多的

eat a...diet 吃一种……的饮食

...sth. can be seen from... 从……中能够看出……

better-off ['betə(r)'ɒf] *adj.* 较富裕的

open-minded ['əupən'maɪndɪd] *adj.* 思想开明的

in the past year 在过去的一年

Q *Why do you think some people choose to be vegetarians?*

A: Well, I suppose the reasons are manifold. The first one that comes to mind is some people consider only eating vegetables healthier, because such a diet may help reduce the risk of diseases like cancer. Also, it's believed by some that animals shouldn't be killed for food. My mum, for example, is a Buddhist and she thinks animals and humans are equal and killing and eating them is morally wrong.

词汇 **Key Words**

consider sth. healthier 认为……更健康	be killed for food 被杀供人食用
reduce the risk of diseases like cancer 降低患癌症这样的疾病的风险	Buddhist ['bʊdɪst] *n.* 佛教徒
	morally wrong 道德上错误的

Q *Why do you think fast food is popular nowadays?*

A: Well, as far as I'm concerned, first of all, it might be because most people today, especially those living in the city are always in a hurry, and they don't have enough time to go home and spend a couple of hours cooking a decent meal and eating. Another reason might be that fast food just somehow appeals to people, especially children and teenagers, because of all the sweet and fatty stuff. Actually, I'm not quite sure whether this is the reason, but take me for example, I used to have a sweet tooth when I was a child. So did many of my friends. We always went to McDonald's and KFC together.

词汇 **Key Words**

in a hurry 急匆匆的	appeal to sb. 吸引某人
a decent meal 一顿不错的饭	have a sweet tooth 喜欢吃甜食

Q *How do you think the way we eat will change in the future?*

A: Well, how do I think...Honestly, I've never thought about it before...I suppose we will eat more and more junk food like hamburgers, French fries, hot dogs and so on, because with a large number of people flocking to cities, the competition in the job market is gonna be more and more fierce. In that case, we'll find it harder and harder to make time to enjoy cooking. Some people might think that if they spend too much time eating, they'll probably lag behind those who only have a burger for lunch and then go back to work. Well, this is only my assumption. Hopefully, it'll never happen.

词汇 **Key Words**

flock to 涌向	assumption [ə'sʌmpʃn] *n.* 猜想
lag behind 落后	

🎙 Study, language, education, skills

Q *Do you think students need to relax when they study?*

A: Well, in my opinion, when students are studying, they shouldn't feel too relaxed, because if they are, they won't be able to focus on what they're doing and the results won't be satisfying. However, after a student has studied for some time, he or she definitely deserves a rest and needs to do something to unwind. This will help the student study more productively later.

词汇 Key Words

satisfying ['sætɪsfaɪɪŋ] *adj.* 令人满意的

deserve a rest 应该休息

productively [prə'dʌktɪvlɪ] *adv.* 高效地

Q *Why do more and more Chinese people go and study abroad?*

A: Haha, I sure know a lot about this coz I'm taking this IELTS test in order to go and study in the UK. I believe one of the fundamental reasons is that it's a great opportunity for people to be immersed in a foreign language, especially English, because most Chinese students choose to study in English-speaking countries like the UK, the United States, Canada and Australia. Being surrounded by this language allows them to learn it more easily and quickly. On top of that, the overall experience of living and studying in a foreign country, absorbing another culture and acquiring another language will set those students apart from other people when they're trying to find a job. My cousin, for example, studied in Canada for three years and it didn't take him long to land a well-paid job after returning to China. I hope it'll be the same for me when I come back.

词汇 Key Words

be immersed in... 沉浸在……中

be surrounded by... 被……所包围

on top of that 除此之外

absorb [əb'sɔ:b] *v.* 吸收

acquire [ə'kwaɪə(r)] *v.* 获得

set sb. apart 使某人显得突出；使某人显得与众不同

land a well-paid job 找到一份薪水高的工作

Q *How can people learn a language if they don't live in the country where it's spoken?*

A: Well, there are many ways to learn a language. Firstly, watching movies and TV programmes is quite effective. I've been learning English for over 10 years and all I do is just watch an American movie and then repeat all the lines over and over again. In my opinion, it's one of the best ways because I've improved dramatically since I started doing it. As well as this, you can always find native-speakers who live in your country and practice with them.

词汇 Key Words

effective [ɪˈfektɪv] *adj.* 有效的

repeat all the lines over and over again 不断重
复所有的台词

improve dramatically 大幅提高

Q *What do you think is the ideal age for learning a foreign language?*

A: As early as possible! It's scientifically proven that children learn language much faster and a lot more easily than adults. I believe this is because kids are better at imitating sounds and so they pick up pronunciation faster than older people. Since pronunciation is a major part of a language, children have their natural advantage in learning a foreign tongue over adults. Take my cousin for example, who speaks English like a native speaker. She is so good at this language because she started off super young. When she was a kid, she was exposed to this language coz she watched English cartoons every day. I wish it had been the same for me.

词汇 Key Words

be scientifically proven 被科学证明的

imitate sounds 模仿声音 / 发音

a major part of sth. ……的重要组成部分

have (an) advantage over... 相对于……更
有优势

tongue [tʌŋ] *n.* 语言

be exposed to... 接触……

Q *Do you think parents should force their children to learn musical instruments?*

A: No, obviously not. Parents shouldn't force their children to do anything. Wait, sorry, I take that back. If it's Chinese, math or English, if children don't want to learn these subjects, then they should be forced to spend time on them, because they're all compulsory subjects that allow people to survive in today's world, in any workplace. However, as for music, some people are born to be musicians, whereas some just don't have a musical ear. For them, it's simply a waste of time to learn music or musical instruments. They should put in the time to learn the things they like and do well in.

词汇 Key Words

obviously not 显然不是

I take that back 我收回刚才的话

workplace [ˈwɜːkpleɪs] *n.* 工作场合

as for 至于

be born to... 生来就要……

have a musical ear 擅长音乐，有音乐天赋

a waste of time 浪费时间

Q *Why do some parents want their kids to be homeschooled?*

A: Well, honestly, not a lot of parents in China do this, so I'm not quite sure if everything I'm gonna say is correct, but um, off the top of my head, I suppose it might be because their kids don't get along with other students. Perhaps they just can't fit in with the other kids at school. Another possible reason I can think of is that some parents are not quite satisfied with the education at school. I guess this might be the primary reason why some parents homeschool their children.

词汇 Key Words

fit in with sb. 和某人相处融洽

the primary reason 首要原因

be satisfied with 对……感到满意

Q *Do you think high school students should learn skills that will be useful in the workplace?*

A: Well, no, I don't think so. It's because high school should be the time when students acquire basic knowledge about different aspects of our life, such as chemistry, biology, history and geography. It should be until college when they learn the skills that will be useful in the workplace. What students learn in high school should be the foundation of everything they learn in college. Without proper and sufficient preparation at high school, they might not be able to learn practical things well later. For example, if a student wants to major in mechanical engineering, he or she has to learn math well at high school.

词汇 Key Words

basic knowledge about different aspects of our
    life 关于我们生活不同方面的基础知识

proper and sufficient preparation 适当和足够
    的准备

foundation [faʊn'deɪʃn] *n.* 基础

major in mechanical engineering 主修机械工程

Q *What kinds of skills do you think are the most useful in everyday life?*

A: Well, the first thing that comes to mind is the skill of how to use the computer. The computer is an essential part of our lives and we can't live without it. We use it at work and school. It's also used by people to search for information and we can do many things online to relax. It's necessary in every aspect of our life. Apart from that, communication skills are also extremely important because we're in a society where we always have to socialise and interact with others. If we are not able to communicate with people properly, then a lot of work can't be done.

词汇 Key Words

can't live without it 生活离不开它	socialise ['səʊʃəlaɪz] *v.* 社交
in every aspect of our life 在生活的每个方面	interact with sb. 与某人互动
communication skills 沟通技巧	

🎤 Emotions, changes, experiences

Q *Why do people get nostalgic?*

A: Oh, that's a very interesting question. I had thought about it before, but I couldn't think of a reason, until one day, I read a book saying all human beings have this innate ability to gradually forget sad things over time. Everyone experienced sorrows and hurtful things,

but we've forgotten most of them, and what we do remember are those joyful moments. The bad things that happen now and have happened recently, we remember them very clearly, so we naturally believe that we suffer more than we did before. This is why people tend to be nostalgic, I think.

词汇 Key Words

nostalgic [nɒ'stældʒɪk] *adj.* 怀旧的	over time 随着时间的推移
think of a reason 想到一个原因	hurtful ['hɜːtfl] *adj.* 伤感情的
innate [ɪ'neɪt] *adj.* 与生俱来的	joyful ['dʒɔɪfl] *adj.* 令人开心的
gradually ['grædʒuəlɪ] *adv.* 逐渐地	

Q *In what situations do people tell white lies?*

A: One situation that comes to mind is when someone gets a new haircut and it doesn't look very good. Most of the time, friends just tell this person that their hair looks good. People do this because they don't want to hurt others' feelings. Plus, we often tell children that their dreams can always come true, but in fact, sometimes, we can't reach our goals. For example, I read in the news yesterday that an Australian girl with Down syndrome wants to be a supermodel. Her mom just tells her that she can do whatever she wants, as long as she works hard. I'm sure everyone knows that she might not be able to realise her dream, but telling a white lie here is essential.

词汇 Key Words

while lie 善意的谎言

Down syndrome 唐氏综合征

hurt one's feelings 伤害某人的感情

realise one's dream 实现某人的梦想

Q *Do you think lying is a crime?*

A: Well, it depends on what kind of lies you tell. If it's just a white lie, like the ones I talked about just now, it's definitely not a crime, because if it were, many people who mean to do a good deed would be in prison. However, if you trick other people into buying your counterfeit products, it's a crime. Also, if you tell lies in order to get out of paying taxes, you should definitely be punished.

词汇 Key Words

do a good deed 做一件好事

counterfeit ['kaʊtəfɪt] *adj.* 假的

in prison 坐牢

get out of paying taxes 逃税

trick sb. into doing sth. 欺骗某人做……

Q *Do changes always lead to a positive result?*

A: Not necessarily. Sometimes, the results of a change are positive. For instance, you move to another city where the traffic is much better than your previous city and you tend to be in a better mood on the way to and from work every day. However, at times, you don't always get what you want. We often hear stories where some people quit their jobs and find work at another company, only to find that they can't fit in there. Although they might earn a bigger salary, I don't think they are necessarily happy that way.

词汇 Key Words

not necessarily 不一定

find work 找到工作

previous ['priːvɪəs] *adj.* 之前的

earn a big salary 赚一笔不错的薪水

be in a better mood 心情更好

that way 那样的话

on the way to and from work 在上下班的路上

Q *Why is it difficult for some people to make a change in their lives?*

A: Well, there could be tons of reasons. The first one that comes to mind is that they're afraid of change. You know, for some people, their life is already pretty good and in that case, they just don't wanna change the status quo, because they fear that they might lose everything. If you live a decent life and someone tells you that you can make a fortune if you invest in a small company, but there's a chance that you might end up losing all your money, I guess it'll be pretty hard to make that decision, right? To be honest, in my view, this is understandable and um, I would probably choose not to make that change. Um, sorry, I don't think I can think of another reason at the moment.

词汇 Key Words

status quo 现状

live a decent life 过体面的生活

make a fortune 赚一大笔钱

invest in a company 投资一个公司

there's a chance that... 有一种……的可能

understandable [ˌʌndə'stændəbl] *adj.* 可以理解的

Media, TV, news

Q *Do you think negative information in the news will have a negative influence on people?*

A: Yes, I think so. The coverage of some negative information really has an adverse effect on people's everyday lives. Let me give you a couple of examples.

One is that there has always been some news about plane crashes and because of this, some people have become much more apprehensive when they fly somewhere. Another example is that from what I've read before, if there's a lot of news about car accidents, then it's likely that there will be even more of them within a short period of time. Sorry, I've forgotten why. But of course, some people claim that negative information never affects them, even subconsciously. I believe that may be true too.

词汇 Key Words

the coverage of... 对……的报道

have an adverse effect on... 对……有不良影响

plane crash 飞机失事

apprehensive [ˌæprɪ'hensɪv] *adj.* 担心的；忧虑的

within a short period of time 在很短的时间内

subconsciously [ˌsʌb'kɒnʃəslɪ] *adv.* 在潜意识层面

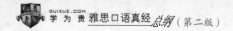

Q *How are television programmes now different from those in the past?*

A: Well, I think there have been quite a lot of changes. For starters, there have been many more entertainment programmes such as variety shows, talk shows and talent shows. By contrast, in the past, say 30 or 40 years ago, the vast majority of what we saw on TV were news programmes. Another difference is that there are loads of programmes every day on health now. I suppose it's because modern people generally lead a sedentary lifestyle and are not as active as before, and therefore we are less fit. Health programmes are very important in today's society.

词汇 Key Words

variety shows 综艺节目

talk shows 谈话节目

the vast majority of... 绝大多数……

lead a sedentary lifestyle 过一种久坐不动的生活

active ['æktɪv] *adj.* 活跃的；经常运动的

Q *How do TV programmes affect people?*

A: They have an effect on people in various ways. The most obvious is that TV programmes help us pass the time and unwind. In my case, I'm fanatical about some reality shows. They help me take my mind off things and I feel relaxed when watching them. Plus, some programmes are educational and not only can school children gain a great deal of knowledge from them, but adults can learn something from certain programmes too. Of course, those that feature violence may have an adverse effect on kids and teenagers.

词汇 Key Words

educational [ˌedʒʊˈkeɪʃənl] *adj.* 有教育意义的

feature ['fiːtʃə(r)] *v.* 以……为特色

violence ['vaɪələns] *n.* 暴力

图书在版编目 (CIP) 数据

雅思口语真经总纲/刘洪波，杨帅编著. -- 2版
. -- 北京：中国人民大学出版社，2023.8
ISBN 978-7-300-31978-0

Ⅰ.①雅… Ⅱ.①刘… ②杨… Ⅲ.①IELTS-口语-
自学参考资料 Ⅳ.①H319.9

中国国家版本馆CIP数据核字（2023）第135661号

- 本书中所有理论、概念均系作者原创，如果引用需注明出处。
- 本书著作权归作者所有，出版权归中国人民大学出版社，任何复印、引用均需征求著作权人
  及出版权持有人同时同意。

雅思口语真经总纲（第二版）

刘洪波　杨帅　编著
Yasi Kouyu Zhenjing Zonggang（Di-er Ban）

出版发行	中国人民大学出版社	
社　　址	北京中关村大街31号	**邮政编码**　100080
电　　话	010-62511242（总编室）	010-62511770（质管部）
	010-82501766（邮购部）	010-62514148（门市部）
	010-62515195（发行公司）	010-62515275（盗版举报）
网　　址	http://www.crup.com.cn	
经　　销	新华书店	
印　　刷	唐山玺诚印务有限公司	**版　　次**　2019年1月第1版
开　　本	787mm×1092mm　1/16	2023年8月第2版
印　　张	14.75	**印　　次**　2024年4月第5次印刷
字　　数	309 000	**定　　价**　59.80元

封面无防伪标均为盗版

版权所有　　侵权必究　　印装差错　　负责调换